A Rough Ride to Redemption

Benjamin Franklin Daniels. Drawing by Jack DeMattos.

A Rough Ride to Redemption

The Ben Daniels Story

ROBERT K. DEARMENT AND JACK DEMATTOS
Foreword by William B. Secrest

UNIVERSITY OF OKLAHOMA PRESS : NORMAN

This book is published with the generous assistance of
The McCasland Foundation, Duncan, Oklahoma.

Library of Congress Cataloging-in-Publication Data

DeArment, Robert K., 1925–2021
A rough ride to redemption : the Ben Daniels story / by Robert K.
DeArment and Jack DeMattos ; foreword by William B. Secrest.
p. cm.
Includes bibliographical references and index.
ISBN 978-0-8061-4112-1 (hardcover) ISBN 978-0-8061-9479-0 (paper)
1. Daniels, Ben, 1852–1923. 2. Peace officers—West (U.S.)—Biography.
3. United States marshals—Arizona—Biography. 4. Frontier and pioneer
life—West (U.S.) 5. West (U.S.)—Biography. 6. Roosevelt, Theodore,
1858–1919—Friends and associates. I. DeMattos, Jack, 1944– II. Title.
F595.D18D43 2010
363.28′2092—dc22 [B] 2009028669

The paper in this book meets the guidelines for permanence and durability
of the Committee on Production Guidelines for Book Longevity of the
Council on Library Resources, Inc. ∞

Copyright © 2010 by the University of Oklahoma Press, Norman,
Publishing Division of the University. Paperback published 2024.
Manufactured in the U.S.A.

All rights reserved. No part of this publication may be reproduced,
stored in a retrieval system, or transmitted, in any form or by any means,
electronic, mechanical, photocopying, recording, or otherwise—except as
permitted under Section 107 or 108 of the United States Copyright Act—
without the prior written permission of the University of Oklahoma Press.

Contents

List of Illustrations	vii
Foreword, by William B. Secrest	ix
Acknowledgments	xiii
Introduction	xv
1. Twice at the Door of Death, 1852–1878	3
2. Convict, 1879–1883	10
3. Dodge City Lawman, 1884–1886	22
4. The Killing of Ed Julian, 1886	34
5. The Daniels-Vaden Affair, 1886	41
6. Lawman of Lamar and the Battle of Cimarron, 1887–1889	52
7. Cripple Creek, 1889–1898	66
8. Rough Rider, 1898	82
9. The Marshalship Quest and the Spectral Past, 1899–1902	102
10. Prison Superintendent, 1904–1905	124
11. U.S. Marshal, 1905–1909	134
12. The Final Years, 1909–1923	161

Afterword	189
Notes	193
Bibliography	221
Index	235

Illustrations

Benjamin Franklin Daniels (drawing by Jack DeMattos)	*frontispiece*
"Dutch Henry" Born	12
Wyoming Territorial Penitentiary	18
Dodge City, 1882	23
Wedding picture of Ben Daniels and Annie Laura Ware	54
Ingalls, Kansas, about the time of the Gray County Seat War	58
Saloon scene in Cripple Creek, Colorado	68
Rough Riders Ben Daniels and Sherman Bell in Florida	91
Charge up San Juan Hill	96
Theodore Roosevelt and his Rough Riders atop San Juan Hill after the battle	97
Daniels's first commission as U.S. marshal	112
Cowboys at President Roosevelt's inaugural	132
Bat Masterson	137
Formal portraits of U.S. Marshal Ben Daniels	149
Gravestone of Annie Laura Daniels	152
U.S. Marshal Ben Daniels in Tombstone, Arizona, 1906	156
President Theodore Roosevelt greeted by Ben Daniels, Fred Dodge, and others at Denver, 1910	167
Ben Daniels, mining, 1918	178
Theodore Roosevelt in last known photograph, 1919	179
Ben Daniels in last known photograph	186
Grave of Ben Daniels	187

Foreword

WAY BACK IN THE 1960s, when I first began writing articles for the western magazines, I tried to come up with subjects that would catch an editor's eye. In those days there were many professionals in the business, writers who wrote under various other names to increase their sales. I was just an amateur then (still am). There were half a dozen western magazines in the 1960s, and much of their output was endlessly recycled stuff-stories about the Daltons, Jesse James, Butch Cassidy, "Wild Bill" Hickok, the Earps, and other big names in the frontier days. Oh, they would add a few adjectives and a lot of suppositions, but seldom anything really new.

It seemed to me that there were many little-known characters passed over by writers, and foremost among these was an obscure fellow named Ben Daniels, who showed up in many places of dramatic action, from the Indian troubles of buffalo days to old Dodge City and the Kansas county seat wars and Roosevelt's Rough Riders in the Spanish-American War. When I started researching him I found a many-faceted character who would be well worth the further effort to discover what he was all about. I was well satisfied with my Daniels article that appeared in *Frontier Times* (April–May 1969), although it ran a little long. So far as I know, however, it was the first attempt at a biography of this obscure frontier character.

My old pal, Jack DeMattos, resurrected Daniels for a series he did called "Gunfighters of the Real West," which appeared in *Real West* (September 1979). Jack, a skilled researcher, had added to what was already known of Ben and was impressed with the Daniels story to the extent that he later authored a manuscript entitled "Daniels and Roosevelt," dealing with the correspondence between Daniels and Theodore Roosevelt. DeMattos's cumulatve efforts now had added significantly to the literature of Ben Daniels's life and times.

When another masterful researcher, Bob DeArment, was casting about for a colorful but little-known Western character for a second volume of his *Deadly Dozen: Forgotten Gunfighters of the Old West*, Ben Daniels seemed a likely inclusion. DeArment, also a pal of long standing, recalled my old Ben Daniels article in *Frontier Times*. He contacted me concerning the use of my old research material as a starting place. I sent the material along and looked forward to an even more enhanced version of the Daniels story. I would not be disappointed, but I was surprised by the next development in the Ben Daniels story.

Bob was well aware of his good friend DeMattos's work on the Daniels story and the wealth of new research he had done in the Harvard Library and other sources. When Bob contacted Jack concerning his project, DeMattos now suggested that instead of adding Daniels to the characters in the second volume of *Deadly Dozen*, they collaborate on a new, full-length biography of the colorful frontiersman. "Great idea!" replied DeArment—and the rest is history (or will be!).

The completed book is a wonderfully thorough job of research by two of our finest western historians. I was genuinely fascinated by the great mass of new materials that was discovered and utilized by the authors. But I was particularly charmed by the fact that the project was initiated in California, my home; enhanced further in Massachusetts, where Jack DeMattos lives; then regenerated in a final biographical form by DeArment in Ohio. It has, indeed, been an interesting example of the collaborative efforts of three friends spanning the country over a period of nearly forty years. Is western history great, or what?

One final observation on the saga of Ben Daniels: is it time to rethink our concept of the face-to-face shootout as epitomized by Wild Bill shooting Dave Tutt on the Spingfield Square? To be sure, it sometimes happened that way, but more often it was a saloon brawl or some kind of ambush scenario. An oft-used trick was to come up behind your enemy, call his name, then shoot as he started to turn around. This satisfied the ethics of the "Code of the West," but was hardly fair, although it happened countless times during frontier days. And it happened so fast that witnesses could report whatever suited their point of view.

But what if someone shot another in the back, *without* first calling his name, as Ben Daniels reportedly did to Ed Julian? What if you were convinced your enemy was going to kill you any way he could, forcing you to be constantly on the alert for an ambush and seldom able to relax your guard? In this situation it was natural for both opponents to seek a confrontation to get it over with, one way or the other. And if you were shy a few scruples, shooting a potential assassin in the back to guarantee your own life might not be such a bad thing.

Or, in the heat of the moment, did Ben just forget to call out Julian's name?

William B. Secrest
Fresno, California

Acknowledgments

MANY INDIVIDUALS OVER the years have aided in the gathering of the story of Ben Daniels, and the authors would like to recognize their contributions here.

Foremost, of course, is William B. ("Bill") Secrest of Fresno, California, whose seminal research into Daniels's life was the inspiration for this book and to whom it is dedicated. Another who helped mightily was Wallace Finley Dailey, curator of the Theodore Roosevelt Collection at Harvard University. Others who contributed in the tracing of Daniels's Kansas adventures included Carol Jenkner, Bob Knecht, Roger Myers, Joseph G. Rosa, and Joseph W. Snell. Larry Brown of Cheyenne, Wyoming, helped uncover details of the Wyoming period. Information on Daniels's Colorado activity was provided by Barbara Dey of the Colorado Historical Society; David Dougherty of the Lamar, Colorado, police department; and Janice Prater of the Denver Public Library. Arizona historians Glenn G. Boyer, Jeff Morey, Robert F. Palmquist, and the late Al Turner aided in the Arizona research. The authors also want to thank Anita Vaden Page, whose investigation into the life of John Vaden was very beneficial in revealing that story.

Introduction

THE MORE ONE STUDIES the history of the gunfighters of the early West, the more one becomes aware of those seemingly peripheral characters who, upon closer examination, turn out to be every bit as fascinating as their more celebrated peers. Perhaps no one typifies this unsung breed of gunfighter better than Benjamin Franklin Daniels, who has somehow failed to attract the attention of yarn-spinners and serious historians, and no biography of the man has been published until now.

The irony is that Ben Daniels probably typified the journeyman gunfighter every bit as much as many of those whose lives have been chronicled in many books and whose names have become well known. It wasn't until some forty-six years after Daniels's death that he was rescued from undeserved obscurity by the publication of a lengthy magazine article sketching out for the first time the man's noteworthy career.

William B. Secrest, the young researcher and writer who wrote that article, knew that the story of Ben Daniels was indeed a rip-roaring one. Bill Secrest quickly recognized that Daniels was far more than just an occasional footnote in the lives of more celebrated gunmen, the role to which he had been relegated before Secrest's landmark study. The authors of this book made that recognition also, and here for the first time is Daniels's full story.

Until the end of his life, Ben Daniels was at the center of the action—whether that action was on the buffalo ranges of Texas, the uproarious cowtown of Dodge City, the mining boomtown of Cripple Creek, or the Battle of San Juan Hill. The story of his rise from outlaw and convict to presidential protégé and high-ranking officer of the law is a remarkable one, certainly a "rough ride to redemption."

A Rough Ride to Redemption

Chapter 1
Twice at the Door of Death
1852–1878

[Daniels's] life has been fraught with many adventures and even dangerous phases and has been closely connected with some characteristic aspects of frontier development.
—James H. McClintock

A RECURRENT PATTERN in the history of Old West gunfighters, particularly those who worked in law enforcement, was the good guy/bad guy ambiguity. One of the most remarkable examples of this antipodean incongruity was the career of Benjamin Franklin Daniels, who served a prison term for theft and killed at least one and perhaps several more people under highly questionable circumstances. And yet the man wore the badge in four states and territories, received the plaudits of a president of the United States, and was awarded one of the highest law enforcement positions it is possible to achieve.[1]

Daniels was a native of Illinois, a state that produced more than its share of celebrated frontier lawmen; "Wild Bill" Hickok and Wyatt Earp were born there, and Bat Masterson, although born in Canada, was reared and schooled in Illinois. "Born of sturdy Welsh and Scottish parentage"[2] on November 4, 1852, in LaSalle County, Daniels was one of nine children of Aaron Daniels, and his wife, Maria.[3]

Aaron Daniels appears to have had some of the adventurous spirit later evidenced by his son, for he left his growing family when gold rush fever swept the land in 1849 and went west to find his fortune in the gold-rich streams of California.[4] He was back by early 1852 and fathered another child, Benjamin, in November of that year.

About 1854, when Ben was still a baby, terrible tragedy struck the family. While the father was away on business, the dread disease cholera struck the Daniels homestead. A neighbor chancing to stop by the isolated farmhouse one day was appalled to find Maria Daniels and all her children dead or dying. As Ben later told the story, his mother and all his siblings died within two days, and a coffin had been prepared for his tiny body when someone, discovering that he was still alive, resuscitated him with a good dose of brandy.[5] Actually, census records show that two sisters, Elizabeth and Maria, survived the calamity along with their younger brother.[6]

Aaron Daniels, after the tragic loss of his wife and most of his children, married the widow of a wagon maker named Christian Stickley. Esther Stickley was the mother of four small boys. Soon three more children were born to this marriage, and young Ben grew up with four stepbrothers, two half-sisters, and one half-brother.[7]

In 1863, when Ben was eleven, Aaron Daniels moved his family to farmland near Ottawa, Franklin County, in eastern Kansas. Five years later Ben, now a strapping youth of sixteen, almost six feet tall, big-chested, and broad of shoulder, decided he was a man and a man who did not care much for farm work. Like many another young blade of the time, he bid his family good-bye and headed for Texas to become a cowboy.

Little is known of his life as a cowpuncher other than he told close friend James H. McClintock many years later that he ran cattle on the range.[8] Veteran cowboy Sam W. Wormwood confirmed this, saying he worked cattle with Ben from 1868 until 1871.[9] Newspapers later reported that during those years he participated in some of the earliest drives of Texas longhorn cattle to the markets in Kansas.[10]

In 1871, at the end of one such drive, Daniels turned up in Wichita, Kansas, a community just emerging as a booming cow town. There he learned of a burgeoning new industry developing on the plains of western Kansas—the hunting and killing of buffalo for their hides—and he decided to get in on that excitement. He drifted on west to a raw new town catering to the buffalo hide trade. First called Buffalo City, the little burg would later become world famous as Dodge City. Here Daniels met many of the other buffalo hunters who would play important roles in his later life: the Masterson brothers—Ed, Bat, and Jim—Fred Singer, and Bill Tilghman.[11]

Due to his reticence to talk or write about his youthful activities, we know little more about the life of Ben Daniels as a buffalo hunter than we do of his cowboy experiences. He did mention to McClintock that he had hunted buffalo in Texas and "had trouble with the Indians."[12] Later newspapers and writers reported that at the age of eighteen[13] he had been an Indian fighter and scout for the U.S. Army.[14]

The extent of his adventures as a fighter of Indians appears to be his participation in a joint campaign of the buffalo hunters and the army against Comanche raiders in the spring and summer of 1877.

In March of that year Daniels was one of some sixty hunters camped near Rath City, a tiny settlement on the Double Mountain Fork of the Brazos River. The "city" consisted of a store, two saloons, a dance hall, and a few tents and dugouts.[15]

When word reached the town that Indian raiders led by Comanche chieftain Black Horse had attacked a hunters' camp,[16] killing and scalping a well-liked hunter named Marshall Sewell, a group from Rath City went back to the scene and buried Sewell's mutilated body. They followed the Indian trail until a mixed-blood named Spotted Jack was wounded in a brief skirmish. Seeing they were greatly outnumbered, the party returned to Rath City, where they learned that the Indians, numbering about 170,[17] had plundered a number of hunters' camps.[18]

On March 4 a retaliatory force of buffalo hunters, including Ben Daniels,[19] organized to go after the Comanche raiders. There were forty-six avengers in all, twenty-six of whom were mounted on saddle horses; the rest rode in wagons. The noted buffalo hunter Jim White was elected captain, but the second night out he began bleeding from the lungs and had to return to Rath City. Jim Smith then took command.

For two weeks the hunters followed the Indian trail westward and, according to a story related by one of their number and published in the *Dodge City Times* a few months later, underwent severe suffering. They exhausted their provisions and had to leave their wagons and lead the horses, who had grown too weak to carry them. But the trail was fresher, and "over the last morsel of food every hunter registered a solemn vow not to taste food again until they had made Indian blood flow on the ground like water."[20]

After two days without food the hunters came upon the Yellow House Canyon camp of the Indians they had been trailing. Although outnumbered, they attacked, driven by hunger and a thirst for revenge. Here the narration, aided no doubt by the pen of the newspaper editor, grew passionate: "Desperate hate lent strength to steady their aim of the well tried buffalo guns in their emaciated hands. Each hunter felt himself to be a fell destroyer. Some of them were severely wounded but they laughed at the pain and their aim was more deadly than before." The battle raged all day. When night fell, the Indians "gathered up their dead and wounded and silently stole away, leaving gore enough to fully quench the hunters' thirst for revenge. The number of killed and wounded Indians could not be ascertained. Only a few hunters were wounded and none killed."[21]

Actually, the hunters suffered three casualties, including Joe Jackson, who had been a skinner for the murdered Sewell. Jackson received a bad wound and a few days after the party got back to Rath City, on March 27, died from its effects.[22]

In May James Harvey led another force of about twenty-four hide hunters out of Rath City in pursuit of Black Horse's band, which had continued to attack the outlying camps, killing hunters, destroying hides, and stealing stock. Two months later a unit of about sixty black cavalrymen under Captain Nicholas Nolan of the Tenth U.S. Cavalry left Fort Concho, Texas, to assist in the effort. The cavalrymen and the hunters joined up at Double Lakes, where they established a supply base. The combined force searched unsuccessfully for Black Horse's band, which had scattered in the arid wastes of the Llano Estacado. The hunt was abandoned as lack of water became a major concern. After two days without finding the life-sustaining liquid, the two parties split up. The buffalo hunters headed southwest where they did find water, but Nolan's cavalrymen turned back for Double Lakes and dry-marched another thirty-eight hours before reaching their destination. In all his men and animals had gone some eighty-six hours without water. Four of his men were dead or missing, and he had lost twenty-five horses and four pack mules.[23]

These forays against the Indian marauders the hunters called "Forlorn Hope," but in the end they proved successful. The hunters were able to recover much of their stolen stock, and Black Horse and his band, tired of the harassment, returned to their reservation in Indian Territory.[24]

Shortly after this Indian-fighting episode, Ben Daniels went through another life-threatening experience. Having barely escaped death from the dread disease of cholera as a baby, he was stricken on the buffalo range with another deadly sickness—smallpox—and nearly died. As a fellow buffalo hunter named J. E. Dickson related it years later, the story revealed a compassionate side of Daniels's nature that many may not have recognized. "Back in 1877," said Dickson,

I was out in west Texas, one hundred and ten miles west of Fort Griffin, hunting buffalo for the hides. The only settler out that way was old man McCamey, who had a shack covered with bull hides and ran a sort of trading store. The shack and a dug-out in the bank of a creek about seventy-five yards away were the only signs of life for a good many miles.

One day a bull team came into the store with a load of hides and on top of the load was a sick man. It didn't take long to see what ailed him—he had the small-pox. None of the folks around the store would go near him—they were afraid of catching the disease—but he managed to crawl off the load and into the old dug-out in the creek bank.

Two days later a new buffalo hunting outfit came in, led by a big young fellow named Ben Daniels. When Ben heard that there was a sick man down in the dug-out and that he had been there without grub or care for two days, nothing to it but Ben must go right down there to look after him. He found him lying in the dirt in one corner, half naked and all crazy he was so sick. Ben fixed up a bunk for him and nursed him the best he could for three days until he died. Then the boys dug a grave up on the hill and Ben buried him. Nobody knew what his name was. But they called him "Buck" and marked his grave that way.

Two days later Ben came down sick himself. It seemed that an epidemic must have hit that country for before we knew it, there were five of us down with small-pox, and all crowded into that little dug-out. There was not a doctor within a hundred miles, but McCamey

dug up an old fellow who had the disease before and was immune, to nurse the bunch. For beds we drove stakes in the ground and hung bull hides over them. They were not very smooth, but beat lying on the ground. Our medicine was wild gourd root boiled up into a kind of black tea, and say—quinine is altar-of-roses compared to that stuff for sweetness. But it did the work and in two months all five of us were well. I remember one day along towards the end of our siege, when we were sitting up playing cards, some eastern chap came driving along with a fine rig and came up to the dug-out to ask directions for getting to Fort Griffin. Ben told him to stay away, that we had the small-pox, and, honest, that fellow broke down all the small brush for ten miles in his hurry.[25]

Soon after his recovery Daniels left the buffalo range. By 1878 the southern herds roaming the plains of Kansas and Texas had been fairly well decimated by the onslaught of the hide men, and Daniels and other hunters had to look for other lines of work. Many of those with whom he had associated, men of grit and determination familiar with guns and danger, including Pat Garrett, John Poe, the Masterson brothers, Bill Tilghman, Tom Nixon, Neal Brown, and Fred Singer, turned to law enforcement in the raucous new towns of Kansas and New Mexico. Daniels in time would also follow the life of a lawman as a lifelong profession, but when first leaving the buffalo range he went in a different direction.

After the great buffalo hunt some of the hunters chose to make their living by means directly opposed to the badge-toters; they turned to outlawry, principally the stealing of horses. Ben Daniels, to his eternal regret, followed this route.

Chapter 2
Convict
1879–1883

> On Saturday last Sheriff Christy and Deputy Sheriff Payne, procured the arrest of a man named Daniels . . . , supposed to be the partner of the infamous Dutch Henry. He was first arrested in Wyoming Territory for stealing Government mules, but shot the two officers who had him in charge and made his escape.
> —*Dodge City Times*, September 13, 1879

SOMETIME IN 1878 Ben Daniels showed up in Dodge City,[1] the town that had been the chief outfitting and marketing point for the buffalo hunters during the great bison harvest, but now was becoming a major cattle town, with thousands of longhorns arriving after the long drive up the trail from Texas to be loaded into railroad cars for shipment to the East. He found that the Masterson brothers, friends from the buffalo ranges, had already taken law enforcement positions in Dodge. W. B. ("Bat") Masterson, although only twenty-five years old, had been elected sheriff of Ford County and headquartered in the town. Ed Masterson held the post of city marshal until shot down and killed by drunken cowboys in April 1878. Jim Masterson was on the city police force. The town was full of other former buffalo hunters—tough, gun-handy types like Fred Singer, Wyatt Earp, Bill Tilghman, Neal

Brown, Tom Nixon, and many others—eager to pin on badges when the opportunity arose. Daniels might have stayed on in Dodge and begun the law enforcement career he was destined to pursue, but for some reason, perhaps daunted by the competition he faced, he chose to move on and soon drifted into outlawry, a choice that would haunt him most of his life.

For some of the former buffalo hunters—hardened frontiersman, familiar with animals and weapons, and used to traveling great distances across the plains—the transition to horse thievery came easily. A few, like "Buffalo Bill" Brooks, came to an early and ignoble demise at the end of a rope,[2] but others, like "Hurricane Bill" Martin and "Dutch Henry" Born, perhaps more clever, pursued their criminal vocation for years and gained from westerners a kind of grudging admiration.

The name of Ben Daniels has never been associated with Martin, whose operations were confined primarily to the Chisholm Trail region,[3] but Daniels hooked up for a time with Dutch Henry Born, the most notorious captain of horse thieves then active on the Great Plains.[4]

Dutch Henry, the son of German immigrants, was born on July 2, 1849, in Manitowac, Wisconsin. Details of his early life are hazy. He reportedly fled west after being accused of killing a man in Michigan. After taking odd jobs around the Kansas army camps, he eventually hired on as a civilian scout, working with such frontier notables as John Smith, Ben Clark, "California Joe" Milner, and "Wild Bill" Hickok.[5] Later, while cooking for the camp of hide buyer Mike Bedell at Kit Carson, Colorado, he befriended Bill Tilghman, who remembered him as a slight, dark-eyed young fellow about his own age, who spoke with a decided German accent.[6]

In 1872 Born turned to buffalo hunting and while encamped along the Arkansas River near Fort Lyon on the eastern plains of Colorado was attacked by a party of Cheyenne.

"Dutch Henry" Born, horse thief extraordinaire, with whom Daniels was allied during his short criminal career. From the R. K. DeArment Collection.

Struck three times by arrows, he received an ugly leg wound that would plague him the rest of his life. He managed to repel the Cheyenne, but they ran off with his stock. Left without a mount and suffering from his injuries, he laboriously hiked to the camp of another hide hunter, where he got transport to the fort. He reported his loss to the commandant, but that officer refused him help and accused him of "stirring up the Indians." Enraged, Born stole back that night and appropriated a pair of government mules to replace the ones he lost and, as punishment for the army officer, rode off with his personal mount, a particularly fine horse. Some time later the commandant received a letter from Born, admitting his theft and announcing his decision to exact vengeance on both the U.S. Army and the Indians by preying on their horse remudas: "Do not blame the Indians or anyone else. For I alone stole your mules. After I hauled my hides, I sold them. I'm keeping the horse for he is a fine saddler. If you want him just come down to the Cheyenne country. I'm going there to collect one hundred ponies and one scalp. Signed: Dutch Henry."[7]

Thus began the outlaw career of Dutch Henry, horse thief extraordinaire. Starting with three accomplices, his brother Jake and former scouts Sam Walker and Charles Christy, he eventually, at the height of his notoriety, headed up a loose-knit gang of horse thieves reputed to number in the hundreds, whose depredations extended across the Great Plains as far as Nevada.[8]

Born reportedly was one of the twenty-eight hide hunters who fought off an attack by hundreds of Indians at the famous Battle of Adobe Walls in the last week of June 1874.[9] But by that time he had already established a frontier-wide reputation as a horse thief, and it is more likely he was the "Henry Born" arrested in Ellis County, Kansas, by Sheriff Alexander Ramsey on June 15 after "an exciting chase" during which he was wounded again. Charged with stealing government mules, the accused was taken to Hays City and thence to Topeka.[10] This was only a few days before the Indian battle down in the Texas panhandle, and if the Henry Born arrested in Kansas was indeed "Dutch Henry," as seems likely, he could not possibly have been in the Adobe Walls fight.

The horse thief who would become legendary as the "Rob Roy of the Plains" escaped this scrape as he did a number of others in his career.[11] He suffered a stab wound during another arrest on June 16, 1876, at Russell, Kansas, and an assassination attempt while in jail, but was freed again or escaped.[12]

Three months later newspapers reported a "haul of horse thieves" by county lawmen and U.S. Army personnel near Hays City, Kansas. They arrested a dozen, including two women, all believed members of the "Dutch Henry Gang," and confiscated fifty-one head of horses and mules and three wagons. Born and one of his principal lieutenants, identified only as "Slapping Jack," evaded capture.[13]

Near Red Cloud, Nebraska, officers arrested Born in July 1877, but he was freed for lack of evidence or escaped once more.[14]

"Dutch Henry is the most noted horse thief on the border," proclaimed the *Dodge City Times* in June 1878. "[He] has stolen more horses, been captured oftener, wounded oftener, broken jail oftener, and has been through more thrilling adventures than any other man in the west. His name is a by-word in Kansas, and it is earnestly hoped that he will be brought to justice."[15]

In December 1878 officers in Trinidad, Colorado, spotted him consorting with a pair of well-known toughs from Dodge City, "Prairie Dog Dave" Morrow and "Mysterious Dave" Mather. The officers placed him under arrest and notified authorities in Dodge. Sheriff Bat Masterson had Ford County horse theft warrants for the outlaw, and he went to Trinidad in January 1879 and brought Born back to Dodge for trial. A Dodge City paper described the man who by now was a frontier celebrity as "rather a genteel looking man for a horse-thief, road-agent and murderer. He has black hair and eyes, black mustache, long face and Roman nose. His eyes are bright and penetrating, and indicate quick intelligence. He is dressed in a good suit of black, white shirt and other corresponding clothing."[16] In another edition the paper noted that "Dutch Henry has become famous in the western States and Territories, and has made many bold and successful escapes from justice. He has broken jail and escaped from officers no less than three times within a year."[17]

In a two-day trial held later that month in Dodge, Dutch Henry was acquitted to the consternation of everyone, including the judge. Perhaps the jury had been swayed by the eloquence of Born's defense lawyer, Harry Gryden, who orated at length on his client's heroic feats on the frontier.[18]

Once again Dutch Henry was freed, but he did not enjoy his liberty long. A month later Deputy U.S. Marshal C. B. Jones nabbed him in Wichita and turned him over to Shawnee County authorities.[19] The *Denver Tribune* commented:

There are very few people at all acquainted with the crime calendar of the West who have not heard of "Dutch Henry," who has ranged in his depredations all over the western slope. . . . He is known to all who own large herds of horses or mules, and is known only to be dreaded. . . . [He] has been shot and cut from top to toe, from Dakota to Texas, but [is] still the same reckless and powerful man he was in the beginning. He seems to be entirely devoid of fear. . . . He is a fine shot and uses the lasso to perfection.[20]

Taken to the federal court of Judge Isaac C. Parker at Fort Smith, Arkansas, to answer for his crimes against the government, Dutch Henry was convicted and sent to prison.[21]

With their leader finally in the toils, members of his horse theft operation began to be picked up at a number of locations across the plains. In July James M. Riley, better known by his alias, "Doc" Middleton, the leader of a large gang that may have been affiliated with Dutch Henry, was captured in Nebraska after a heated gunfight with officers.[22] In Palo Pinto County, Texas, another gun battle between lawmen and horse thieves in August resulted in the death of one outlaw and the capture of several others.[23]

Ben Daniels, who contemporary newspapers alleged was associated with the "Dutch Henry Gang," perhaps even a "partner" of the infamous outlaw,[24] fell afoul of the law in September. Officers took him into custody, charging him with the theft of government mules some time earlier. It was said that he and another man had stolen mules from a pack train being taken by Quartermaster Perry Organ from Camp Carlin, an army supply depot near Cheyenne, Wyoming, to Fort Laramie. The thieves heated "skillets red hot, applied them to the sides of the mules and thus obliterated the government brands. The mules were then sold and Daniels and his pal skipped out." The other man (who may have been Dutch Henry himself) disappeared, but Daniels was arrested.[25]

According to rather sketchy newspaper reports, Daniels managed a sensational escape from the members of the military who had him in custody, shooting two in the process, one of whom, an army lieutenant, later died.[26]

Daniels then fled to Ford County, Kansas, and, apparently determined to abandon the outlaw life, filed a land claim near Dodge City.[27]

Someone may have informed on him, for on September 8, 1879, U.S. marshal for Kansas, B. F. Simpson, issued a warrant for his arrest on the mule theft charge and turned it over to Ben's old friend, Bat Masterson, who was now sheriff of Ford County and a deputy U.S. marshal. With the assistance of H. B. Van Voorhis, another deputy marshal, Masterson took Daniels into custody without incident and conveyed him to the federal court at Larned in Pawnee County.[28]

"The arrest of a horse thief who had killed an army officer and stolen ten mules from the government, created considerable excitement at this place," said the *Larned (Kansas) Optic*. Strangely, the paper described the robust Daniels as "a small man," and added that he didn't appear to have half the "cussedness" that had been attributed to him.[29]

Daniels was arraigned before U.S. Commissioner P. C. Hughes on September 20 and, based on affidavits sworn to by soldiers from Fort Lyon,[30] was additionally charged with the murder of a Nineteenth Infantry lieutenant in 1874. He was held under bond of $2,000 to answer the charges at the November session of federal court at Cheyenne.[31]

At the trial held in November before District Judge J. W. Fisher, prosecutors Layman and Carroll, after digging into the facts of the case and learning that other evidence tying Daniels to criminal activity as early as 1874 was lacking and believing that the soldiers' identification of him, now five years old, would not hold up in court, dropped the murder charge and concentrated on the lesser offense of larceny, the theft of five government mules. The court-appointed law firm of Kinkaid and Riner represented Daniels. In a trial lasting but one afternoon, a jury convicted the defendant, and the judge sentenced Daniels to two years in the territorial prison at Laramie and fined him $1,000.[32]

Wyoming Territorial Penitentiary as it appeared during Daniels's incarceration. Courtesy of the Wyoming State Archives and Historical Department.

On November 29, 1879, Ben Daniels entered the Wyoming Territorial Penitentiary as Convict No. 88.[33] He must have made a deep impression on the officer who conducted him in shackles from the Cheyenne jail to his new place of confinement, for Deputy U.S. Marshal W. R. Schnitger, who was given that assignment, recalled Daniels vividly some twenty-three years later, and described his charge as "six feet tall, raw-boned, of a powerful physique. He had a very prominent nose, a defective right ear, the lobe of which was missing, I believe, and [was] pox marked.[34]

Daniels's lawyers found an error in the judicial proceedings and filed an appeal, and the court ordered a new trial. Meanwhile Daniels languished in his prison cell.[35]

During this period while awaiting his second trial, Daniels had an opportunity to regain his freedom. On April 7, 1880, five inmates of the prison engineered a bold escape. They were led by Charles Wilbert, a dangerous convict serving a ten-year stretch for manslaughter who on an earlier occasion had attacked Warden A. J. House with a knife and almost killed him. Wilbert was joined in the breakout by George Taylor (also serving time for manslaughter), Robert Hamilton, Myron M. ("Buffalo Sam") Blair, and Charles ("Kid) Condon. According to news reports, Taylor, Blair, and Hamilton all urged Daniels to join them in their bid for freedom, but he declined and remained in his cell.[36]

After more than eight months in various lockups Daniels was brought to the Laramie County jail at Cheyenne for his second trial. There, on June 1, 1880, he was enumerated in the U.S. Census for Wyoming.[37]

As it turned out, his lawyers did him no favors by securing a second trial. He was convicted again on June 10, 1880, and the judge in the case, J. B. Sener, slapped him with an even stiffer sentence, three and a half years.[38]

Reassigned as Convict No. 97, Daniels was described in the prison records as "a large strong built man weighing 165 pounds," measuring five feet ten inches in height, with a fair complexion, dark brown hair, and brown eyes. "He has," the report continued, "a thin face, large roman nose, bushy eyebrows and ears that stand straight out from his head. Nose has been broken and the lobe of his right ear is missing. The letters B. D. are in Indian ink on his right arm. A small scar under the right knee and a small scar on the left knee. A large round scar on the left shoulder blade. He is pock-marked slightly on the body and considerably on the face. Has had small pox [sic]." He professed a Methodist church affiliation and a "common" education.[39]

The pockmarks on his face and body, of course, were remnants of his bout with smallpox back in Texas. But the broken nose, body scars, and missing earlobe were lasting souvenirs of Daniels's belligerent disposition and propensity to brawl. The missing lobe of his right ear intrigued many who knew him, including Theodore Roosevelt, who came to know and greatly admire Daniels, and remarked on the damaged ear in one of his books.[40] A newspaper dispatch in 1916 referred to Daniels as a "half-eared gent of belligerent proclivities who lost part of his aural appendage when he got between another man's molars as they happened to come together."[41] Bill Tilghman, curious about that disfigured ear, asked Ben once how he came to lose part of it. "In a fight," was Ben's typically terse response, saying nothing more on the subject. Tilghman, among others, noticed that Daniels was self-conscious about the disfigurement and took pains when having his photograph taken to turn his left side to the camera so the tattered ear would not be visible.[42] Years later enemies of Daniels would claim that one of his ears had been mutilated deliberately to brand him as a horse thief, an allegation that was, of course, unfounded.[43]

His next of kin, Daniels told prison officials, was a sister living in Osage County, Kansas. This was apparently his sister Maria, one of his two siblings who survived the cholera disaster. She had married a man named John S. Edie and in 1880 was living at Valley Brook Township, Kansas, with her husband and two children. The fact that Daniels did not name his father, who was still alive and farming at Key West in neighboring Coffey County, Kansas, suggests that Ben had left home at an early age because of conflict with his father and that their differences had still not been resolved.[44]

Daniels's conduct in prison was good, and after three years and two months incarceration he was released, with his sentence reduced by four months to reward his good behavior. On August 28, 1883, he walked out of Wyoming Territorial Penitentiary and headed for the friendlier climes of Dodge City, Kansas.[45]

Chapter 3
Dodge City Lawman
1884–1886

Daniels was every inch a gunfighter and he had made a big reputation as a killer, when the people, following a happy custom, decided that it would be better to have such a man as a peace officer than a destroyer.
—*Dallas Morning News*, August 17, 1903

FOLLOWING HIS RELEASE from the Wyoming penitentiary in August 1883 Ben Daniels headed straight for Dodge City, where many of his friends from buffalo hunting days had established themselves as law officers. It is evident that during his long months in prison Daniels had pondered the direction of his life up to that point and concluded he had taken the wrong trail, a trail that could only lead to another jail cell or perhaps the end of a rope. He determined now to step over that dim line separating outlaws from lawmen, pin on a badge, and become a hunter rather than one of the hunted. It was a path he would follow to the end of his life.

Dodge City, he found, was just returning to normality after the conclusion of the nationally publicized "Dodge City War." In May 1883 a political faction that had taken control of the municipal and county government, led by Mayor Alonzo B. Webster and Sheriff George Hinkle, drove Luke Short and several other gamblers out of town. Short retaliated by calling on a number of his friends from the western sporting community to come to his aid. A coterie of cold-eyed gunmen, including Bat Masterson and Wyatt Earp, descended on Dodge in June, completely intimidating Short's adversaries, and the dispute was resolved without bloodshed.

When Daniels arrived in early September he found that some of his old friends were no longer in Dodge. Ed Masterson had been killed in a shootout with drunken Texas cowboys back in 1878. Bat and Jim were now in Colorado, as was Wyatt Earp. But many he had known since buffalo hunting days, including Fred Singer, Howell P. Myton, Tom Nixon, Bill Tilghman, and Neal Brown, were still on hand. Singer was Hinkle's undersheriff, and Myton was a deputy. Jack Bridges, a former deputy U.S. marshal and a particular pet of Mayor Webster, held the position of city marshal, and "Mysterious Dave" Mather was his assistant. Nixon, Tilghman, and Brown were still around, but, being aligned with the betting, booze, and brothel brethren, currently held no law enforcement jobs as their political supporters, called the "Saloon Gang" by their opponents, were currently out of power.

As was typical of westerners, who famously believed that a man's previous history was private, to be divulged only voluntarily, Dodge City folks did not inquire about where Daniels had been or what he had been doing the past three years, and Daniels, a tight-lipped man by nature, did not volunteer that information. Whether out of shame, remorse, or simply the belief that it was no one's business, Daniels kept hidden his record as an ex-convict for years. In the future, however, the story of his criminal past would be widely publicized and threaten to deprive him of his most cherished ambition.

Tilghman told him to be patient, that since the Luke Short imbroglio the Webster crowd was growing in public disfavor, and expected administration changes at the November

Dodge City as depicted in 1882, the year before Daniels settled there. Courtesy of the Kansas State Historical Society.

election would open up a law enforcement job opportunity. While he waited for the political climate to change, Daniels tended bar in the saloons and concentrated on the study of the pasteboards; professional gambling was to become an important source of his income in the coming years.

As predicted, the voters of Ford County threw out the incumbents in November 1883 county and April 1884 municipal elections.

In November Pat Sughrue, one of a pair of identical twin lawmen and a Luke Short supporter, defeated Fred Singer, who had been Hinkle's undersheriff, in the contest for Ford County sheriff. Sughrue appointed Thomas J. Tate to the post of undersheriff and his twin brother, Michael, and Bill Tilghman as deputies. Like their boss, all had staunchly supported Luke Short in the recent "war," and opposed Webster and Hinkle. Later Sheriff Sughrue added Ben Daniels to his deputy roster, and Daniels was presented with the first of the many badges he would wear throughout his life.[1]

In the municipal elections held five months later the voters elected George Hoover, a prominent member of the "Gang," to the office of mayor. Other "Gang" leaders, including former mayor James H. ("Dog") Kelley and William H. Harris, business partner of Luke Short, took seats on the city council. At the first meeting of the new city council held two days after the election, Mayor Hoover proposed the appointment of Bill Tilghman as town marshal and Tom Nixon as assistant. Both nominees were quickly approved.

Several months passed before Daniels could land a city law enforcement job, but when the cattle season heated up in earnest late in June he did receive an appointment as a special policeman.[2]

The month of July 1884 would prove to be particularly momentous for Dodge City, its lawmen, and Daniels personally. City leaders that year planned a grand Fourth of July celebration that included foot races, horse races, and shooting matches, topped of with a real Mexican bullfight. Members of the sporting fraternity of both sexes headed for Dodge City from as far away as New York and New Orleans. Daniels and the other local cops were kept busy maintaining order and collecting license fees from whiskey peddlers, prostitutes, and gamblers. On the big day Daniels was assigned the unenviable job of separating respectable women from the prostitutes. Said Marshal Tilghman: "We just roped a dividing line and posted Ben Daniels to separate the sheep from the goats."[3]

The night following the big event a gunfight in the perceived tradition of the frontier West erupted in A. B. Webster's Old House saloon. About one in the morning Texas cattleman K. B. ("Bing") Choate, full of red liquor, pulled out a revolver that he had failed to check according to city ordinance and, plainly spoiling for a fight, loudly announced to the crowd, "I am the fastest son of a bitch in town." Sticking the pistol back in his pants, he focused his attention on gambler Dave St. Clair, cursed him, prodded him with a cane, and challenged him to draw. St. Clair rose from his gambling table, looked at Choate, and said, "You have been punching my neck and stomach with that cane, and you have been shaking your gun pretty freely. I'll take the pistol from you and shove it up your ass."[4]

Both men pulled their guns. St. Clair fired first. His bullet struck Choate and whirled him around. The cattleman dropped to the floor, but struggled to his knees and was leveling his cocked pistol at St. Clair when policeman Daniels burst through the doorway and kicked the gun from his hand. Choate died within moments, and Daniels and other officers arrested St. Clair. At a hearing witnesses corroborated the gambler's claim that he fired in self-defense, and he was released.[5]

Daniel M. Frost, editor of the *Ford County Globe* and judge of the police court, criticized Mayor Hoover and his police force for failing to enforce strictly the ordinance against "the carrying of deadly weapons and particularly the six-shooter" within the city limits. The mayor, he said, should "see to it that all those not officers of the law (and perhaps some of them) be made to lay aside their shooting irons while in the city."[6]

Only two weeks later Frost's contention that some of the city's lawmen were dangerous—if not to the general public, at least to each other—was confirmed when former assistant marshal "Mysterious Dave" Mather and his successor, Tom Nixon, went at it with six-shooters. There had been bad blood between the two for some time, and on the night of July 18 Nixon took a shot at "Mysterious Dave." Narrowly missing Mather's head, the bullet threw splinters from the Opera House Saloon into his hand, and the blast left powder burns on his face. Sheriff Sughrue, quickly on the scene, disarmed and arrested Nixon before further damage was done, but only three days later Mather took his revenge, shooting Nixon dead only a few feet from the spot of the earlier gunplay.

Nixon's sudden demise left the assistant city marshal position open, and Bill Tilghman wasted little time in appointing Ben Daniels to the job, swearing him in to the $100-a-month position on July 24.[7]

Dave Mather was acquitted for the Nixon killing and soon left town. But, according to Zoe Tilghman, Bill's wife, he held a grudge against Nixon's pals in Dodge and returned to exact revenge against Tilghman; Daniels; Dr. A. S. Chouteau, an outspoken Nixon supporter; and perhaps others. "He brought with him a veritable arsenal," she wrote, "six-shooters, a rifle, shotgun, and a supply of ammunition,"[8] and rented an upstairs room in a lodging house, accessible only by means of an open, outside stairway. But, anticipating Mather's murderous intentions, the targets of his wrath took turns watching that stairway. Mather could not even come down for food without plunging into a deadly line of fire. He was brave, but not foolhardy. He held out for nearly a week.

Then, at last, a white handkerchief waved cautiously from the window. Ben Daniels, who was "on duty," kept his gun ready, while Bill Tilghman and Dr. Chouteau moved nearer, to hold parley. If Mather would come down the stairway with his hands up and no weapons about him, they would escort him to the station for the next train, east or west. He would promise never to come back. Mather agreed, and so it was carried out.[9]

On August 4 Officer Daniels was involved in a shooting affair that fortunately resulted in no fatalities or serious injuries. A cowboy, furious after losing his money at a gambling table in the Opera House Saloon, got into a shouting match with the dealer, a young man named Hart.[10] Both used some sulfurous language. The cowboy started to leave, but at the doorway pulled a six-shooter from his boot and began firing at Hart. After three inaccurate shots he turned and ran, pursued by Assistant Marshal Daniels, who fired five or six equally ineffective shots in his direction and failed to catch the man. "The only blood that was drawn," according to the newspaper account, "was when young Hart went through the back window. He was going at such a speed through that he received but slight injuries."[11]

The remainder of the cattle shipping season passed without gunplay, but the city police had some difficulty controlling the many "soiled doves" who had swarmed into Dodge. Only three days after the Opera House Saloon shooting two of the demimonde got into a row over "a mutual lover," and Bertha Lockwood stabbed Sadie Hudson "in three different places;

one wound pretty near the spinal column under the back bone, one a little forward, and one in the breast." A surgeon dressed the wounds and deemed them "quite deep, but not necessarily mortal."[12]

A few days later the officers were called to resolve another battle between two sporting women over a disputed lover. Since they gave their names as "Ollie Hart" and "Mollie Hart," both evidently claimed the affection as well as the surname of the young house gambler who had almost been perforated a few nights earlier. As recounted in the *Dodge City Democrat*, the women claimed "the right of possession to the heart and necessary appendages" of Hart, and sought to settle the matter by a "free-for-all cat fight."[13]

The rest of the cattle shipping season passed without incident, and with the departure of the Texas cowboys and the violence-prone sporting crowd that followed them, the lawmen of Dodge could relax during the winter months. But with the beginning of the new season of 1885 the troublemakers were back in force, and in May Daniels had a little tussle with another pugnacious doxy. As a newspaper reported: "Miss Fannie Nash, a soiled dove of color, who has been in the habit of giving Ben Daniels a little chin music, was caught up by him last Monday [May 11] and put in the jug. Ben was a little afraid of getting his eyes scratched out, so encircled his arms around her and walked her off in a pleasing manner."[14]

Of course belligerent males could face off on occasion also, as noted in an August item: "A little 'scrapping match' took place on Front street last Monday evening. The combatants were promptly given quarters in the 'cooler' by Marshal Daniels."[15]

Some claimed that Daniels sometimes overstepped his authority as an officer and could be brutal with those he disliked. One of these was Jacob C. ("Jakey") Bloom, who had a candy and cigar store in Dodge and alleged that Daniels entered his store and "for no reason whatever . . . abused [him] shamefully." Daniels and Bloom would meet again in Cripple Creek, Colorado, and Bloom would seek revenge by badmouthing Daniels at every opportunity.[16]

Daniels provided a public service that cast him in a much more favorable light in May when a circus, S. H. Barrett's New United Monster Railroad Show, appeared in Dodge. A German couple, almost hysterical with fear and dread, came to Daniels, saying their little boy was missing and that they believed he had been "stolen" by the circus people. Daniels tracked the boy's movements, discovered him fast asleep in a neighbor's house, and returned him to his grateful parents.[17]

Dodge City's leading merchant, Robert M. Wright, who replaced Hoover as mayor of Dodge in April 1885, kept both Tilghman and Daniels, favorites of his, in their positions. He would later write:

Tilghman . . . was marshal under me, when I was mayor of Dodge City, and Ben Daniels was his assistant. No braver men ever handled a gun or arrested an outlaw, and Dodge never passed through a tougher time. . . . It did seem like every bad and desperate character in the whole West gathered here; and when we would drive out one lot, another set would make their appearance. But Tilghman was equal to the occasion. He had many narrow escapes, and many desperate men to deal with; and Ben Daniels was a good second.[18]

On the night of November 28, 1885, an oil lamp exploded in a Dodge City saloon, setting off a devastating fire. Members of the city's fire department were called on for heroic efforts to battle the conflagration while the police strove to protect the homes and businesses from looters. James McClintock later repeated a story told him by Ben Daniels about that catastrophe that was illustrative of Daniels's bellicosity:

As the fire raged Daniels spotted a Texas cowboy helping himself to some candy from a store. He let the sweet-toothed fellow off with a stern warning that if caught looting again he would be arrested and tossed into the calaboose. An hour later Daniels found the herder back, packing a six-shooter and making "bad talk." Following through on his threat, Daniels arrested and disarmed the man and marched him off to jail. The night was cold, and the rudely built jail had no stove. When two of the man's friends approached Daniels and offered to go his bond, Daniels said if they would put up fifty dollars to assure his appearance the next morning and take him home and keep him there all night he would be released. The men consented and appeared in the morning with the cowboy.

Daniels charged him with carrying concealed weapons and turned the money that had been put up for his bond over to the judge. The man pled guilty, and the judge fined him fifty dollars and costs, which he paid without a murmur, but immediately said: "Mr. Marshal, if you will lay off your gun I will show you how quick I can lick you," whereupon the marshal threw his six-shooter across the table to the judge and jumped over the railing after the Texan, whereupon ensued a hot fight in which the stove was thrown over and the furniture broken, while the judge stood on top of his table swinging the six-shooter and demanding peace in the courtroom.[19]

When the cowboy cried "uncle" and admitted he was whipped, Daniels let him up. Turning to the judge, Daniels entered a complaint against himself for disturbing the peace and was fined $25. He then entered an identical complaint against the Texan for the same offense. The judge fined him the same amount. "Afterward," said McClintock, "Mr. Daniels' fine was remitted."[20]

The fire wiped out an entire block of Front Street and gutted the store of Bob Wright. The distraught mayor, believing rumors that the blaze had been deliberately set by prohibitionists led by attorney Michael W. Sutton, his political enemy, went to Sutton's home at four in the morning and pumped four shots into the house. No one was injured, but charges of felonious assault were lodged against Wright, and Marshal Tilghman had the distasteful task of arresting his boss and benefactor. The charges were later dropped, but the affair presaged an end to the Wright administration.[21]

That winter Ben Daniels had an experience that must have been embarrassing to him, but proved to be even more painful to an innocent bystander. While he was spending a convivial hour in the Long Branch Saloon on the night of January 21, 1886, his six-shooter fell out of his pocket, struck the floor, discharged, and "a colored man was shot through the fleshy part of the leg."[22] As a pistol wielder of experience, Daniels should have been careful to keep the hammer of his six-shooter on an empty chamber to prevent just such an accident. But then he wasn't the first or only highly regarded gunfighter to make the same mistake. Ten years earlier the famous pistoleer Wyatt Earp had the same ignominious accident while serving on the police force of Wichita and almost shot himself, as the bullet passed through his coat. The incident was embarrassing enough for Wyatt that he requested Stuart Lake, his biographer, to omit the story from his book.[23]

Following the disastrous fire of November 1885 leading to Mayor Wright's attack on the house of Mike Sutton and its embarrassing repercussions, the political winds changed again in Dodge City and Ford County. Bill Tilghman, sensing the rising discontent of the electorate, resigned as city marshal in March 1886, a month before the election. The mayor and council accepted his resignation, but did not name a replacement pending the outcome of the voting.[24] For a month Ben Daniels was the chief law enforcement officer in the town and had every expectancy of being awarded the marshalship after the election. But the voters in April returned Ab Webster to the office of mayor, and Webster immediately relieved Daniels of his duties and appointed T. J. Tate city marshal and I. J. Collier assistant marshal.[25]

Seething with rage at this turn of events, Ben Daniels five days later shot a man dead.

Chapter 4
The Killing of Ed Julian
1886

As cowardly murder as was ever committed. . . . Daniels slipped up behind Julian and shot him dead.
—Charles Belson, 1902

Julian needed killing but not in that way.
—O. H. Simpson, 1926

SOME TIME BEFORE LOSING his lawman's job, Ben Daniels had taken over ownership of a combination saloon, gambling house, and dance hall in Dodge. The Green Front, as it was called, was on Locust Street, south of the railroad tracks that split the town from its northern, "respectable" side and the southern district devoted to recreational facilities for the cowboy trade. From the start the Green Front seemed to attract the rowdiest of the cowpunchers, all of whom were notorious for the exuberance of their celebrations after long, hard months on the trail.

Several businessmen with establishments neighboring the Green Front had protested to the owner about the noise emanating from the place. Most vociferous in his complaints was the proprietor of a nearby restaurant, a Civil War veteran and all-around tough character named J. E. ("Ed") Julian.

Seventeen months earlier, in November 1884, Bill Tilghman had arrested Julian when he got into a brouhaha with some Texas boys, knocking two of them to the floor before the others escaped and fired several shots through the windows of the restaurant. Julian was fined $10 and costs for his part in that altercation.[1]

On another occasion Sheriff Pat Sughrue, following a breakout from the county jail, found one of the escapees hiding under Julian's bed. He accused the restaurant proprietor of complicity in the escape, but Julian denied the charge, and in an apparent conciliatory gesture, invited Sughrue to have a drink on the house. But when Sughrue approached the counter, Julian pulled a gun from a shelf and threw down on the sheriff. As Julian was pulling the trigger, Sughrue swung his arm, knocking the gun upward. The bullet ripped through the brim and crown of his hat, and powder burned the side of his face. Julian cocked the gun again, but before he could pull the trigger Sughrue grabbed his hand, and the gun and the hammer fell on the sheriff's thumb.[2]

The feisty restaurant owner had friends in the new city administration that took the reins of Dodge City government in the spring of 1886, and when Daniels lost his position as assistant marshal, Julian used his connections to try and close the Green Front saloon by means of an injunction. As Heinie Schmidt, Dodge City newspaperman and historian, put it, this act triggered "one of the bitterest feuds and most wanton killings in the turbulent life of our city. The feud centered around two well known frontier characters, J. E. Julian and Ben Daniels, whose violent tempers and blazing guns wrote a black chapter in the city's history."[3]

Following a "stormy" session in court, "in which both men abused each other in vile language," a judge dismissed Julian's injunction request, but this only intensified the feud between the two men. Storekeeper Jacob C. ("Jakey") Bloom, certainly no friend of Daniels, said that "after the hearing of the case, the men quarreled again, while neither was armed. Both swore that they would shoot on sight."[4] This exchange was before witnesses, which, under the unwritten, but universally understood, Code of the West, gave each of the adversaries the right to kill the other without warning.

According to Schmidt, word quickly spread throughout Dodge that Julian had sworn to kill Daniels and two of his friends. When they heard of the threat, the three targeted men drew straws to see who would dispose of the dangerous Julian. Daniels drew the short straw. Stationing himself outside Julian's door, he called him out, shot him when he emerged, and pumped four more bullets into his body as it lay on the sidewalk.[5]

In 1926 veteran Dodge City physician O. H. Simpson wrote his version of the affair. He said the basis for the killing was more than a quarrel over the noisy Green Front clientele and that more than three men were committed to Julian's demise.

The custom of the day, said Dr. Simpson, was for a gambling house proprietor to pay 40 percent of his winnings to anyone who would steer a "sucker" to his game. Julian sent a "sucker" to the Green Front who quickly lost $400 to Daniels's game. But at payoff time Daniels gave Julian 40 percent of a much smaller sum. When Julian found out he had been cheated a quarrel resulted. Julian threatened to get out an injunction invoking the state prohibition law and closing Daniels's saloon. Up to then, the doctor said, the prohibition laws had been ignored in Dodge City.

"The 'gang' realized that Julian had the necessary nerve to back his threat and believed that once an injunction had been sworn out and served it would be the beginning of the end," so in an emergency council of war members the "gang" concluded that Julian must be die. "Nine broom straws were placed between the leaves of a book. One was shorter than the others. Each man took a straw and Daniels drew the short one and was automatically selected to perform the unthinkable task."

Simpson said he was an eye-witness to the drama's finale: "Daniels stationed himself in front of the first business house east of Julian's place and waited for an opportunity to act. Julian came out for some change and started [for the] hardware store. . . . Julian failed to see Daniels and the latter shot him three times in the back. Julian needed killing but not in that way."[6]

Editor Daniel M. Frost of the *Globe Live Stock Journal* said nothing of a drawing of straws, reporting only that on the evening of Thursday, April 15, at about six o'clock,

a shooting scrape took place . . . two doors west of Ed. Julian's restaurant, the latter gentleman being the victim in the affray, and his antagonist, ex-assistant city marshal Ben Daniels. Four shots were fired, all by Daniels, all of which took effect on Julian. While Julian was found to be armed, he, however, did not get to fire a shot; there is much diversity of opinion in the matter, some claiming it to have been a deliberate murder, while others assert it to have been justifiable. The evidence taken at the preliminary trial does not fully sustain either. It is a well known fact that that these parties had been bitter enemies to each other for a long time, and both had made threats against each other. . . . It appears that no one could have prevented this tragedy, not even our officers, no matter how vigilant they might have been, the bitterness that existed between them was almost certain to bring them together sooner or later, and as many predicted, that one or the other, or perhaps both, would be mortally wounded, if not killed outright.[7]

At the preliminary hearing before Justice of the Peace Harvey M. McGarry, bond of $5,000 was set for the appearance of Daniels at the next term of court, but at the insistence of County Attorney Benjamin F. Milton, who argued Daniels was a likely flight subject, McGarry raised the amount to $10,000.[8]

The trial of Ben Daniels, charged with the murder of Ed Julian, was held in November 1886 before Judge R. G. Cook.[9] James T. Whitelaw and L. L. Ady of Newton represented Daniels. Colonel Thomas S. Jones, Captain J. H. Finlay, and Benjamin F. Milton prosecuted. Witnesses to the shooting testified one after another that when Julian appeared on the street, Daniels, standing in front of his saloon, opened fire without warning. His first shot struck Julian in the back, and three more followed at close range as Julian lay on the ground. Although Daniels went at once to find the marshal and surrender, it seemed to be a clear case of premeditated murder. The only argument put forward by the defense lawyers was that Julian had made death threats against Daniels on previous occasions, and he "appeared to be reaching for a gun" when Daniels shot him. They put two men on the stand who swore they saw Julian reaching for a gun before Daniels shot him. But, said Dr. Simpson, both men were actually hunting jackrabbits outside town at the time of the killing. "I'll never forget," he added, "how pleased the gang was when the undertaker found that Julian had a gun underneath his shirt."[10]

The *Globe Live Stock Journal* reprinted Judge Cook's charge to the jury in its entirety and summed up the closing arguments of prosecution and defense.[11] The jury retired and deliberated the rest of that day and evening, and into the small hours of the next morning. The first ballot found the jurymen evenly divided, with six for conviction and six for acquittal, but gradually the tide turned as one by one those in favor of conviction changed their minds. At four in the morning they returned to the courtroom to announce a verdict of acquittal.[12]

As there was little doubt that a deliberate and cold-blooded murder had been committed, the deciding factor in the case seemed to be that unwritten Code of the West, and the unsavory and pugnacious reputation of the victim. Perhaps the jury concluded in the end that Ben Daniels had done the city a favor by eliminating Ed Julian and refused to punish him for that act.

Dodge City historian C. Robert Haywood has posited an additional explanation for the surprising verdict:

Daniels had been a popular peace officer and he represented the lawman's role in the minds of many citizens. Sheriffs, marshals and policemen were upholders of the right, right being interpreted as what was best for the community as a whole. Lawmen were killed and maimed in the streets of the cattle town as part of their job. By the same standards, law enforcers "in the line of duty" killed more individuals than any other western type. They were understood to be men who had to make quick and fatal judgments and consequently could be forgiven a certain amount of bloodletting indiscretion. In the courts of law they stood as people's champions. In defense of former Marshal Daniels, Whitelaw only had to show that Daniels had stood in danger of assault. Julian's past record made that a likely circumstance and Finlay was unable to overcome community prejudices. With predictable certainty, Finlay lost and Daniels went free.[13]

The killing of Ed Julian by Ben Daniels was very controversial at the time and remained so for many years afterward. Sixteen years later, when Daniels was nominated for an important federal law enforcement position, Senator Joseph R. Burton of Kansas queried Bob Wright about the case. "Was Ben Daniels justified and exonerated for killing a man at Dodge City some years ago?" he asked.

Wright answered by telegram: "Daniels was fully justified in killing Julian. It was a case of self-defense. He was acquitted by a fair and impartial jury." But then he added the gratuitous and erroneous comment, "Daniels was assistant marshal of Dodge City at the time."[14]

After reprinting this exchange from the pages of the *Kansas City Journal*, the editor of the *Dodge City Democrat* chipped in with his version of the story:

> Daniels came out of his saloon and called to [Julian] and before Julian could turn to face him, Daniels fired a shot at him, which entered his right side and came out over his heart. Julian fell backward but before he reached the sidewalk Daniels fired a second shot which also hit Julian. Daniels then walked up to Julian as he lay on his back and deliberately fired two more shots into his body. The editor of this paper was the first person to reach the body of Ed Julian which was yet quivering, and helped to carry it into his restaurant. The body was searched and no weapon of any kind was found on his person.
>
> Julian never expected to be killed as openly as it was done, his fear, if he had any, was that he would be shot at night out of some dark corner.
>
> The Daniels case was tried in the District Court of Ford County. In those days justice was very loose and it was a hard matter to get a jury who would convict one of the gang. Some of the witnesses who had testified at the Coroner's inquest were gone and with a jury fixed for the occasion Daniels was acquitted and he soon left Dodge City.
>
> Mr. A. B. Webster, who is now dead, was mayor of the city at the time of the killing, and had been elected on the Anti-Gang Citizen's ticket and had appointed as his marshal Thomas Tate. Mr. Julian had taken a prominent part in the election of Mayor Webster and was hated by the gang, of which Daniels was one of the leaders.
>
> Ed. Julian . . . was ordinarily quiet and a sober man and had gained the respect of the best people here. . . .
>
> Feeling ran high for a few days after the killing of Julian and threats of lynching were made by many. Mayor Webster expressed himself very forcibly against Daniels during that time as Julian was a personal friend of Mayor Webster.[15]

Chapter 5
The Daniels-Vaden Affair
1886

The grand jury investigated the killing of Vaden and refused to find a bill of indictment against Daniels. Sometime afterward, Daniels left the country and the last news I had of him he was in New Mexico and doing well.
—John Warren Hunter, 1912

Ben Daniels was never indicted for the killing of John Vaden. He went to Arizona and remained there. Later he became a very efficient officer of the law and made a good reputation for himself.
—J. Marvin Hunter, 1941

BEN DANIELS HAD BRUTALLY dispatched Ed Julian in Dodge City, all right, but, strangely, he has been credited with (or blamed for) another killing hundreds of miles away in Texas during the same time period.

The man he is said to have killed was named John W. Vaden, and, if ever a man needed killing, John W. Vaden qualified. He has been described accurately as "an undisputedly hard rascal, one with a sour and sorry reputation [who] once rode with the nit-wits, half-wits, and misfits making up Ben Bickerstaff's menagerie of Reconstruction era outlaws and racists and bushwackers."[1]

Vaden's faults were many and grievous, and in the end he got his due. His violent passing is only remembered today because of the name of the man who finally snuffed out his light. And therein lies a mystery.

Born in Alabama in 1849, John W. Vaden grew to manhood in northeast Texas and became caught up in the turbulence of the Reconstruction period after the Civil War. In 1868 he reportedly killed a man in cold blood in Hopkins County, Texas, for no reason other than the man's well-known allegiance to the Union during the great conflict. But the victim was very popular in the community, and Vaden barely escaped the wrath of an angry mob.[2] He has been identified as a member of the Ben Bickerstaff gang who murdered many blue-coated soldiers and African Americans during those tumultuous years.[3]

Concho County, Texas, sheep rancher John A. Loomis, for whom Vaden worked in later years, recalled his employee opening a pouch he carried and proudly displaying the dried ears of three blacks he said he had killed. Loomis accounted Vaden "a reckless, dangerous man when he was drinking."[4]

Vaden was tried for one of his murders in Hopkins County, but was acquitted, and prosecutors dropped other charges pending against him.[5]

Marriage to a thirteen-year-old bride in 1877 seemed to have had a positive effect on Vaden, and for a short period he turned from outlawry to law enforcement, doing service as a Texas Ranger and a justice of the peace.[6] He fathered three children, but even this added responsibility did not prevent him from returning to his lawless, bullying ways. At an election contest in Menardville, he brandished a rifle, threatening to kill anyone who wouldn't vote his way. John Warren Hunter, a resident of Menardville, remembered seeing him, in a fit of rage, smash the windows of the courtroom where the votes were counted because the election was not going his way. The county judge and deputy sheriff were present but did nothing, said Hunter, because "no one wanted to take the risk of being killed."[7]

Vaden was arrested twice in Somervell County, Texas. Charged with rustling, he was convicted, but an intimidated judge fined him only a dollar. He beat an aggravated assault case on a legal technicality.[8]

John Loomis described Vaden as "a former outlaw . . . , a tall, powerfully built fellow who never referred to his past" (except when displaying the ears of three of his victims apparently).[9] It was not long before Vaden's bullying, sadistic nature became apparent. "During our first year at the ranch," said Loomis,

a young half-witted fellow drifted in and I let him stay around the place because I felt sorry for him and he was able to do a few odd jobs for me.

For some reason John Vadon [sic] began riding him pretty hard and making fun of him. One day when I happened to be in the house the boy came in, picked up a shotgun and asked for some cartridges. I asked him what he was going to do with the gun and he calmly said he was going to the barn to kill John Vadon. I took the gun away from him and talked him into a different frame of mind. Then I hunted up Vadon and told him he had had a narrow escape from death, for the boy had just enough sense to do what he said he would. . . . I made up my mind right then to get rid of the Vadons.[10]

The last time Loomis saw Vaden he was acting as a sheriff's deputy at Eagle Pass in Maverick County, Texas. The rancher found it amusing "to think of what a lively enforcement officer the little town had secured for itself."[11]

In the summer of 1886 Vaden opened a saloon in Ballinger, a new railroad town in Runnels County, Texas. On August 6 he got drunk and went on a drunken tear. Grabbing a Winchester rifle, he shot out the lamps in his own saloon and then proceeded to the Palace saloon to continue his campaign of destruction. Frank Bornan, the Palace bartender, intercepted him, and the two engaged in a scrap in which the combatants suffered no more damage than bloodied noses and blackened eyes.[12] Lawman John Thomas Hill stepped in to break up the fight and went down with a bullet accidentally discharged from Vaden's rifle. A newspaper reported that Vaden, "being well filled with snake medicine, accidentally shot his friend, Tom Hill, through the left foot, which probably will necessitate amputation."[13] Hill lost more than his foot; he lost his life, for he died from complications resulting from the surgery.[14]

A sense of responsibility for the death of his friend, like marriage and fatherhood, did not moderate Vaden's disgraceful behavior. On October 7, 1886, he went on one of his drunken rampages at Fort McKavett, Menard County, and his violent career came to a sudden end when he attempted to bully a man who would not be bullied.

Vaden at the time was a deputy under Sheriff J. W. Mears.[15] A bartender in F. Mayer's saloon in Fort McKavett, a man named Ben Daniels, also held deputy sheriff papers.[16]

Up until that fateful Thursday the two deputies had apparently gotten along without difficulty; Daniels had been a guest for dinner in the Vaden home only the day earlier.[17] Later in the evening of that same day a number of men were gathered in Sam Wallick's store awaiting arrival of the Menardville mail hack. There they were regaled by John Vaden, well into his cups and unusually loquacious about his murderous history. A quarter century later John Warren Hunter vividly recalled that boastful recitation:

> *Vaden began by relating his experiences with the Mexicans while in the sheep business and the number he had killed. He reverted to the earlier years of his career and told of the men he had killed in north Texas; of the raids and adventures and scoutings he had engaged in while with Ben Biggerstaff [sic] and others. He recounted his achievements on the race course and in the gambling houses and told of the unfair methods he employed to win success. . . . He seemed not only boastful, but exultant, over the death of men whom he had slain.[18]*

D. T. Priest had known Vaden for years. After listening to this recital, he turned to Sam Wallick and muttered: "John Vaden is going to kill somebody tomorrow or else somebody will have to kill him. I know him better that any man in McKavett and you can mark my words. He is in one of his dangerous moods."[19]

Priest was absolutely correct. The next day Vaden got liquored up and went on one of his rampages.

John Warren Hunter witnessed the whole affair and in a newspaper account some years later recounted what transpired: "Vaden entered [Mayer's] saloon and began to abuse Daniels. He set about to smash furniture and to create a rough house generally. He threw a billiard ball at Daniels, which barely missed his head and crashed into a large mirror behind the bar. Bystanders interfered, and Vaden swore he would go home, only a few steps away, and get his gun." Finding that his wife had hidden the weapon,

> *Vaden picked up a set of brass knucks and put them in his pocket, saying something about what he would do to Daniels with these knucks. Meantime, Daniels had closed the saloon, buckled on his pistol, and went into an old corral at the back of Mayer's store, where, in order to avoid Vaden, he remained until three o'clock that evening.*

> Finding the saloon closed and Daniels gone, Vaden next went into Wallick's store and picked up a long shaft or wooden handle to which was attached an iron hook used in that day by merchants to take down tinware from overhead. With this and without provocation he began to thrust a Mexican, who had called to get his mail, and to tear his clothes. The Mexican said something about such treatment, whereupon Vaden flew into a rage and would have killed the fellow but for the intervention of Sam Wallick and others. He next turned his attention to the horses hitched . . . on the little square, and it seemed to afford him great amusement thrusting and lacerating these poor animals just to see them jump, kick and surge. . . . Groups of men were broken up, chased around and scattered with the same gusto and the same weapon. Brave fearless men there were in those groups, but they knew John Vaden and they did not care to kill him or take chances on being killed. . . .
>
> He had the boys jumping sideways for Sunday, when Ben Daniels came in view. . . . As he turned the corner of the building . . . , he found himself facing, and within twenty feet of Vaden, who at once made a dash at him as if to prod him with the sharp iron of his pole. Daniels drew his pistol and told him to desist, but Vaden gave no heed to the order and continued to advance, Daniels giving back and repeating his warnings. Finally Daniels opened fire, four shots going wild. The fifth struck Vaden about the collar bone and produced instant death.[20]

A special bulletin from Fort McKavett to the *San Angelo Standard Times* told the story much as Hunter described it twenty-six years later, adding only that after being hit, "Vaden walked about 20 yards and fell dead, [saying] 'Daniels, I would not have done you this way for anything.' Daniels mounted his horse and rode off."[21]

J. Marvin Hunter, son of John Warren, was only six years old at the time of the Vaden killing, but later wrote that this was the first time he had seen a man shot down, and it made a strong impression on him. Daniels, he said, made an effort to avoid the tragedy: "Knowing that Vaden was a dangerous character, Daniels closed the saloon and sought a hiding place in a side room of Sam Wallick's store, where he remained for a greater part of the day."

Vaden meanwhile had sharpened the point of the pole in a blacksmith shop, making it a formidable pike. "Then he went about town looking for Ben Daniels, swearing he would kill him on sight." Later in the afternoon,

Daniels, thinking all danger was past, stepped from his hiding place. Vaden, who was standing nearby with the pike in his hand, immediately spied him and made a rush at him. Daniels side-stepped and started across the street with Vaden following and cursing him, and, getting closer, he made another rush with the pike pole. Again Daniels jumped to one side and as Vaden went past him Daniels suddenly pulled a pistol and fired two shots, one of which struck Vaden in the side and passed through his body. He crumpled to the ground and died in a very few minutes. . . .

Ben Daniels, cool and composed, walked to a hitching rack in front of Wallick's store, where a number of saddled horses stood hitched. Looking these horses over, he selected the best of the lot, and asked some men who were standing on the store gallery whose horse it was, and when one of the men said it was his horse, Daniels remarked: "I am borrowing it for a few days. I will send it back to you within a week," and mounting the animal he rode off at a gallop. He never came back, but he did send the horse back to its owner within the time specified. His reason for flight was probably due to the fact that he feared some of Vaden's friends or relatives there would seek to avenge his death.[22]

John Warren Hunter said that "the killing of John Vaden created no excitement among the citizens. On the contrary, a deep sense of relief seemed to pervade every circle." Vaden was buried the next day in the Fort McKavett cemetery, and "besides his widow and two or three bright little children there were few if any mourners."[23] For many years only a plain stone marked his grave, but recently an engraved headstone has been erected. It reads:

JOHN W. VADEN
2-22-1849 10-7-1886
SHOT IN COLD BLOOD
WHILE UNARMED IN FT. MCKAVETT
BY THE GUNFIGHTER, BEN DANIELS[24]

An inquest into the shooting found that Vaden "came to his death by shots from a pistol in the hand of one Ben Daniels," but a grand jury refused to bring an indictment, and Daniels never stood trial for the killing.[25]

John W. Vaden's brutal and murderous career would be forgotten today but for the name of the man who brought it to an abrupt and inglorious end: Ben Daniels.

The first writer to give the story of this shooting any prominence was John Warren Hunter, who wrote it for the December 12, 1912, edition of the *San Angelo Standard*. He later reprinted it in the November 1924 edition of his magazine, *Frontier Times*. His son and cofounder of *Frontier Times*, J. Marvin Hunter, recounted his version of the story as he remembered seeing it unfold as a child and published it in the January 1941 issue of *Frontier Times*. Prior to all these publications, the subject of this book, Benjamin Franklin Daniels, had received a great deal of national press coverage in the 1902–1907 period, and yet the Hunters, father and son, newspapermen who kept well versed on the doings of important frontier characters like Daniels, never directly stated in their articles that the Ben Daniels of national prominence was the Ben

Daniels who shot and killed John Vaden. John Warren Hunter remarked that after the shooting, "Daniels left the country and the last news I had of him he was in New Mexico doing well."[26] His son, in his 1941 article, was a little more ambiguous, commenting that after killing Vaden, Daniels "went to Arizona and remained there. Later he became a very efficient officer of the law and made a good reputation for himself."[27]

Based on this vague remark and the identical names, later writers have leaped to the conclusion that the Ben Daniels who snuffed out John Vaden's light was the same Ben Daniels who rose from gunfighter notoriety to become a presidential favorite and law enforcement officer of high stature. For half a century Old West historians of eminence have embraced this notion.[28]

All these writers made the seemingly logical assumption that Benjamin Franklin Daniels, buffalo hunter, gunfighter, and noted lawman of Kansas, Colorado, and Arizona, was the same Ben Daniels who ended the violent career of John W. Vaden on October 7, 1886, at Fort McKavett, Texas. A review of the historical record for the relevant period, mid-1885 to mid-1887, reveals, however, that this was impossible.

It is clear that two men named Ben Daniels were active in the western frontier towns at this time. To differentiate, we'll call one "Kansas Ben Daniels" and the other "Texas Ben Daniels."

The activities of Kansas Ben Daniels for the critical period are well documented. We know from Dodge City newspaper reports that as early as June 1884 he was operating as an officer of the law in that town.[29] He was then appointed assistant city marshal on July 24. Reappointed on April 7, 1885, he held the position until April 10, 1886. During this twenty-one month period his peacekeeping activities were mentioned frequently in the pages of the town's newspapers.

By the spring of 1886 he was also operating his Green Front combination saloon, dance hall, and gambling facility in Dodge. This led to his fatal clash with Ed Julian on April 15, 1886. Free on bail, awaiting trial for the shooting of Julian, Daniels continued to operate his saloon until November 17, when he sold it as his trial was about to begin. Three days later, on November 20, he was acquitted in the Julian shooting case.[30]

During this period of Kansas Ben Daniels's well-documented activity in Dodge City, Texas Ben Daniels, hundreds of miles away in Menard County, Texas, was tending bar in Mayer's Fort McKavett saloon and serving as a "constable, or deputy," having been appointed to this post and sworn in on June 9, 1885.[31] Then, on April 5, 1886, five days before Kansas Ben Daniels's position as assistant marshal was terminated, Sheriff J. W. Mears appointed Texas Ben Daniels a deputy of Menard County.[32]

On October 7, 1886, while Kansas Ben Daniels was managing his Dodge City saloon and out on bond awaiting trial for the Julian killing, Texas Ben Daniels shot John W. Vaden to death at Fort McKavett. After a Menard County grand jury failed to indict him for this killing, Texas Ben Daniels remained for a time in Menard County; as late as April 1887 he accepted another deputy sheriff appointment offered by newly elected Sheriff R. R. Russell.[33] Then he disappears from the pages of history.

A review of the clearly established dates detailed above reveals that the actions of the Ben Daniels of Menard County, Texas, including his killing of the notorious John W. Vaden, cannot be ascribed to Benjamin Franklin Daniels of Dodge City. A man could not perform the duties of assistant city marshal and manage a combination saloon, dance hall, and gambling den in Dodge City, Kansas, while concurrently tending bar and serving as a deputy sheriff at a small town in central Texas, hundreds of miles away. It is also significant that when sixteen years later Ben Daniels, lawman of Kansas, Colorado, and Oklahoma, came under intense national scrutiny and criticism for his misdeeds, including his criminal record and the shooting of Ed Julian, there was not one mention of another killing in Menard County, Texas.

Chapter 6
Lawman of Lamar and the Battle of Cimarron
1887–1889

> *Ben Daniels, noted coward, was in the court room Wednesday trying to look brave. He was well loaded with "tangle foot" and succeeded fairly well.*
>
> —Ellis Garten of the *Cimarron Jacksonian*, June 28, 1889

IN FEBRUARY 1887 Ben Daniels rode the cars of the Santa Fe Railroad west from Dodge City to Lamar, a new community just over the Kansas line in Bent County, Colorado. He was accompanied by two of his lawman pals, Pat and Mike Sughrue.[1] Each of the twin Sughrue brothers held a sheriff's commission in Kansas, Pat in Ford County and Mike in Clark County. Exactly what their business was in Lamar is not known, but quite possibly they were checking out a tip that a fugitive for whom they held warrants was holed up in Lamar. Daniels, who never strayed far from law enforcement, was probably along as a special deputy to assist in an arrest if the sheriffs located their quarry. Whether they made an arrest is not known, but the Sughrues soon returned to Kansas. Daniels stayed on, however, when James Talbot, city marshal at Lamar, offered him a job as deputy.

Jim Talbot, described by a Bent County old-timer as "a big husky fellow who always seemed to be where trouble was," had been marshal at Granada, a wild end-of-track town that had been a favorite hangout of buffalo hunters a decade earlier, and Daniels and Talbot probably were acquainted from those days. Talbot was an experienced gunfighter, having killed at least one man in Granada and having been shot several times himself. He was, said the Granada pioneer, "the envy of every kid in the town."[2]

Lamar was not lacking in law enforcement officers. Daniels joined Talbot's other deputies, Ben Hines, M. D. Parmenter, and night watchman Bill Hinan, in the office of the city marshal. Other lawmen in town were a deputy sheriff and two constables. Over the next five months the work of Daniels so impressed city officials that when Talbot left for Kansas on business in July, they appointed the newcomer to the marshal's position in Talbot's absence. That same month Daniels was visited in Lamar by his old Dodge City boss, Bill Tilghman.[3]

Earlier in the year Daniels had given up bachelorhood at the age of thirty-four. For some time he had been carrying on a long-distance romance with a young woman named Annie Laura Ware, whom he always called "Laura." As the poet noted some years earlier, "In the spring when a young man's fancy lightly turns to thoughts of love,"[4] he traveled to Blue Springs, Missouri, where, on March 6, 1887, he and twenty-eight-year-old Laura were married.[5]

The newlyweds returned to Lamar, where Ben resumed his law enforcement duties. In January 1888 he accepted an appointment as a deputy sheriff of Bent County. The *Lamar Register* praised him for his law enforcement service in the town: "Ben never had an enemy so mean as to say he did not make a good officer."[6] Bent County old-timer O. G. Hess attested some years later that Daniels "was quite valuable in quieting the lawless element who frequented this county . . . ; in one case he saved the life of an inexperienced constable

In this wedding picture of Ben and Annie Daniels taken March 6, 1887, Ben, at the age of thirty-four, displays the paunch he would carry throughout his life. *Standing left to right:* the bride, Annie Laura Ware; the groom, Ben Daniels; and Annie's siblings, Susan and John T. Ware. *Seated:* the bride's parents, Belle and John Ware. Courtesy of the Arizona Historical Society.

against a notorious tough, one Milt Smith, in his fearless promptitude in the constable's behalf, and other instances I could tell of a similar kind, where his energy run down and run out law-breakers, some of whom were of the worst stripe."[7]

Next-door neighbors and particular friends of Ben Daniels and his wife were Mr. and Mrs. Jack Flood. Another lawman with a reputation for toughness, Jack Flood was reputed to be handy with his fists as well as with his guns. On one occasion he and a challenger were scheduled to meet in a boxing match, but at the last minute the other man thought better of it and failed to show up.[8] Daniels and Flood often teamed up. They spent ten days together as armed guards at an election in Gray County, Kansas, where an all-out county seat war was looming.[9]

Jack Flood's frequent out-of-town trips troubled his wife, an extremely jealous sort, who became convinced her husband was being unfaithful to her. Arguments between the Floods heightened and culminated in tragedy as Laura Daniels was to discover shockingly. When Jack left on another "business trip," his wife descended into a deep depression. Laura Daniels, after observing no movement at the home of her friend for several days, investigated and found the young woman dead, a suicide from arsenic poisoning.[10]

Another close friend of Daniels in Lamar was Bat Masterson, who lived in the town from July 1887 to the end of November of that year.[11] Although it has been suggested that Masterson was employed on one of the Lamar newspapers (three were published in the town during this period),[12] his career as a newspaperman lay years in the future. While maintaining a lively interest in the politics of Colorado and Kansas, his contributions to the press consisted entirely of fiery letters to the editor as he pursued his career as a professional gambler.

Later chroniclers of Lamar's early history have apparently confused Bat Masterson and Ben Daniels, the two noted Dodge City gunfighters residing in their midst. A Lamar publication celebrating the town's seventieth anniversary in 1957 related a story of how a "gun-toting pedestrian" met a group of twenty or more cowboys bent on carousal at a main intersection in Lamar and announced: "Glad to see you boys. Heard you were coming this way. Also heard about you roping outhouses and stove pipes at Vilas and Springfield and riding your horses into saloons and up to the bars. We have 16 saloons and two red light districts here and all the gambling you want. But there will be no gunplay or monkey-shines here or your horses will go back to your outfit with empty saddles." "My name," he stated to underline his orders, "is Bat Masterson." Evidently daunted by the name, the cowboys quieted down.[13]

Since there is no record that Masterson ever held a law enforcement position in Lamar, the intimidating officer in this anecdote was no doubt Ben Daniels, whose reputation as a quick-triggered gunfighter during this time and at this locale was almost as formidable as Masterson's.

The latter years of the 1880s saw a number of bitterly fought county seat battles in western Kansas, and Ben Daniels was destined to get caught up in the Gray County conflict, one of the most violent.

For promoters of the new towns springing up in western Kansas, capture of the seat of county government was believed to be the key to prosperity, rapid growth, and personal quick fortune. To assure success at the special elections held to select the county seat, the town boomers began importing gunfighters to protect friendly voters and intimidate the opposition. Dodge City, long a stomping ground of notorious gunmen, was a major source of supply. Soon former lawmen and renowned gun-wielders of the Cowboy Capital, men like Bat and Jim

LAWMAN OF LAMAR AND THE BATTLE OF CIMARRON   57

Masterson, Bill Tilghman, Fred Singer, Neal Brown, and Ben Daniels, found their services in demand at high wages.

In newly organized Gray County, just west of Dodge, the towns of Cimarron and Ingalls contended for the coveted county seat prize. Cimarron, first to be founded, centrally located within the county boundaries, and boasting of a larger population, seemed the logical choice. But when New York millionaire Asa T. Soule invested in an irrigation project in that part of Kansas, established a new town called Ingalls as his base of operations, and announced he wanted it as the county seat, the war was on.

In preparation for a special county seat election held on October 31, 1887, Soule's agents called on Bat Masterson, then living in Lamar, Colorado, but who still was considered a man of stature in Kansas business and political circles as well as the sporting element. He was asked to head up a force of gunfighters to look after the interests of the Ingalls faction at the polls. Masterson enlisted former Dodge City officers Tilghman, Singer, Brown, and Daniels, and several other less notable types, including gambler John Sheridan and "Eat-'Em-Up Jake" Murphy, described by one who knew him as "a part-time hired gun, rustler and outlaw."[14]

The editors of the two newspapers in Cimarron minced no words in denouncing the actions of Soule and his agents. George W. Benedict, editor of the *Gray County Echo*, complained that "the Ingalls gang" was importing "a crowd of toughs" to take over the polls and ensure an Ingalls victory.[15] His protests were echoed with even more vehemence by editor Ellis Garten of the *Cimarron Jacksonian*, who denounced "the hired henchmen of Ingalls" as "cutthroats and thieves, curs on our streets, deadly vipers."[16]

On election day the Ingalls gun-packing poll-watchers glared across at an equally dangerous-looking Cimarron crew

Ingalls, Kansas, about the time of the Gray County Seat War. Courtesy of the Kansas State Historical Society.

that included Dodge City gunmen "Conk" Jones, Frank Donohue, "Baldy" Scott, and Ed Prather.[17] Despite the presence of so many gunmen—or perhaps because of it—the election went off smoothly with no incident of violence. When the votes were counted, Cimarron claimed victory, but the Ingalls partisans, charging ballot box stuffing, got an injunction staying the count, and another election was ordered for November 7. This time Ingalls appeared to win in the balloting, but Cimarron took its fight to the courts.

Throughout the year 1888 lawyers for the contending towns waged the legal battle all the way to the Kansas Supreme Court. The justices, unable to sort out charges of fraud and skullduggery thrown from both sides, ordered yet another election. With gunmen from the two competing towns hovering near the polling places, the voting went off without incident on November 6, 1888, and again Ingalls appeared victorious, winning the county seat contest and the important offices of county clerk and sheriff.

But when A. T. Riley, county clerk pro tem at Cimarron, refused to turn over the county records to the newly elected county clerk, Newton F. Watson of Ingalls, Soule's lawyers secured a directive from the Kansas Supreme Court ordering the transfer of the records. Watson took the order to the new sheriff, Joseph N. "Buffalo Joe" Reynolds, and demanded his assistance in taking the records by force. Reynolds demurred, saying a gunshot wound received in a scrape with rustlers had put him out of commission.

Watson then appealed to Bill Tilghman, who agreed to take on the job on the promise of a $1,000 payment to be divided between those participating in the raid.[18] Bat Masterson had departed the area for Denver and was not available, but his brother Jim was in Dodge and signed on, as did other old warhorses Ben Daniels, Neal Brown, and Fred Singer.

Filling out the ranks were three youngbloods from Dodge, George W. Bolds, Edward D. ("Ed") Brooks, and William H. ("Billy") Allensworth. Watson, with his legal papers, would accompany these eight specially deputized Gray County sheriff's deputies, together with Ingalls coal dealer Charles Reicheldeffer, who would convey the raiders in one of his heavy wagons.

On the morning of Saturday, January 12, 1889, the wagon rolled into Cimarron and halted outside the red brick grocery store of Charles J. Dixon, where an upstairs storeroom was serving as a temporary courthouse and repository for the county records. While the other raiders stood guard outside, Watson, Masterson, Allensworth, and Singer entered the building and ran up the steps to the second floor. They held A. T. Riley and J. Q. ("Jake") Shoup, chairman of the board of county commissioners, the only ones in the room, at gunpoint and began removing the records. When Riley requested a receipt, he was told to "go to hell."[19]

Suddenly a shot rang out from below, and the gunfight that would make headlines across the country as the "Battle of Cimarron" was on. No one could be certain who fired that first shot, but aroused Cimarron citizens, recognizing that their improvised courthouse was under siege, took up arms and began shooting at the Ingalls invaders, who returned the fire. Although one newspaper later reported that as many as a thousand shots were fired during the battle,[20] the total was probably closer to forty.[21]

Cimarron resident J. W. ("Will") English was one of the first hit. He went down with a bullet through the heart and died within moments. Charles B. Riley, a Cimarron attorney, later said he personally witnessed the shooting of English and that Ben Daniels was the man who did the deed. He said he saw Daniels "with a large gun and side arms, [shoot] English, killing him instantly. There was no necessity of the killing and Daniels was not being shot at or otherwise molested, but fearing an uprising on the part of the Cimarron people . . . , this man shot one of the leading citizens."[22]

At least one newspaper report also identified Ben Daniels as the man who fired the fatal shot.[23]

Other Cimarron casualties were A. J. ("Jack") Bliss, with buckshot wounds in the neck, cheek, and shoulder; Ed Fairhurst, also struck in the chest by buckshot; and Henry Harrington, whose thumb was shot off. Bliss and Harrington were said to have been fatally wounded in early reports, but both survived.[24]

There were many near misses and close shaves. Two men standing in a doorway across the street from the courthouse saw a shotgun leveled in their direction and dropped to the ground just before a buckshot blast shattered the door. Two bullets ripped Frank Luther's derby hat from his head and left a lock of his hair lodged in the lining. A rifle slug passed through J. B. Munson's overcoat just below the shoulder blade without touching him.[25]

The Ingalls deputies in the street also came under intense fire. They took cover behind the wagon as Cimarron residents of both sexes, numbering as many as two hundred, grabbed weapons and opened up on the invaders.[26] "The bullets began to fly," said George Bolds, like "the frantic buzzing of angry bees." He "saw two women, each armed with a rifle, rush out a side street. . . . Horses were flailing at the air with their hooves, wounded ones were screaming in pain, men were shouting, the air was heavy with gunpowder."[27]

Charlie Reicheldeffer, the driver, struggled mightily to control his frightened horses until a bullet hit him in the hip. He tumbled backward into the wagon bed, struck his head, and was knocked unconscious. The team of horses, freed of rein, bolted, leaving the five Ingalls men—Tilghman, Daniels, Brown, Bolds, and Brooks—exposed to the Cimarron fire. They scrambled after the wagon, trying to reach the cover of an irrigation canal at the end of the street. In its account of the battle the *Cimarron Jacksonian* said the five "scattered like so many birds and run [*sic*] for their lives. [They] would stop at intervals and return fire at some of the citizens, who, crazed and enraged over the killing of [Will English], were 'pumping' lead into them thick and fast."[28]

Ed Brooks fell, shot through the body and both legs. Bill Tilghman hobbled along, having suffered some kind of leg injury.[29] Then Bolds was hit in the leg, went down, got up, and stumbled on a few yards before crashing to the ground again with a bullet in the head. Somehow he got to his feet and, using his Winchester as a crutch, made it to the canal.[30]

Reicheldeffer, meanwhile, had regained consciousness and control of his team of horses. Before passing out again he drove to the canal where Daniels and Brown, who had emerged from their gauntlet run unscathed, placed him in the back with the others and hightailed it for Ingalls.

Back in Cimarron, the four beleaguered Ingalls partisans in the courthouse—Watson, Masterson, Allensworth, and Singer—held out all day under sporadic fire from below. They piled office furniture against the door to prevent a storming of their sanctuary, and, according to one story, when shots were fired from the lower floor up through the ceiling, took refuge atop a steel safe. The Cimarron folks had the invaders trapped, but didn't know what to do with them.

Telegrams describing the fight flew over the wires of Kansas and beyond throughout that day. Another flurry of telegrams between Cimarron and Ingalls finally resulted in Cimarron's agreement to turn over the four besieged men to the custody of Sheriff Reynolds. About six o'clock that evening

Reynolds, Ford County Sheriff Hamilton Bell, and a large contingent of deputies arrived in Cimarron by special train. The residents of Cimarron stood silently and watched as Reynolds disarmed and arrested the four Ingalls fighters and took them under heavy guard to the train for return to Ingalls.[31]

Western Kansas had been plagued by a number of violent county seat battles necessitating the intervention of state militia to preserve order, so Governor John A. Martin was not at all surprised when he received a call for another intervention in Gray County. He dispatched General Murray Myers to the scene, with orders to quell the disturbance. Quickly assembling two companies of the Kansas National Guard, the general accompanied one unit by special train to the embattled county, arriving at two o'clock on the morning following the fight. The second company arrived shortly thereafter. The troops camped between the rival towns and remained two days, but when things quieted on the Gray County front, they returned to their homes on Tuesday, January 15.

While the fight over the seat of Gray County continued in the courts of Kansas, the men who had participated in the abortive attempt to transfer the records were released on their own recognizance to await any legal action against them. Then, on June 12, 1889, six months to the day after the Cimarron battle, Sheriff Reynolds, acting on a complaint filed by Harry Brice and Frank Luther of Cimarron, arrested Watson, Masterson, Singer, and Allensworth, the four men who had been besieged in the courthouse, as suspects in the murder of Will English. At a hearing before Justice of the Peace A. J. Evans, the four waived preliminary examination. Since Gray County had no jail, they were locked up briefly in the Dodge City calaboose before gaining release on bail. Sheriff Reynolds later arrested Daniels and Brown on the same charge. Bolds was living in Ingalls, but for reasons unexplained was not arrested. Tilghman and Brooks had left the country and could not be found. Reicheldeffer was never considered a fighting man, and his participation in the raid was ignored.[32]

"The trial of toughs for the murder of J. W. English will come up for hearing on Wednesday morning of next week," wrote editor Garten of the *Cimarron Jacksonian* with obvious relish. "Ben Daniels, noted coward, was in the court room Wednesday trying to look brave. He was well loaded with 'tangle foot' and succeeded fairly well. . . . Fred Singer, the would-be brave, paraded through the court room today with a gun strapped on him as large as a cannon. This is the way they run things in Ingalls."[33] When the case came to trial Garten wrote: "A 'square deal' is all we ask for and if we get it eight or ten of the most dastardly desperadoes that ever trod the free soil of Western Kansas will be birds behind the iron bars of prison cells in the Leavenworth State Penitentiary. If justice is meted out and the letter of the law complied with the result cannot be otherwise."[34]

Ben Daniels, whom he had called a "noted coward," seemed to be a particular object of Garten's contempt. Daniels reciprocated in kind, although not having a newspaper to express his feelings, he was left to voice his disdain for Garten in the saloons of Dodge and Ingalls. Hearing reports that Daniels was gunning for him, the editor responded in a lighthearted manner: "Ben Daniels, who has been trying for the past eight or ten years to establish a reputation as a 'bad man,' threatens our life. Like a cat we have seven lives, and he had better begin at once if he expects to get done before Christmas. Cold weather is a bad time for funerals and we don't want to put our friends to any trouble."[35]

On June 29 Gray County Attorney George W. Dunn filed a formal "information," charging the six men with the murder of English, but before the case came to trial he dropped the charges against Daniels and Brown. The latter move certainly dismayed editor Garten and Charles B. Riley, the Cimarron lawyer who claimed to have seen Daniels shoot English. Riley had been added to the prosecution team at the request of the widow of Will English and over the strong objections of J. T. Whitelaw, attorney for the defendants, who argued that Riley was an ardent Cimarron partisan who could not conduct an objective prosecution.

The trial of the four who had fought the daylong battle from the courthouse began on July 10 before Judge A. J. Abbott and lasted a week. At its conclusion a jury brought in a verdict of "not guilty," and the four men were released.[36]

Riley was infuriated at the outcome, and thirteen years later was still bitter. The jury, he said, was "intimidated by Daniels and others, who were present during the trial, and after the case was submitted to the jury they made such threats against members of the jury as to practically compel them to bring in a verdict of acquittal." He admitted that the four defendants were innocent of the crime. Daniels, he insisted, had committed the murder, but "was so firmly protected by his friends as to make it more than useless to attempt prosecution."[37]

Whether Ben Daniels was actually responsible for the death of English will never be known for certain. He was not tried for the killing, those who did stand trial were acquitted, and no one was ever convicted of the crime.

Chapter 7
Cripple Creek
1889–1898

Daniels' career at Dodge City gained him such fame as a gun player that when the new and noisy gold camp of Cripple Creek began to boom up, Sheriff Bowers of El Paso County, Col., sent for this famous revolver expert.
—*Dallas Morning News*, August 17, 1903

SEVERAL OF THE MEN involved in the Battle of Cimarron—Ben Daniels, Bill Tilghman, Neal Brown, and Jim Masterson—were caught up in another kind of excitement in the spring of 1889. On April 22, months before the murder case against the Ingalls raiders came to trial, all four of them, along with eight thousand other "boomers," took part in the land rush into Oklahoma Territory. They were at the town of Guthrie in its earliest days and served on the police force there.

In later years Daniels told friends and publicly claimed that he held the office of city marshal at Guthrie. Bat Masterson, believing him, would write that Ben was "marshal of Guthrie, Okla., [a] position he filled with honor to himself and fidelity to the public."[1] A newspaper ad endorsing Daniels for public office in 1916 said that "he was summoned to Oklahoma at the opening of that state and was appointed marshal of Guthrie at the same time holding the appointment of deputy United States marshal for the northern district of Oklahoma."² P. H. Pernot, another boomer, recalled that "Daniels was made a marshal by provisional government of the town and through his fearless execution of its orders, kept as good order as could be found in any Kansas town or best regulated mining camp."³

Actually, the Guthrie city records show that Daniels was on the police force of the town for several weeks in June 1889, but was not city marshal.⁴ It was the practice at the time to award deputy U.S. marshal commissions to local police officers, and Daniels, like his friends Tilghman, Masterson, and Brown, may have received a federal appointment in Guthrie, but it is clear that he held both offices only a short time.⁵

He accompanied Jim Masterson back to Dodge City in July for the trial of the four charged in the county seat war shooting death. When the trial was over, Masterson rejoined Tilghman and Brown in Oklahoma, where the three men remained as lawmen the rest of their lives.⁶ Daniels, meanwhile, went off in a different direction. He turned to the sporting world and the life of the professional gambler, keeping a low profile and his name out of the papers over the next few years.⁷

In the early 1890s W. R. Schnitger, the former deputy U.S. marshal who in 1879 and 1880 had conveyed him back and forth from the lockups of Cheyenne and Laramie, ran into Daniels and noted that he had "gained quite a reputation as a gambler and high-roller."⁸

In 1893 Daniels turned up in the new boomtown of Cripple Creek, Colorado. Following the discovery of gold on a ranch twenty miles from Colorado Springs in 1891, a mountain mining district burgeoned over the next decade to a dozen separate communities with a total population of fifty-five thousand. Cripple Creek, nestled in a valley on the southwest side of Pike's Peak, was the largest of the towns. It would grow by the turn of the century to a population of twenty-five thousand,

The proprietors, their burro mascot, and patrons, including a pair of lawmen, in the White House Saloon of Cripple Creek, Colorado, in the mid-1890s. Courtesy of the Denver Public Library Western Collection.

with eight newspapers, a stock exchange, three banks, sixteen churches, a streetcar line, and scores of clubs, lodges, union halls, gambling houses, and bordellos. During this boom period the doors of as many as seventy saloons remained open day and night. In spite of several devastating fires in the 1890s the town continued to grow and prosper.[9]

Daniels found Cripple Creek to be a sporting man's mecca. It was described by Edith Sessions Tupper, a popular writer of the period:

Three years ago Cripple Creek was a wilderness. . . . Today in the town and vicinity are at least 13,000 people. . . . As I write I look out on the main street. There is a wheel of fortune spinning on the corner yonder. Saloons, gambling rooms, faro banks and dancehouses are in full blast. . . . Here are the names of the prominent joints where the miners throw away their hard earned wages: The Ranch, Clipper, Gold Dollar, Big Dog, Black Bill's Topic, Novelty, Becker's and Dolan's and Mike Whelan's. Some of these are roulette and faro rooms, where green baized tables are presided over by smooth faced, cold eyed gentlemen, who turn the wheel or the cards with an immobility which any self respecting sphinx might do well to copy.[10]

Daniels found all of this excitement and growth to his liking and resolved to make his home in Cripple Creek and pursue his duel professions of gambling and law enforcement. But shortly after his arrival a serious labor dispute erupted that would grab the attention of the nation and involve everyone in Cripple Creek, including Ben Daniels.

Some of the wealthiest and most politically powerful men in Colorado, including J. J. Hagerman, David Moffat, Eben Smith, and Sam Strong, owned the 150 mines operating in the district in January 1894. With the collapse of silver values in the panic of 1893, the demand for gold increased, and the mine owners, in an effort to get more production, announced that beginning in February the standard workday would be lengthened from eight to ten hours. Daily wages, however, would remain at three dollars. The newly formed Western Federation of Miners, of course, furiously rejected this decree, and a strike was called. It began on February 7, 1894, and dragged on for five months.[11]

As a historian of the strike has observed:

Cripple Creek was not the ordinary mining camp, but a newly settled, essentially frontier, district. The men were not of the mining populations familiar to the coal fields—foreign born, ignorant, used to obedience, easily cowed—but of the characteristic frontiersman type, come not so much to find work as to seek a fortune. Rough, ready, fearless, used to shifting for themselves; shrewd, full of expedients; reckless, ready to cast everything on a single die; they were not the kind of men to be caught napping, or to be turned from their purpose until every possible resource had been tried. They would act quickly, shrewdly, and effectively, withal straightforwardly, but with small respect for authority, and none too much for law. Nor were the mine owners generally of the usual capitalistic type. The majority of them were as much frontiersmen as the miners themselves, men who had gained their wealth by successful prospecting, or be lucky buying in the early days of the camp. It was Greek against Greek, similar ideas and strong methods on both sides.[12]

M. F. ("Frank") Bowers, the sheriff of El Paso County of which the district was then a part, was described in a paper of this period as "a typical westerner . . . , of ordinary height, very spare, with sharp thin features [and] a countenance indicative of resolution and firmness."[13] He was also without question the tool of the owners. At their behest he began recruiting deputies, fighting men of demonstrated ability, in anticipation of rough days ahead and likely gunplay.

Daniels was signed up, as were other "knights of the trigger," as a newspaper termed them.[14] Among the new deputies were Frank ("Kid") Wallace, Bob Taylor, and the Crumley brothers—Sherman, Grant, and Newt. All were hard cases, veterans of a dozen boom camps. Bob Taylor was reputed to have killed at least nine men in Missouri, Arkansas, Indian Territory, New Mexico, and Colorado.[15]

On March 16 a group of armed strikers ambushed six of Bowers's deputies, who were unidentified in newspaper reports but probably included the "knights of the trigger" recently recruited. There was a fistfight, shots were fired, and two deputies were injured. Two days later Sheriff Bowers wired the Colorado governor for state militia to help him stem the violence.[16]

Governor David H. Waite, with his wild, flowing white mane and beard, looked like an Old Testament prophet who had survived a strike of lightning. But he was a Populist and a former miner who was sympathetic to the strikers' cause. In 1892, with his public and ill-advised pronouncement: "It is infinitely better that blood should flow to our horses' bridles than our national liberties should be destroyed," he had permanently acquired the epithet "Old Bloody Bridles Waite."[17]

Reluctantly Waite acceded to the sheriff's urgent request and dispatched a considerable militia force under the command of Adjutant General Thomas J. Tarsney—the entire first regiment of the state militia, a portion of the second, a unit of light artillery, and the signal corps—a total of three hundred militiamen, to Cripple Creek. When Tarsney reported back that Bowers's fears were overblown and there was no fighting between the entrenched forces, the governor, furious, immediately recalled his troops on March 20 and castigated the sheriff for misleading him.[18]

For the next two months sensational telegraphic bulletins, most of them untrue, continued to fill the pages of the nation's newspapers:

An explosion at one of the mines, set off by warring parties, had killed eleven and perhaps more.[19]

The strikers had purchased a "rifled cannon," which was on its way to the scene.[20]

Strikers were planning an attack on the deputies in an effort to capture the deputies' "Napoleon," a twelve-pound field piece.[21]

The deputies were prepared to resist the assault with their "Napoleon" and two Gatling guns.[22]

A special train with 150 armed deputies arrived at the town of Victor, only to be met by four hundred strikers, and a gun battle ensued.[23]

Additional rifles and revolvers were arriving daily. One hundred thousand rounds of ammunition shipped from Chicago were expected momentarily.[24]

The entire district was in "a reign of terror," and General W. J. Palmer of the Denver & Rio Grande Railroad, who had a well-known record as a fighter, was taking command of the army of deputies, with General Charles Adams in charge of the cavalry.[25]

Actually there were no life-threatening confrontations during this period, only minor clashes, brawls, and stone-throwing incidents between striking miners and scabs hired by the owners. But store and warehouse owners reported break-ins and the theft of guns and ammunition, which did not bode well for the future.

Both sides made preparations for battle. The mine owners, determined to break the strike, imported hundreds of non-union workers and told Bowers they would subsidize the employment of a hundred or more additional deputies to protect them. Bowers went to Denver and began recruiting ex-policemen and ex-firefighters who hated Waite for defying them in the Denver City Hall War only two months earlier.[26] Scottish-born John Calderwood, the union president, turned over defensive operations to Junius J. Johnson, a miner who had some education in military tactics, having attended West Point for three years before being dismissed for hazing. Johnson and his second-in-command, a tough ex-convict calling himself "Jack Smith," established a camp atop Bull Hill, overlooking the town of Altman, and directed the building of fortifications. They stocked a commissary and drilled the strikers in maneuvers.[27]

On May 24 strikers seized the Strong mine on Battle Mountain above the town of Victor. The next day a force of 125 deputy sheriffs rolled in on a Florence & Cripple Creek train, set up a camp at the base of Bull Hill, and then began an advance on the strikers at Altman. They had no sooner started than "the whole sky over and around the Victor town seemed to explode," as the shaft house at the Strong mine flew three hundred feet in the air. The blast was greeted at Bull Hill, "where wild cheering blended with the echoes." Moments later the Strong steam boiler blew, showering the attackers with debris: "timbers, hunks of iron, pieces of cable, and iron wheels of assorted sizes. The deputies, tough men though they might be, were appalled at such a welcome. They clambered back on the freight cars and the train backed out of the sight of Bull Hill."[28]

In celebration of their victory, the strikers broke into liquor warehouses and stole whiskey enough to inebriate an army. "By early afternoon the half dozen towns in the Cripple Creek district were so many bedlams of drunken men." At the head of a drunken crew "General" Jack Smith, intent on blowing up "every mine shaft and every mine superintendent's house in the district," loaded two wagons with dynamite.

Commander Johnson prevented this worse than idiotic expedition from leaving camp. He ordered Smith to sober up, and then, if he felt like doing something for the cause, to take his gang and chase the retreating Denver army out of the district.

Smith sobered up—a little—then led his mob to Victor town. There, about midnight, they stole a work train. . . . Somewhere in the night out of Victor they caught up with the Denver gang and fought a bloody battle among the boulders. One deputy was killed, and one striker.[29]

The incident convinced the mine owners that even more force was required. On May 26 they met with Bowers and informed him that they would provide sufficient funds to employ twelve hundred more deputies. Bowers departed to begin recruitment throughout the state.

When Governor Waite heard of this new development, he interceded again. On May 27 he issued a proclamation ordering the strikers at Bull Hill to disband. He declared the owners' army of deputies illegal and ordered it to disband as well. Going to Cripple Creek the following day, he visited with the miners, who authorized him to negotiate on their behalf.[30]

On May 30 Waite and Calderwood, representing the strikers, met with mine owners Hagerman and Moffat on the campus of Colorado College at Colorado Springs. A crowd of local citizens, who blamed the governor and union president for the Cripple Creek violence, stormed the building, dragging lynch ropes. Waite and Calderwood were hurried out a rear door and taken by cab to the governor's waiting train, barely escaping the mob's wrath.[31]

CRIPPLE CREEK   75

An agreement to end the strike was reached on June 4, but it was soon apparent that Sheriff Bowers could not control his army. On June 5 a contingent of deputies, including Ben Daniels, moved into Altman and made preparations to storm Bull Hill once more. In an effort to keep the governor ignorant of their offensive, they cut telegraph and telephone lines and locked up reporters. But Waite learned of their plans and again dispatched militia under command of General E. J. Brooks to the battleground.

General Brooks moved troops to the foot of Bull Hill on June 6. As gunfire broke out,[32] Sheriff Bowers, County Commissioner W. S. Boynton, and General Brooks argued over the next course of action. At this juncture, according to a newspaper report, Ben Daniels took advantage of the leaders' indecision to charge the miners:

Daniels showed his nerve during the strike in a way that recalled the Dodge City days. The strikers, headed by veterans of the labor wars of the Couer d' Alenes, under the command of the mysterious "General" Johnson and Jack Smith, were entrenched behind earthworks on Bull Hill. They had cannon and their position was considered impregnable.[33] *But Daniels one morning organized a company of mounted deputies and started out with the avowed purpose of capturing and hanging "General" Johnson. Just at this time the National Guard . . . flung itself between Daniels and the strikers and prevented a conflict which would have been nothing short of a battle on a large scale.*[34]

Brooks had been alerted to Daniels's attack by the warning whistle blown by the miners at the Victor mine. He stopped the advance and directed his troops to occupy fortifications atop Bull Hill. The strikers did not resist the militiamen. By the end of that day Brooks had taken control of Cripple Creek, and his troops began the process of rounding up and detaining Bowers's deputies.³⁵ When the mine owners refused to disband their army, Waite threatened to impose martial law and keep the militia for a month. Faced with paying twelve hundred mercenaries to do nothing, the owners agreed to discharge them.

By June 11 Calderwood and three hundred miners were under arrest. Four were later convicted but quickly pardoned.³⁶ The rest of the miners returned to work, and most of Bowers's mercenaries departed. Newspapers reported that on the way out there was one last skirmish between the factions: "Yesterday afternoon the party of deputies who were discharged started for home [and] were fired upon by a party of miners. . . . The deputies took refuge behind rocks and general firing followed. Two hundred shots were fired, but no one was injured."³⁷

Sheriff Bowers came in for much criticism in the Colorado press for his employment of "hired thugs" to confront the strikers. "One can hardly resist the conclusion that Sheriff Bowers of El Paso County is at best a very poor stick," opined the *Greeley Tribune*. "The miners were in the wrong from the first in resorting to violence to secure their ends, but Sheriff Bowers created sympathy for them when he came up to Denver and enlisted the services of paid brigands to help him enforce the law."³⁸

The *Boulder Daily Camera* reprinted an editorial headed "LAWLESS BOGUS DEPUTIES" that appeared in the *Denver Republican*. Bowers had hired "hoboes and hoodlums, the scalawag element," it said. "Some of the deputies employed by Sheriff Bowers of El Paso county seem to be, if anything, more lawless than the strikers on Bull mountain. . . . Large numbers of them were raked from the slums of this city, and some of them would be more at home in a chain gang than in a sheriff's posse."³⁹

And again quoting the Denver paper in another issue:

*The conduct of the deputies at Cripple Creek has been outrageous. There is no excuse for it, and Sheriff Bowers has shown himself to be either unwilling or unable to control the men under him. Public sympathy has turned against the sheriff's forces, and incalculable harm has been done what was looked upon as the party of law and order before these mercenaries began the high-handed conduct which has characterized them ever since the miners laid down their arms. Instead of preserving the peace the deputies are the cause of trouble and discord.*⁴⁰

Not all of Bowers's deputies left Cripple Creek, of course. Those the sheriff had originally enlisted—Ben Daniels, Kid Wallace, Bob Taylor, and the Crumley brothers—were residents of the town before the strike and had business interests there, primarily in the gambling and saloon industries.

On the night of June 22 seven masked men burst into the quarters of Adjutant General Thomas J. Tarsney, who had remained in Cripple Creek to act as counsel for the arrested miners. The intruders then committed what was universally denounced as an "outrage." They tarred and feathered the general, conveyed him in a hack twenty-five miles out of town, and left him there. Governor Waite immediately posted a $1,000 reward for the arrest and conviction of the perpetrators of the crime, and Bowers and his remaining deputies immediately fell under suspicion.⁴¹

In August a man named Joe R. Wilson, a former Bowers deputy, was arrested in Missouri and confessed to taking part in the assault. Bowers, he said, was the leader, and the sheriff even "released a murderer from jail to assist in the outrage." He said Bowers provided the tar, and a Mrs. Quackenbush "ripped open a pillow to provide the feathers." Others involved were an officer and enlisted man from the militia and two of the Crumley brothers.[42] Bob Taylor was also accused later. The affair ended in what many papers called a farce. A grand jury, after hearing evidence against fifteen of the accused, including Sherman Crumley and Bob Taylor (but not Ben Daniels), failed to hand down indictments, and a judge complied with the district attorney's request to drop the charges.[43]

Some of the men Daniels had worked with during the strike could not stay out of trouble, however. The following spring Bob Taylor, Sherm Crumley, Kid Wallace, and two others, Lou Vannick and James Gibson, were arrested and charged with robbery of a Florence & Cripple Creek train on the night of March 23, 1895. At a preliminary hearing on April 17 Taylor and Gibson were held for the grand jury on bonds of $10,000 each. The others were discharged for lack of evidence, but were rearrested and charged again in May.[44] A trial in July resulted in disagreement by the jury members as to the guilt of the various defendants, and apparently they were never retried.[45]

Most of this crowd shook the dust of Cripple Creek from their boots after this episode, but Ben Daniels and the Crumley brothers stayed on to contribute to the colorful history of the town.

Like Ben Daniels, the Crumleys, sons of a Presbyterian minister, were saloon men and professional gamblers, and, like Daniels, they moved right into Cripple Creek's sporting milieu. Grant Crumley oversaw the roulette wheel at Johnny Nolan's gambling house before opening his own saloon, the Newport, and prospered. He sometimes made the society columns of the local papers, as in July 1899 when the *Cripple*

Creek Morning Times announced: "Grant Crumley early this morning entertained a number of his friends at the Apex. It was a watermelon social and the melons were full of champagne."[46]

About the same time brother Grant was treating his pals to champagne-laced melons, Sherm, along with a cohort named Aaron Purdy, was hauled in and charged with the theft of a lot of giant powder from a hardware store.[47] They beat that rap, and apparently no one ever found out if Crumley and Purdy intended to use the explosive in a train robbery or some other nefarious scheme.

In August 1901 both brothers made the news when on a single night Sherm was shot and wounded and Grant killed a man in an apparently unrelated incident. In a gambling dispute a man named William Tromback shot Sherm in the thigh, though the wound was not serious.[48] A few hours later Grant shot and killed another man in another argument over a bet. This shooting grabbed the attention of the nation's press, not only because a fatality resulted but also because the victim was an important personage in Cripple Creek, millionaire mine owner Sam Strong.[49]

The shooting occurred about six o'clock on the morning of August 22 in Grant Crumley's Newport saloon and gambling house. Strong, accompanied by his father-in-law, John B. Neville; his private secretary, Clarence A. Fitch; and attorney Charles Prentice, had been drinking and gambling in the resort all night. According to witnesses to the shooting, Neville and Crumley got into a heated argument, and Strong, thinking his father-in-law in danger, pulled a "thirty-two hammerless gun." Crumley jerked a sawed-off shotgun from behind the bar and blasted the mining man full in the face, blowing the top of his head off. Despite this horrendous wound, Strong's heart continued to beat for a full hour and a half before finally stopping. Crumley submitted to arrest by an officer and was held in the city jail without bail. Tried in November 1901, he was acquitted by a jury after four hours of deliberation.[50]

Ben Daniels, who had sided with these tough characters during the strike, managed to avoid law problems, concentrating instead on mining speculation, something that would be a major interest for him the rest of his life. While his wife became active in community activities, he joined the Elks lodge and took employment as both a deputy sheriff and night marshal of West Cripple Creek. When several of the various camps merged to form the city of Cripple Creek, he was promoted to police captain. All the while he speculated in mining ventures. The future looked bright, both for the mushrooming community and Ben and Laura Daniels.

Then calamity struck. On December 7, 1897, the Cripple Creek fire chief, a man named Allen, brought a series of charges against Daniels before the city council. Quick to jump on this was a man who had waited years to take his revenge against Daniels. Jacob C. ("Jakey") Bloom, the candy and cigar store owner who had charged Daniels with physically abusing him back in Dodge City, now had a jewelry business in Cripple Creek, sat on the city council as an alderman from the third ward, and led the attack on the police captain.[51]

There were twelve allegations in all, the most serious of which was that Daniels had been implicated in a robbery at the National Hotel the previous October. He was also accused of false imprisonment and extortion of prisoners. The charge was made that he "consistently and continually" failed to discharge his duties and was "a person wholly disqualified for holding any office whatever upon the police force."[52]

At a hearing on December 10 the city council heard testimony supporting the charges. The most fascinating allegation concerned a "certain poker table devised for cheating at cards" that had reportedly been stolen from the swank establishment of gambling kingpin Johnny Nolon. The table ended up in the possession of Police Captain Ben Daniels, who, when asked how he acquired it, said that he had found it in an abandoned mine. Clabe Jones, a former officer under Daniels, testified:

I had heard of this poker table and I wanted to get possession of it. I was on the police force at the time and had several conferences with Mr. Daniels about buying the table; he offered it to me for $100, then $75, and then said I could have it for the amount of my warrant. I declined this proposition. He then said he would give me the pattern for the table for $50. This table had a peculiar contrivance; there were two pegs under the table, by touching one of these pegs with the knee, up would come the concealed cards and down goes the other cards. [This produced laughter in the council chambers.] I saw the table at Mr. Daniels' house. He showed me how it worked. I tried it and it worked right enough for me [more laughter]. Yes, it was highly satisfactory [still more laughter] and I thought it was worth the money.

Under cross-examination, Jones expounded on the beauties of that remarkable table. It was, he said, "a peculiar device for winning at cards. I did not see how it was possible for any man to lose with that table [more mirth from the councilmen]." "Yes, I always did have a hankering for that table. I was trying to buy it before it was stolen."[53]

Daniels, of course, vehemently denied the allegations. The council voted to suspend Daniels pending further investigation,[54] but seemed to have no great desire to pursue the matter further, especially when Daniels told them he was quitting the town to join the Klondike gold rush. As it turned out, he did not go to Alaska, but, impelled by dramatic far-off events a few months later, left Cripple Creek to head off in the exact opposite direction.

Chapter 8
Rough Rider
1898

Ben Daniels [is] Cripple Creek's contribution to "Teddy's Terrors." . . . The regiment of rough riders will have no more efficient man. A man utterly devoid of fear, unexcelled as a horseman, a dead shot with rifle or revolver, trained by years of hard work in the saddle and on the trail of marauding Indians, he will make his mark even among the thousand men chosen for just such attributes.
—Cripple Creek Morning Times, May 17, 1898

I speedily found that [Benjamin Franklin Daniels] was one of the men in whom I could place entire trust and whom I could use in the most hazardous and responsible service. A more gallant, more loyal and more trustworthy soldier never wore the United States uniform.
—Theodore Roosevelt, December 8, 1905

ON FEBRUARY 15, 1898, the American warship USS *Maine* blew up in Havana harbor in Cuba. Led by newspaper publisher William Randolph Hearst, the nation was swept up in a wave of patriotic war fervor unprecedented in American history, culminating on April 25 in a declaration of war on Spain. It would be a popular conflict, quickly and decisively won, with relatively few casualties, and it would vault into national prominence a hitherto obscure forty-year-old politician whose stone visage in a later day would adorn a mountain in South Dakota along with those of George Washington, Thomas Jefferson, and Abraham Lincoln. He was also destined to play a major role in the future of Ben Daniels.

Theodore Roosevelt was a native New Yorker and Harvard graduate who had gone west in the 1880s to experience the vigorous life of a cattle rancher in Dakota Territory and regain his failing health. Revitalized, and ever afterward a staunch proponent of the vigorous life, he had returned east to pursue his political career, but never forgot the tough, hard-bitten western characters he had come to know and admire.

When the war with Spain broke out Roosevelt held the position of assistant secretary of the navy, but he quickly resigned to take the lead in forming a regiment of western fighting men to be called the U.S. First Volunteer Cavalry. Offered command of the unit, he declined, but accepted a commission as lieutenant colonel under an experienced warrior, Colonel Leonard Wood. But from the first it was Roosevelt who was identified with the regiment, which soon came to be known far and wide as "Teddy's Rough Riders."[1]

Ben Daniels was forty-five years old in the spring of 1898, a little long in the tooth for a combat cavalryman, but this did not deter him from rushing off to offer his services to his country by joining the "Rough Riders." That decision led to association with several influential men who would have a profound effect on the rest of his life. Gaining the respect and friendship of the future president of the United States, Theodore Roosevelt, was of course the most important benefit Daniels derived from his war experience, but it helped also that he came to be known and admired by other Rough Riders, principally Alexander O. Brodie and James H. McClintock.

Brodie was a West Point graduate who went to Arizona to fight in the Apache Indian wars and was one of General George Crook's most highly regarded scouts. He resigned from the army in 1877 to pursue cattle interests in Kansas and mining investments in the Dakota and Arizona territories. Arizona governor John N. Irwin in 1891 appointed him first commander of the National Guard of the territory. When the Rough Rider regiment was formed in 1898, he became second-in-command to Colonel Roosevelt, with the rank of major. He was wounded at the Battle of Las Guasimas and later promoted to lieutenant colonel. One of the first political appointments Roosevelt made after becoming president was awarding Alexander Brodie the office of Arizona governor.[2]

As governor, Brodie was in a position to advance the career of Ben Daniels, another Rough Rider he and Roosevelt both admired, and he did.

James Harvey McClintock was a native Californian who went to Arizona in 1879 and gained some military experience working in the adjutant general's office at Fort Whipple during the later stages of the Geronimo campaign before entering into his lifelong profession of journalism. Enlisting in the First Volunteer Cavalry Regiment in 1898, he was given a captaincy and command of B Troop. Like Brodie, he was wounded at Las Guasimas and thereafter walked with a limp. After becoming governor of Arizona in 1902 Brodie made McClintock a colonel in the First National Guard Infantry. In later years McClintock was appointed state historian and wrote a monumental three-volume history of the state in which he extolled his friend and fellow Rough Rider, Ben Daniels.[3]

When it became known in Cripple Creek in May 1898 that Daniels was going off to fight in Cuba, the town's newspapers, having completely forgotten his recent embarrassment, apparently, hailed him and his patriotism. Under a headline praising him as a man with a "record for daring" who was "not afraid of anything that walks," the *Morning Times* said:

> Ben Daniels left last night for San Antonio, Tex. He goes as Cripple Creek's contribution to "Teddy's Terrors," the cowboy regiment raised by Wood and Roosevelt for service in Texas. Ben goes as a scout.
>
> Ben has a record. To those who do not know him well, Ben Daniels is a cold, passionless, secretive man, who goes about his business of thief-catching as relentless as a blood hound, and hardly less certain of results.
>
> But to the half dozen men in camp who know him in reality, he is a man who never deserted a friend, and would go to any lengths to serve one. Likewise he never forgets an enemy. To the few who have ever seen an exhibition of his skill, he is known as a wonderful marksman. The old-fashioned, single-action Colt is his favorite arm, and few men in the West are more expert with it. With either hand he can shoot with marvelous rapidity and no less marvelous aim. He has had a long and varied experience in the west. He was marshal at Dodge City when that town was known as the wildest and woolliest of a wild and woolly west and was in those days a close companion of Bat Masterson. He has been tried for years as a scout on the frontier against Indians, and a pursuer of cattle rustlers. He was in Oklahoma during the rush from the border. He also held the position of marshal of Lamar, in this state, in the boom days of that town.
>
> He came to Cripple Creek in the early days, and before consolidation was night marshal of West Cripple Creek, and was afterward captain of police of the city of Cripple Creek, resigning last winter to go to Alaska. He afterward changed his mind and did not go.
>
> Ben has had many an encounter and many a hair-breadth escape—and many a harrower—in his career. Indians, cattle thieves, and outlaws of every class have attempted his life, and it is said that he has sent no less than seventeen of them to their accounting.
>
> In person Daniels is of giant proportions. Over six feet tall, he has the black hair and keen, piercing black eye of an Indian, and the

same aquiline nose of that race. His strength is enormous, and his nerves of steel.

The regiment of rough riders will have no more efficient man. A man utterly devoid of fear, unexcelled as a horseman, a dead shot with rifle or revolver, trained by years of hard work in the saddle and on the trail of marauding Indians, he will make his mark even among the thousand men chosen for just such attributes.[4]

At San Antonio on May 21 Daniels enlisted in K Troop, First Volunteer Cavalry, giving his residence as Colorado Springs, Colorado.[5] Other enlistees from the Cripple Creek–Colorado Springs area included Walter Cash, Alonzo Bainter, Charles Wilson, William Underwood, Horace K. Devereaux, who would be awarded an officer's commission in K Troop, and, most notably, Sherman Bell, who had served with Daniels as a sheriff's deputy during the miners' strike of 1894 and had later been a deputy under Daniels on the Cripple Creek police force.[6]

It was later reported that Roosevelt offered Daniels a commission as captain in the regiment, but he refused.[7] This hardly seems likely, as Daniels had only three known previous interactions with the military, and two of the three were negative in nature. He may have served briefly as a civilian scout for an army detachment in the Yellow House Indian engagement back in 1877. Soon after that he was caught stealing government mules from an army post and reportedly shot one or more soldiers in making his escape. As one of a force of strikebreaking mercenaries during the Cripple Creek labor troubles of 1894, he had acted in opposition to the Colorado militia. Daniels was recruited, performed his service, and was mustered out of the Rough Rider regiment as a private.

But he did get the attention of Theodore Roosevelt, who, in his book on the campaign in Cuba published a year after the conflict, remarked on the recruit with the damaged right earlobe:

> *Some of the best recruits came from Colorado. One, a very large, hawk-eyed man, Benjamin Franklin Daniels, had been Marshal of Dodge City when that pleasing town was probably the toughest abode of civilized man to be found anywhere on the continent. In the course of the exercise of his rather lurid functions as peace officer he had lost half of one ear—"bitten off." It was explained to me.*
>
> *Naturally, he viewed the dangers of battle with philosophical calm. Such a man was, in reality, a veteran even in his first fight, and a tower of strength to the recruits in his part of the line.*[8]

Roosevelt seemed intrigued by that damaged ear. In a magazine article written some years later he quoted this exchange he had with Daniels about it:

"Now, Ben, how did you lose that half of your ear?"

"Well, Colonel, it was bit off."

"How did it happen, Ben?"

"Well, you see, I was sent to arrest a gentleman. And him and me mixed it up, and he bit off my ear."

"What did you do to the gentleman, Ben?" Roosevelt asked.

"Well, Colonel, we broke about even," Daniels admitted.

Roosevelt said he then "forbore to inquire what variety of mayhem he had committed on the 'gentleman.'"[9]

Daniels, with his varied experience on the plains and in the mountains of the West, typified the type of fighting man Roosevelt admired and was eager to lead. He said that it was these kind of men who "made up the bulk of the regiment and gave it its peculiar character." Drawn primarily from the western states and territories, the Rough Riders were, in Roosevelt's words, *a splendid set of men, these South westerners—tall and sinewy, with resolute, weather-beaten faces, and eyes that looked a man straight in the face without flinching. They included in their ranks men of every occupation; but the three types were those of the cowboy, the hunter, and the mining prospector—the man who wandered hither and thither, killing game for a living, and spending his life in the quest for metal wealth.*

In all the world there could be no better material for soldiers than that afforded by these grim hunters of the mountains, these wild rough riders of the plains. They were accustomed to handling wild and savage horses; they were accustomed to following the chase with the rifle, both for sport and as a means of livelihood. Varied though their occupations had been, almost all had, at one time or another, herded cattle and hunted big game. They were hardened to life in the open, and to shifting for themselves under adverse circumstances. They were used, for all their lawless freedom, to the rough discipline of the round-up and the mining company. . . . [Many] were sheriffs, marshals, deputy-sheriffs, and deputy-marshals—men who had fought Indians, and still more often had waged relentless war upon the bands of white desperadoes. . . .

They were to a man born adventurers, in the old sense of the word. . . .

The men in the ranks were mostly young, yet some [like Ben Daniels] were past their first youth. These had taken part in the killing of the great buffalo herds, and had fought Indians when the tribes were still on the war-path. . . . Some of them went by their own name, some had changed their names, and yet others possessed but half a name, colored by some adjective, like Cherokee Bill, Happy Jack of Arizona, Smoky Moore, the bronc-buster . . . , and Rattlesnake Pete. . . . Some [like Ben Daniels] were professional gamblers, and, on the other hand, no less than four were or had been Baptist or Methodist clergymen—and proved first class fighters, too, by the way. Some [like Ben Daniels] were men whose lives in the past had not been free from the taint of those fierce kinds of crime into which the lawless spirits who dwell on the border-land between civilization and savagery so readily drift. A far larger number had served at different times in those bodies of armed men with which the growing civilization of the border finally puts down its savagery.[10]

Joining the Rough Riders to take part in the Cuban campaign were a number of notable western figures, many of whom received officer commissions:

William Owen ("Buckey") O'Neill, an Arizona sheriff and mayor of Prescott, was captain of A Troop and became the most famous casualty of the war when he was killed by a Spanish sniper at Santiago.

William Henry Harrison Llewellyn, New Mexico lawyer and Indian agent, renowned for running the notorious horse thief "Doc" Middleton to ground, was captain of G Troop.

George Curry, former sheriff of Lincoln County, New Mexico, and future governor of that territory, captained H Troop.

Charles L. Ballard, lawman of Roswell, New Mexico, who only recently had actively pursued the notorious "High Five" outlaw gang in that territory, was Captain Curry's second lieutenant in H Troop.

Thomas H. Rynning, onetime cattle driver to Dodge City, Indian fighter in the frontier cavalry, and future captain of the renowned Arizona Rangers, was a lieutenant in B Troop.

Alexander O. Brodie of Arizona, a West Point graduate and cavalry officer on the western frontier, was commissioned a major in the Rough Rider regiment and later, when Roosevelt was promoted to full colonel, became his second-in-command. In later years Brodie, one of three regimental officers Roosevelt, as president, appointed to governorships, would play an important role in the future of Ben Daniels.

Not all the Rough Riders were westerners, however. The commander of K Troop, where Daniels was assigned, was

Captain Woodbury Kane, a New York City man who had been a close friend of Roosevelt at Harvard. When Roosevelt arrived at San Antonio he found his college chum cooking and washing dishes, but he quickly changed that, and Kane was soon wearing captain's bars.[11] First Lieutenant Joseph A. Carr of K Troop was also an easterner, hailing from Washington, D.C. The other officer, Second Lieutenant Horace K. Devereaux, a Princeton graduate and a friend of Daniels from Colorado Springs, qualified as a true westerner.

At Camp Wood, a hastily constructed training area near San Antonio, the recruits were issued their uniforms, "slouch hats, blue flannel shirts, brown trousers, leggings and boots, with handkerchiefs knotted loosely around their necks," and their weapons, Model 1896 Krag-Jorgensen .30–40 caliber bolt action repeating carbines. Many also wore holstered single-action Colt revolvers.[12]

It was here, according to a later writer, that Daniels showed his contempt for conventional superstition: "While his troop was in camp at San Antonio numbers were given to each of the company but no one could be found who would accept No. 13. Mr. Daniels, however, took the number."[13]

After only a few days of close order drill, men of the regiment entrained for Tampa, Florida, their embarkation point. On June 7 eight of the twelve troops of the regiment, including Ben Daniels's K Troop, boarded the transport *Yucatan*, bound for Cuba. A severe lack of transport, however, necessitated leaving most of the horses and four troops of the regiment behind. This meant, as Daniels and the other Cuba-bound westerners learned to their disgust, they would be forced to fight as dismounted cavalry.

For seven miserable days the Rough Riders in overcrowded quarters suffered from the heat and poor food and water aboard the ship. Finally, on June 14 the *Yucatan* sailed

Two former Cripple Creek lawmen, Ben Daniels and Sherman Bell, now members of the U.S. First Volunteer Cavalry, await transport from their camp in Florida to Cuba. Note Daniels's "chewed-off" right earlobe. Courtesy of the Arizona Historical Society.

out of Tampa harbor, its destination the Cuban port town of Daiquiri. Landing there on June 22, the troops almost immediately began a march toward Santiago, the regimental objective.

Two days later the initial land battle of the war was fought at Las Guasimas, and the regiment suffered its first casualties, eight killed and thirty-four wounded. Buckling under intense Rough Riders pressure, the Spaniards retreated toward Santiago with the Americans pushing hard behind.

It was during this advance that Sherman Bell, while suffering severe pain from an aggravated rupture, caught the attention of Roosevelt. Bell's hernia would normally have made him unfit for combat duty, said Roosevelt, "but he was so excellent a man that we decided to take him. I do not think I ever saw greater resolution than Bell displayed throughout the campaign. In Cuba the great exertions which he was forced to make, again and again, opened the hernia, and the surgeon insisted that he must return to the United States; but he simply would not go."[14]

William McGinty, a Troop K cowboy from Stillwater, Oklahoma Territory, related "the rest of the story" about Sherman Bell's hernia and the part Ben Daniels played in it.

At a stream where the troop got its drinking water Bell slipped and fell, severely aggravating his rupture. Four doctors were unable to help him and decided to send him to the general hospital at regimental headquarters. McGinty said he and Ben Daniels volunteered for the job.

They shot him full of morphine and told us we had better get him to the hospital before the drug played out. We put him in this two wheel cart we had rigged up. The back-band of the harness was padded like a saddle, and it fitted right on the mule's back, so the lift and weight was mostly on the mule's back. . . . Ben Daniels walked behind, while I sat up in the back of the cart with a rifle in my hands. We had to go through a very spooky part of the jungle. . . . The walking was mighty hard, and it was hot, too, and in a short time Ben was just rolling in sweat. I kept telling him we would have to hurry, but he would get behind, and I would have to pull up and wait. . . .

We fussed back and forth all the time. The road was rough . . . going down that mountain pass to the hospital. I kept whipping the mule trying to hurry, and Ben kept telling me I would kill Sherman Bell if I didn't slow up. But I knew that if we didn't get there before the morphine played out we would have lots of trouble. I didn't pay much attention to Ben's hollering, for he was having a time holding onto the cart, and couldn't do much anyway.

That old cart hadn't been greased for many a month and the wheels would squall out plenty loud every time they turned around. And there we were going down the mountain lickety-split, the wheels squalling, and Ben Daniels trying to hold on, yelling above the noise for me to "take it easy." Sherman Bell's head was about a foot or more lower than his feet, the way we had laid him in the cart, and the morphine had relaxed his body so that he took each bump with the cart. . . .

We reached the Hospital before the drug played out, and I gave a note from our doctors to the head doctor there. Ben and I took it easier going back to the camp. . . . I told our Doctor Thorp how Ben had griped about jarring Sherman Bell so much, and he told me he didn't think it made much difference, as he didn't hold much chance for him anyway.

Some time after the war McGinty ran into Sherman Bell at a hospital in New York City, and Bell credited McGinty and Daniels with saving his life in Cuba. "The doctors told me," said Bell, "that trip down the mountain side was what saved my life. My head being lower than my feet, and I being relaxed, the jolts along the rough mountain side worked that rupture slowly back until when I reached the hospital the doctors did not need to operate, or do much else, since I was already on the road to recovery."[15]

On the high ground approaches to Santiago the Spanish made a stand and poured down heavy fire on the advancing Americans. The Rough Riders dug trenches, which protected them from most of the fire, but Spanish sharpshooters in the surrounding jungle continued to inflict casualties. It was here that Ben Daniels distinguished himself. As Roosevelt told it,

> *I chose out some twenty first-class men. . . . They were to slip out into the jungle between us and the Spanish lines before dawn next morning and there to spend the day, getting as close to the Spanish lines as possible, moving about with great stealth, and picking off any hostile sharp-shooter who exposed himself in the trenches. . . . Daniels and [Henry K.] Love were two of the men always in the front of any enterprise of this nature.*[16]

A newspaper would later credit Daniels with taking a leadership role in the elimination of the sniper harassment: "Colonel Roosevelt asked Daniels if he would undertake the task of routing the sharp-shooting gang. Daniels . . . organized a company and successfully performed [the job]."[17] It was probably Daniels's success in this sniper eradication operation that impressed the colonel and made him remember and admire the big Colorado lawman with the mangled ear. Daniels "endeared himself to Roosevelt" through bravery, hard work, and devotion to duty.[18]

Rough Rider Arthur Crosby, who became a nationally acclaimed hero of the Cuban campaign after being wounded twice and receiving a commission, related a similar story about Daniels, whom he described as a "cowboy, marshal, scout, and what-not from the west." On the second day of the troop's engagement with the enemy, said Crosby,

> *Daniels paused for a moment from his dare-devil fighting, mopped the perspiration from his brow, and remarked: "Well, boys, this is my fourteenth fight, but it about the fiercest thing I ever staggered against." Then he quickly raised his rifle and fired. Down from a tree, two or three hundred yards away, tumbled a Spanish sharpshooter*

who had been picking off our men. "That's the tenth fellow today," said Daniels, coolly as he touched his rifle.[19]

On June 30 Leonard Wood was relieved of his command of the First Volunteer Regiment and promoted to brigadier general, with responsibility for the entire Fifth Corps. At the same time, Roosevelt was promoted to full colonel and given command of the Rough Riders. The next day he led his troops in an attack on an elevation called "Kettle Hill," and then the famous assault up San Juan Hill, a battle that would be immortalized by the facile pen of famed journalist Richard Harding Davis and the skilled artistry of Frederic Remington, both of whom observed the San Juan Hill battle as war correspondents.

Ben Daniels took part in all these skirmishes and battles of the Cuban campaign, from the fight at Las Guasimas on June 24 to the assault on San Juan Hill on July 1 and the siege of the city of Santiago that began on July 3 and lasted until the Spanish surrender two weeks later.[20]

In July Ben's wife, Laura, who was living in Kansas City, Missouri, during her husband's absence,[21] received a letter from Lieutenant Devereaux, written from a New York hospital where he was recovering from a wound received in the San Juan Hill fight.[22] Devereaux assured her that Ben was all right and that he "was one of our best men, and was one of the heroes of the San Juan fight."[23]

A few days later Laura received another letter, this one from her husband in Cuba. Waxing uncharacteristically voluble, Daniels in this epistle related some of his battle experiences. Laura turned the letter over to a local newspaper, the *Kansas City World*, which published it.

In a preface the paper summarized Daniels's record: "Well known in the West, he was marshal of Dodge City, Kan.,

The only known photograph of the Rough Riders' fabled charge up San Juan Hill, July 1, 1898. Courtesy of the National Archives.

Theodore Roosevelt and his Rough Riders atop San Juan Hill after the battle. Courtesy of the National Archives.

when that town was at its wildest; he was a boon companion of Bat Masterson; he is noted as an Indian scout; he helped preserve order during the opening of Oklahoma; he was marshal of Lamar, Colo. and was captain of the Cripple Creek police until shortly before he enlisted." After including the incorrect information that Daniels was "chief scout with the Rough Riders," the paper described him as "a man of enormous strength, utterly devoid of fear, unexcelled as a horseman, a dead shot with rifle and revolver, and a man who will make his mark among a thousand men with just such attributes." Other papers, including the *Morning Times* of Cripple Creek, picked up the story and reprinted it.

"The last letter I wrote to you," Daniels began,

was on the transport on the other side of Key West. We were on the boat sixteen days until we were all starved to death nearly, and then we landed. We laid over until the next day at 4 o'clock and then we rolled up our blankets and walked twelve miles that night. We were all tired and worn out and some of the boys did not get through until late in the night. I kept right up with the command.

It rained all the time and we were wet through and through. At daylight we started on the march again with all our wet clothes on our backs and when the sun came up it was very hot and the boys kept falling out of the ranks overcome by the heat.

We were marching along a bushy ridge, and the underbrush and cactus and trees were so thick that we could not see ten steps on either side.

Well, there was a surprise in store for us. We had marched about four miles when the order to halt was given and to keep still.

In about two minutes, My God, it looked as if there were a Spaniard behind every bush, and they all commenced firing at us at a distance of 50 feet. The next order the captain gave was:

"Charge the right flank!"

You ought to have seen us go into that brush after them, everybody a-shooting. Our charge surprised them, and they retreated. We fought two hours and 40 minutes and gained the day.

There were about 4,000 Spaniards and 900 of us, and I think we crawled out of a very small hole. We killed 119 of them and wounded 800 more. Our loss was 27 dead and about 50 wounded.

We camped there two days and buried our dead, and then we buried the Spaniards and then we advanced three miles and went into camp again. At daylight we turned loose on them with artillery and they answered with bomb shells and were cutting us all to pieces. One shell burst within twenty feet of us and crippled seven or eight. One of them was within twelve inches of me when he was struck with a piece of shell. I picked him up and turned him over to a Red Cross man, and then I rejoined my troop. We moved over about a mile and then we got into it in great shape.

About 15,000 Spaniards, it seemed, turned loose on 5,000 of us. They were in rifle pits and behind breastworks and we had to charge them in their stronghold. To do this we had to cross a smooth, grassy valley about 300 yards wide under their terrific fire. Our men were falling on all sides, but we kept on and took that hill and the next one, about 600 yards away.

We fought almost constantly for three days and two nights and every one of us was played out. While some slept the others fought.

This is a very mountainous country. It looks like the Rocky Mountains. No matter how hot it is, it is always cool in the shade of a tree because of the closeness of the sea.

I am going to send you some flowers that grow in trees here and are very pretty. I could write a hundred pages to you, but I guess I'll wait till I see you, and then it will take me a year to tell you all. That is, if I ever get back and I have been in the front ranks all the time.

How do the papers speak of the Rough Riders?

Ben Daniels

PS: Whoop! What a long letter for me to write. Just make me a leather medal.[24]

On July 17, 1898, two weeks before Daniels's letter appeared in the Cripple Creek paper, the Spanish surrendered. The capitulation came none too soon for the American forces in Cuba, as an epidemic of jungle fever in various forms—malaria, yellow fever, dengue fever, and dysentery—was devastating their ranks. Of the 771 Americans who died in the Cuban campaign, disease was the cause of death of 514.[25]

More than 1,500 fell victim to the tropical disease, including Private Ben Daniels. The entire regiment of Rough Riders, able-bodied and malaria sufferers alike, boarded the transport *Miami* for the States on August 7 and debarked eight days later at Montauk Point, New York, where Daniels was hospitalized until September 1, when, having cheated death from disease for the third time, he rejoined his unit. On September 15 the now famous Roosevelt Rough Rider regiment was disbanded at Camp Wikoff, Long Island.

As their colonel stood before them for the last time, the men of the regiment presented him with a gift, a bronze by Frederic Remington of a cowboy on a bucking horse. Roosevelt, dewy-eyed, spoke:

I am proud of this regiment beyond measure. I am proud of it because it is a typical American regiment. The foundation of the regiment was the cow puncher, and now we have got him here in bronze....

No gift could have been so appropriate as this bronze of Frederic Remington. The men of the West and the Southwest—horsemen, ridemen and herders of cattle—have been the backbone of this regiment....

Outside of my own immediate family I shall never show as strong ties as I do toward you. I am more than pleased that you feel the same toward me....

Boys, I am going to stand here, and I shall esteem it a privilege if each of you will come up here. I want to shake your hands—I want to say good-bye to each of you in person.[26]

Daniels was mustered out at New York City on October 3 and presented the princely sum of $145.71 for his four-month service in the war.[27]

Chapter 9
The Marshalship Quest and the Spectral Past
1899–1902

To appoint as United States Marshal a man who is a professional gambler, with a record of whiskey selling and murder, is a blow to good government from which this territory will not recover in many years.
—Pastor R. A. Rowland

You did a grave wrong to me as well as to yourself when you failed to be frank with me and tell me about this blot on your record. —Theodore Roosevelt to Ben Daniels

AFTER LEAVING THE ARMY Daniels joined his wife in Kansas City and went to work as a guard for Wells, Fargo & Company. His supervisor was Fred Dodge, another veteran of the western towns who had worked with many of Daniels's lawmen friends, including Bat Masterson and Bill Tilghman.[1]

In May 1899 Daniels dropped in at his old stomping ground of Cripple Creek and was extolled as a hero by the press. "HE WAS OUR ROUGH RIDER," proclaimed the headline in the *Morning Times*: "BEN DANIELS HELPED TO MAKE THIS DISTRICT FAMOUS; HE FOUGHT IN CUBA; LED THE COLORS OF HIS REGIMENT IN THREE HARD FIGHTS."

B. F. Daniels . . . is back in the metropolis of the greatest gold mining camp on earth after an even year's absence. . . . Ben Daniels was one of the Rough Riders and as such he has helped to make Cripple Creek famous. He was in every battle fought in Cuba by his regiment. . . .

Ben Daniels received a royal welcome yesterday from all who knew him and people who had not been friendly in the past were simply delighted to grasp the hand of a man who fought not only gallantly, but heroically on San Juan Hill, and who had received especial praise from his commanding officer.

"Cripple Creek looks good to me," said Mr. Daniels last night, and it was quite a time before the man who is a real hero would say more. Question after question brought out the story and finally he broke out by saying: "Colonel Roosevelt is the greatest man in America."

This, in a manner, loosened the tongue of "the man who never talks," and Mr. Daniels related several little incidents to prove that his first assertion was correct. He has the greatest esteem for Col. Wood, who was at the head of the regiment, and declares that he is the coolest and most fearless man that he has ever seen. But, it appears, that Colonel Wood was quiet, while the dear old Teddy, who has a million namesakes today, was a dashing sort of a boy—wanted to be after the enemy with a whoop and a yell—regular Indian fashion—and that caught Ben, for he has fought the red divvies, off and on, the greater part of his life.

"I came out without a scratch," he said last night, "but many a good man fell by my side. I was in every engagement in which our regiment took part, and we were in the very thickest of it from start to finish. We had three hard fights, but that day on San Juan hill and later on in front of Santiago was something to chill the blood in a tropical climate. Many a good man went down, but he went down facing the enemy. I cannot say too much for the men who carried the Stars and Stripes into Cuba—they were Americans and as such they did their country proud.

> That is the longest speech Ben Daniels ever made in his life, but all the world knows that he has only told a little part of the truth in the sentences that appear above.
> No man in the service was more gallant or more brave in front of an enemy than our Ben Daniels. . . .
> While Mr. Daniels is with us now, it is not assured that he may remain permanently, as he has not so far fully outlined his policy. He comes back the same genial, unassuming man that he was before the war. He is as cool and quiet and collected as ever.[2]

A few days later the paper reported that Daniels was the only member of the Elks lodge from Colorado to volunteer for the Rough Rider regiment, and the Elks of Cripple Creek honored him by granting him a life membership for his heroism in the war.[3]

But Daniels did not remain in the Cripple Creek district. After working for the express company out of Kansas City a little over a year, he resigned in December 1899 to make another geographical and career move. Perhaps drawn to one of the last remaining outposts of the vanishing frontier, he relocated at Nogales, Arizona, a small town on the Mexican border that still retained the look and atmosphere of the Old West. There he gambled professionally, invested in mining ventures, and acquired part ownership in herds of cattle grazing on both sides of the national line.

When enumerated by federal census-taker Edward E. Noon on June 6, 1900, Daniels said he earned his living as a "quartz miner," but had not been employed for seven months. He maintained his interest in law enforcement, joining posses in pursuit of cattle rustlers and train robbers who were thick down in that border country.[4]

It was during this period that he watched with great interest the meteoric political rise of his wartime leader, Theodore Roosevelt. Soon after returning from Cuba as a war hero, Roosevelt had been elected governor of New York State. In March 1899, while still living in Missouri, Daniels wrote his former commander, congratulating him on his election. Roosevelt penned a warm response, saying that he considered Daniels, Sherman Bell, Horace Devereaux, and the others who came down to San Antonio from Colorado in May 1898 "on the whole better than any other group of its size that joined the regiment." He said he was "getting along pretty well as Governor," but sometimes thought leading the charge up San Juan Hill was easier, and added: "At any rate, I enjoyed myself more there in spite of the fever and the canned beef. We had a pretty good time, take it all in all, in the old regiment, didn't we? Give my warmest regards to Mrs. Daniels and to any of our comrades whom you meet."[5]

Roosevelt had hardly settled into the governor's office when powerful men in the Republican Party, fearful that his maverick political views and growing celebrity posed a threat to their grip on the party, nominated him for the dead-end position of vice president under President William McKinley, running for reelection in 1900. As the politicos planned, the McKinley-Roosevelt ticket won an easy victory that November.

On November 16 Daniels sent a congratulatory telegram to the vice president–elect and received a quick response. Roosevelt, addressing Daniels as "Marshal," said he appreciated nothing more than receiving the best wishes of the men of his old regiment and invited Daniels to call on him if he ever was in his vicinity.[6]

On March 4, 1901, President William McKinley was inaugurated for his second term. It was not an exciting occasion for Roosevelt; the vice presidency had little to offer a man of his ambitious temperament. Beyond presiding over the

Senate when it was in session, there were no real duties attached to the office. Roosevelt feared that his political career was over. Not since Martin Van Buren, in 1836, had a vice president succeeded a president through election. Presidential death in office by illness and assassination had caused the ascension of four vice presidents to the presidency between 1841 and 1881, but Roosevelt refused to consider that possibility.

Out in the remote village of Nogales in Arizona Territory Ben Daniels saw in the rise to power and show of cordiality on the part of his former commander an opportunity to advance his own ambitions, and he began to lobby for a federal appointment, preferably the prestigious position of U.S. marshal for Arizona Territory. After Roosevelt's election he first broached the subject in a letter that has not been preserved, but Inauguration Day in March 1901 provided him a follow-up opportunity.

In a letter addressed to "Dear Colonel," a title he said he felt more comfortable with, Daniels apologized for not attending the inauguration ceremony, which would have afforded him "one of the happiest moments" of his life. He had, he said, been "mixed up in some mining property" that required his attention.

"I wrote to you," he reminded Roosevelt,

in regards to a Government position. Now if it will [inconvenience] you in any way, don't assist me, but if you think of any other position that would be better for me than the one I asked for, and you feel as though you could assist me in getting it, please notify me.

Now I suppose you are flooded with letters from your Rough Riders in regards to getting some position. If so, and it is asking too much of you to help me, please drop my name, and help some more worthy person.[7]

Roosevelt was unable to aid Daniels at this time, but at four o'clock on the afternoon of September 6, 1901, both his and Daniels's prospects changed dramatically when President McKinley, attending the World's Fair in Buffalo, New York, was shot by an anarchist, Leon Czolgosz. Eight days later McKinley died, Theodore Roosevelt was sworn in as the twenty-sixth president of the United States, and everything changed for the nation and certainly for the cynical manipulators who thought they had disrupted Roosevelt's meteoric political rise.

Daniels could hardly wait to press his case for the job he coveted with the man who now had the power to make that appointment. The new chief executive had barely settled into the White House when Daniels wrote him, raising the U.S. marshal appointment issue again. In a letter dated October 20 and addressed this time to "Dear President," he reminded Roosevelt of a current scandal about Chinese entering the country illegally across the southern border. "It may be," he suggested rather clumsily, "that a removal of the US Marshal [for Arizona Territory] will be urged and if so and that Office is Declared vacant, I would like to get the appointment to that place if you have not been Spoken to by any one else that you would rather have there." It was signed, "As ever your cincere [sic] Friend, B. F. Daniels."[8]

To aid him in his campaign, Daniels in December had several of his friends write letters of support. Dodge City and Ford County, Kansas, official H. P. Myton said he had known Daniels since 1878 and found him to be "a man of good ability and good nerve . . . , entirely fearless . . . , not afraid of anybody, [and still] a gentleman."[9]

Wells Fargo Special Officer Fred Dodge affirmed that he had known Daniels a number of years, the man had worked under his supervision, and he had "never found him wanting in any respect."[10]

Daniels's request was by no means the only one Roosevelt received from members of his regiment. As early as July 1901, when he was still vice president, he had written W. H. H. Llewellyn, a former Rough Rider captain and currently attorney general of New Mexico Territory:

I have had great trouble through men of the regiment writing me for positions. Sometimes they are unfit and I turn them down; but there are plenty of them who are fit for the positions they seek but who cannot expect to get them because there are others with greater capacity or greater influence. . . . I have asked for so many favors for men of the regiment that I am positively ashamed to go to a single department in Washington. Yet each trooper not unnaturally when he writes to me thinks that his own is the only case, and that if I chose to, I can surely do anything he wants.[11]

Roosevelt had already decided to reward his former Rough Rider with the Arizona marshal position when the first stirrings of a serious problem with the appointment hit his desk in the form of a Secret Service memo, implying there were skeletons in Daniels's closet that might embarrass the president if made public.

Roosevelt had his secretary turn the memo over to Attorney General Philander Chase Knox, asking for his recommendation.[12] When Knox raised no objections the president called Daniels to Washington and on January 6, 1902, informed him personally that his name would be presented to the U.S. Senate as the replacement for the current U.S. marshal for Arizona, Myron H. McCord, a McKinley appointee. Roosevelt assured Daniels that Senate confirmation was only a formality and the job was his.[13]

When it reached the press the announcement caused no little surprise in some quarters of the West. Newspapers pointed out that McCord, as a matter of protocol upon McKinley's death, had tendered his resignation, but expected to be reappointed. He was a man with impressive credentials. He had been governor of the territory, but at the outset of the war with Spain resigned to become colonel of the First Territorial Regiment, made up of cowboys from Arizona and New Mexico, an outfit that unfortunately remained stateside and never saw combat. As editor of the *Phoenix Gazette*, McCord was positioned to attack the man who coveted the job he wanted for himself and used that advantage expertly in the coming months.

Another aspirant for the job was James H. McClintock, an Arizonan who had captained B Troop of the Rough Riders and suffered a severe ankle wound at the Battle of Las Guasimas.

Daniels, on the other hand, had only been a private in the war. In addition, he was known as a lifelong Democrat, not the party of the president.[14]

It soon became apparent that Senate confirmation of Daniels's appointment was not assured. No sooner had word of Roosevelt's selection hit the news wires than telegrams of protest began pouring into senators' offices. Some Republicans showed displeasure because they believed Daniels was affiliated with the Democrat Party, but most complaints came from clergymen and religious people who objected to a professional gambler being given such an important position. In a telegram to Senator George F. Hoar, chairman of the Senate Judiciary Committee, a prominent resident of Nogales, Arizona, charged that Daniels was a faro dealer whose trip expenses to Washington had been paid by the town's gamblers. The appointment, he said, was "an insult to the decent people of the Territory."[15]

The pastor of the Methodist Episcopal Church of Phoenix fired off a telegram and a follow-up letter calling Daniels "a professional gambler with an unsavory reputation." He said that the president, with his "experience in Western life," should know

> that those who represent the principles of righteousness in civic government [i.e., clergymen like himself] have an uphill fight under the most favorable circumstances. And to appoint as United States Marshal, a man who is a professional gambler, with a record of whiskey selling and murder, is a blow to good government from which this territory will not recover in many years.
>
> Surely there are a sufficient number of good men and true who can worthily represent the dignity of the United States in this Territory, without appointing a man who, whatever may be his personal qualifications, is identified with the basest elements of society.[16]

Daniels was not without defenders. Among the many telegrams of support pouring into the White House were two from residents of Phoenix who blamed McCord and his friends for the attacks on Daniels. C. H. Robinson stated flatly: "McCord is making the fight against Daniels. McCord is abominable, of all Federal appointments his is the worst."[17] Isaac T. Stoddard, acting governor of Arizona, said he had been "assured by leading businessmen and Republicans of nd elsewhere that charges against Daniels are not warranted by the facts. Protests being made are based on rumors circulated by disappointed politicians and irresponsible parties."[18]

Roosevelt ignored the fulminations and protestations from friends and enemies of Ben Daniels and continued to push for confirmation of his nominee. Viewing the situation, the editor of the *Washington Post* commented rather acidly:

> Some one said the other day that all of the Rough Riders who were not in jail were seeking office. Here is a story of a Rough Rider

who sought office, but who may find there is many a slip 'twixt the cup and lip: Ben Daniels was recently appointed Marshal of Arizona. He was a Rough Rider, and in President Roosevelt's story of that famous regiment his name is mentioned with high praise for his courage. It was quite natural that when Mr. Roosevelt became president, Daniels should sign for the flesh pots of Federal office. He came to Washington, asked for the marshalship of Arizona, was greeted with open arms and was granted the place.

Unfortunately, however, when Daniels hurried off to see his old commander, he had been running a faro bank. In Arizona this is a legitimate and popular occupation, but somehow or other there happened to be several moral and tender souls who thought the United States Marshal ought not to be associated with the gambling business. They have objected quite forcibly to Senator Hoar, the Chairman of the Judiciary Committee, and it may be that Mr. Daniels will not be confirmed.[19]

The Judiciary Committee, over the objection of Senator Hoar, did pass the nomination, however, and it went to the floor of the full Senate, which confirmed the nomination on January 21.

Roosevelt signed the document officially naming Ben Daniels as U.S. marshal of Arizona on January 30. Two days later he wrote Daniels, advising him of his confirmation but reminding him that Senate approval had only been attained after the president had given his "personal guarantee" of his appointee's "honest, efficiency and courage," and his assurance that Daniels would conduct his life "on the highest plane of citizenship, public and domestic." He reminded Daniels that "a great many scoundrels, men who have violated the laws, and men of vicious and seditious temperament," would be watching and eagerly hoping he would make some slip, as well as "upright and intelligent citizens" who viewed him with suspicion. He admonished Daniels, saying:

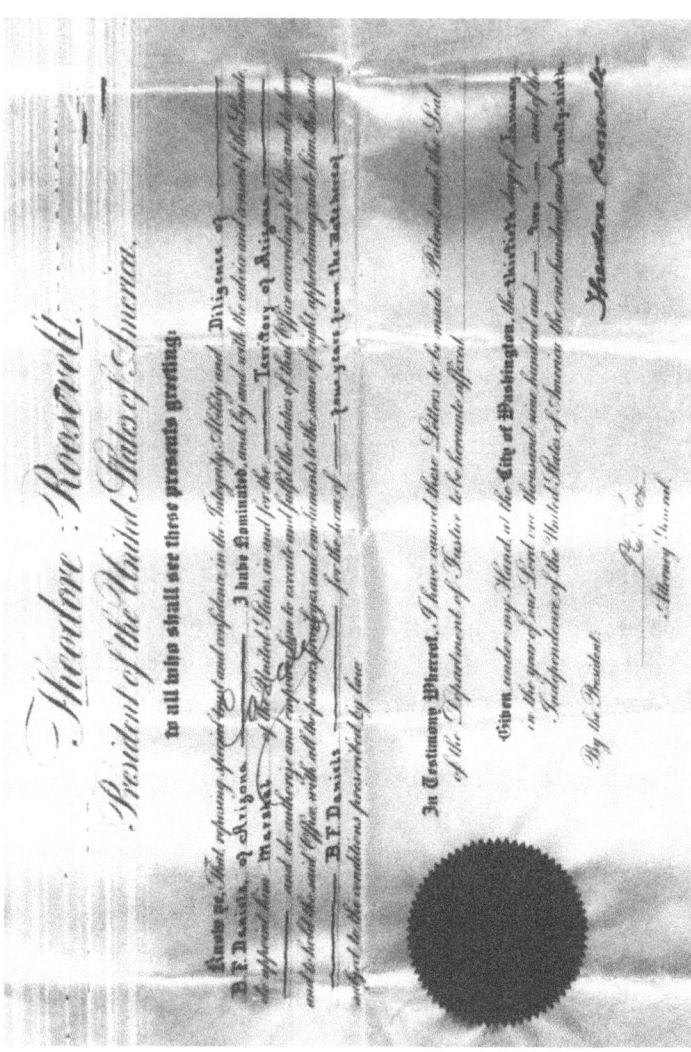

The word "cancelled" is written across Daniels's first commission as U.S. marshal. Courtesy of the National Archives.

Now I wish you to feel to the fullest extent the weight of your responsibility, not only to the Government and yourself, but to me. You are bound in honor to make my judgment good. You have been my close comrade in days of risk and hardship and danger against a violent criminal, against an anarchist or mob leader; I know I can count on you always.

I have not the slightest anxiety as to your integrity or courage; but I want to warn you that you must be ever on your guard to do nothing that could be misconstrued by those who wish you ill, into an act that would reflect discredit upon you, and upon me for appointing you.

I want you to keep on touch with men like Colonel Brodie, Captain McClintock, and Secretary of State Stoddard, and above all I want you to remember that the one way in which you can reward me is to carry on the work of your office on the very highest plane of efficiency and integrity.[20]

But the affair was not ended. Some senators opposed to the nomination angrily charged that the floor vote on the confirmation had been rushed through during the absence of a number of interested members. At an executive session of the Senate called to consider the matter, Senator Hoar argued that Daniels's commission already had been issued, rendering it impractical to adopt Colorado senator Henry Moore Teller's motion to reconsider the vote by which it had been confirmed.[21]

Up until this point charges against Daniels concerned his unsavory past as a professional gambler, but a bombshell allegation was tossed into the controversy on February 5 when a report reached Washington from Cheyenne claiming that Roosevelt's appointee had served time in a Wyoming prison. Joseph Ohl, Washington correspondent for the *Atlanta Constitution*, a paper politically opposed to Roosevelt's Republican administration, leaped on the story, quoting the Cheyenne dispatch: "Great surprise has been caused here at the receipt of the news from Washington that the senate on Thursday last confirmed the nomination of Ben Daniels, if that is really his name, as United States marshal of Arizona. His career as swindler, gambler and desperado was known to certain people in Washington before his appointment, but it seems hardly creditable that the senate committee on the judiciary, who passed upon his nomination, knew that he has a prison record as a convict." Ohl went on to sketch out (inaccurately) Daniels's later career:

> When Daniels served his penitentiary sentence he lived for two or three years at Denver, employed by the most disreputable bunco men and gamblers and was the leader of a "brace" game of faro. He afterwards took himself to La Junta, Colo., where he distinguished himself on one occasion by holding up a faro game with a gun, and robbing it of $600, for which little stunt he was driven out of La Junta.
>
> Daniels then moved on to Cripple Creek, alternately served on the police force and acted as stool pigeon for the crooked gamblers of the place. It is understood that an effort will be made to have Daniels' commission withheld until his past record can be more fully ventilated, in the hope that a republican can be found to serve as marshal of Arizona who is not a convicted felon.
>
> It is given out by his friends that the president had no inkling of this phase of the man's past, but as this dispatch intimates, it was certainly known to some people in Washington who might, if they love the president as much as they protest, have placed the facts to his ears.
>
> Just what will be done about it is not known. The republican politicians of Arizona are understood to resent the appointment, and it is possible some of them may file charges with the department of justice which will lead to investigation and possible removal, though how this can be brought about at this stage of the proceedings it is

difficult to understand. Daniels has the commission, and if he is wise enough to carry himself straight as an official, it looks as if the republican organization, the administration, and the people of Arizona will have to stand it.[22]

The story was further clouded by another dispatch from Cheyenne quoting unnamed police authorities of that city who were convinced that the Ben Daniels incarcerated at Laramie in 1879 was not the same man as the Roosevelt appointee, and that "friends of the Arizona Daniels living in Cripple Creek who have known him for over twenty years deny emphatically that he has any prison record."[23]

When he learned of the Daniels prison allegation for the first time, Roosevelt immediately instructed Attorney General Knox to wire the U.S. attorney at Cheyenne, T. F. Burke, for particulars about the man who had served prison time there. He also telegraphed Daniels, ordering him to refrain from entering into discharge of his duties until the matter could be resolved.

But only days after Roosevelt penned his letter to Daniels more sordid events in the past history of his appointee became public. When a photograph of Daniels appeared in the *Denver Republican*, former U.S. deputy marshal W. R. Schnitger came forward to affirm that the man pictured was without a doubt the same man he had guarded during his trials back in 1879 and 1880. "I cannot be mistaken," he told a reporter for the *Cheyenne Leader*. "I knew Daniels well and I recognized the picture at a glance. . . . I was the man who took Daniels to prison when he was sentenced and also brought him back for his second trial. The picture bears such a strong resemblance that there is no doubt in my mind as to his identity."[24]

Then, on February 12, Attorney General Knox received a letter from U.S. Attorney T. F. Burke of Cheyenne with an abstract of the Daniels Laramie prison record, which left no doubt that the president's appointee was indeed a former convict.[25]

The newspapers picked up the story, and once again protests flooded Washington. A man named Augustus Curtius of Denver, Colorado, wrote Roosevelt, advising him that to his personal knowledge Daniels, "while running a dance hall in Dodge City," killed an unarmed man named Julian "in the most brutal manner . . . , but because of the lawless conditions then existing in the west was not convicted" of the crime. While employed as a fighter in the Gray County Seat War he killed "a defenseless farmer" in Cimarron, Kansas. Prior to these crimes he had been a horse thief and "the lower part of one ear [was] removed to brand him as such." Throughout the West he had always been considered "a very dangerous man."[26]

There were also letters and telegrams of support from friends of Daniels, many of whom were influential men in Arizona. Pima County Superintendent William Angus; S. W. Drachman, president of the Tucson board of education; H. N. Seigfreid, general manager of the Tucson Electric Company; L. C. Hughes, editor of the *Tucson Daily Star* and ex-governor of Arizona; and Thomas S. Wilson, former U.S. attorney, all expressed their belief in the integrity and worth of Ben Daniels. Wilson took the trouble to write a letter to the *Arizona Star* in defense of Daniels. "As there is no man who can truthfully say that he ever knew me to gamble to the value of one cent, or even to make a bet of any kind, or that I ever took a drink in a saloon," he stated,

I can not be accused with sympathizing with gambling or saloon keeping, yet I have no sympathy with those who attack a man like

Ben Daniels because dire necessity drove him to dealing faro to get his daily bread. I do not know Daniels personally and I have not endorsed him for the office to which he aspires, yet from all I have heard of him he is a brave, honest man and would make a good marshal. Daniels' record, though he may have dealt faro, is far above that of a large number of those who have held federal offices in Arizona, and is clean and white as compared with some of those who hold federal offices in the territory now. . . . Arizona will not be disgraced or even discredited by the appointment of Ben Daniels as marshal. He will make a good officer.[27]

Even the renowned western artist and sculptor Frederic Remington, who had known Daniels while serving as a war correspondent in Cuba, wrote the president on behalf of the former Rough Rider. While acknowledging that perhaps the man had been a gambler and convict, he reminded Roosevelt that he had also been a "brave soldier [who] has tried to live down his past," and "a lot of his critics in cold blood wouldn't do what he did in hot blood in a disinterested way for the public good." His advice was for the president to ignore the complaints of a bunch "of old nosey women—superannuated Senators and Democrats," and hold fast with his selection.[28]

But when Roosevelt learned that Senator Teller had taken up the fight to keep Daniels from the marshalship and was about to refer the matter back to committee, he reluctantly bowed to the political pressure and asked Daniels to resign. His letter reveals his disappointment in the man who, he now believed, had not been completely straightforward with him: "You did wrong in not being frank with me. You put me in the position of unwittingly deceiving my friends in the Senate. It may be that if you had told me all of the circumstances before your nomination, I could have sent in your name anyway, but as things are it is impossible, I regret to say, for you to act as Marshal. I must therefore ask you to send me at once your resignation. I am more sorry than I can say to write you this letter."[29]

Roosevelt's letter crossed in the mail with a response from Daniels about the allegations against him. In another letter written five days later the president acknowledged receipt of the Daniels missive, and, while making clear his disappointment in his friend's behavior, admitted he still admired him, and offered advice for the future:

> I am sure that you are telling me the truth, and that you would be a first class Marshal. I like you and trust you, and would employ you without hesitation in my private business. But, as you must now see, you did a grave wrong to me as well as to yourself when you failed to be frank with me and tell me about this blot on your record.
>
> It may be that if you had been frank and told me about it, and I had looked into it, I could have stood by you and sent in your name; but it is not possible for me to have you assume the duties of Marshal under the circumstances as they actually are. You put me in the attitude of unwittingly deceiving the Senate and of establishing a precedent which was bound to return and plague me. So I must ask you to send in your resignation.
>
> Now, Sheriff, I want to say a word most earnestly to you. This is a hard blow to you, and you can best show the stuff that is in you by the way you bear it. If you weaken and do anything of which you and your friends have cause to be ashamed, you will justify all that your enemies say of you, and you will wreck yourself forever.
>
> If you stand straight and go about your duty as a man, you will do for yourself what no one else can do for you—you will give the lie to your enemies and you will put yourself in a position where in the future the men who believe in you will be able to repose trust in you and use you in a responsible position.
>
> Your friend and old Colonel, Theodore Roosevelt.[30]

Daniels wrote a terse note of resignation on February 25, 1902, and followed up with a letter in which he expressed his appreciation for Roosevelt's continued belief in him and apologized for not telling the full story, "a very delicate subject," in the beginning. Although admitting the loss of the job had been a "hard blow," Daniels said he would never weaken, as he was "not made from that kind of material." It was his intention to live in the future as he had in the past, "honorable and upright in all my dealings with my fellow man," and to "look every one square in the face," which, he added, was more than some of my enemies could do. "And, you can believe me that I will always be your friend, although the friendship of one who has been painted so black as I have been, may not amount to mutch [sic].[31]

While the *Arizona Daily Republican* called the Daniels affair "a situation unique in the history of federal appointments,"[32] political foes of Roosevelt seized the opportunity to further embarrass the president by painting Daniels in the worst possible colors. Under the headline "OUT OF PRISON INTO OFFICE" newsman Joseph Ohl reprinted his entire Wyoming prison record.[33] Other papers castigated him as "an ex-convict, a hold-up man, and a brace game gambler."[34]

Jacob C. ("Jakey") Bloom, the man who had accused Daniels of "abusing" him back in Dodge City and had been a leader in the effort to discredit him at Cripple Creek, now ran a jewelry store in Denver. He gave an interview to a reporter for the *Denver Republican* in which he heaped scorn on Daniels, describing him as a murderer and a gambler. While admitting that Daniels and Ed Julian had sworn to shoot one another on sight, he still maintained Julian's killing had been cold-blooded murder:

> Julian walked out on the sidewalk in front of his place. He had a $10 note in his hands and was going across the street to change it. Daniels saw him and ran out of his own place. Julian did not see him and was unaware of his danger. Daniels waited until he reached the edge of the sidewalk, and then shot him through the head. As Julian fell, Daniels walked up beside his prostrate body, and pointing his revolver downward, emptied the remaining four chambers into Julian's body. The bullets were forty-five caliber, and Julian was probably killed by the first one. . . . Daniels was arrested for this murder, tried and acquitted.

Bloom said Daniels killed his second man (English), whom he described as a "German hotel keeper" at Cimarron in the Gray County Seat War. At Cripple Creek he "worked in different gambling houses . . . and made his living running faro banks." He said he had heard that Daniels had saved the life of Teddy Roosevelt at the San Juan Hill battle and believed it, "as he would do anything for a friend."[35]

Perhaps to avoid humiliating meetings with Arizona friends after these widely published disparagements of her husband, Laura left Nogales to stay with relatives in Missouri, while Ben departed for New Mexico. The *Atlanta Constitution*, whose editorial staff was not friendly to Roosevelt, suggested that Daniels left "to chase down a certificate of good character."[36] The paper took every opportunity to needle the president and Daniels over the botched appointment:

"Hon. Ben Daniels feels aggrieved that he had to go all the way to Washington City to find out what a real rough house really is."[37]

"Ben Daniels has got a say coming but his vocabulary has also developed a sag in the explanatory section."[38]

"Hon. Ben Daniels seems to have faced himself as readily as the man who thaws dynamite on a kitchen stove."[39]

"Ben Daniels must have gone very deep into the chaparral to recover his composure. He hasn't been heard from since he hit the grit."[40]

"Hon. Ben Daniels has not yet returned from the jackrabbit regions. He'll probably get back in time for the Rough Rider convention."[41]

According to a story in the *Fort Worth Register*, some senators used the Daniels appointment debacle to have some fun at the expense of the president. At a dinner Senator Mark Hanna remarked that Senator Nathan B. Scott had found Roosevelt's "standard."

"How's that?" asked Roosevelt innocently.

"Why," responded Hanna, "Scott says every time he went to see you about an appointment you told him you would appoint any one he would recommend, but the man must be up to your 'standard.' Now he says he has found it." Everybody was all attention, and Hanna continued. "Scott says it's Ben Daniels." Everybody laughed and none more heartily than the president. Senator Scott never takes anyone to the White House now that the president does not tell the "standard" story. It is also told that Senator Hoar, who investigated the case of Daniels when his nomination was before the senate, found that the charge that Daniels had run a faro bank was not true, and shortly after Daniels appeared before the committee and acknowledged that he had been a faro dealer. Members of the committee tell this on Mr. Hoar.[42]

On March 10 Laura wrote Roosevelt from Kansas City, describing the bad financial straits in which the Daniels found themselves, and asking if the president could appoint Ben to some other position. As was his practice, Roosevelt answered promptly, saying he knew the situation was "very, very hard" for the two of them, and suggesting Ben take a deputy's job under U.S. Marshal McCord.[43] This was forwarded to Ben Daniels, whose response to Roosevelt showed clearly his contempt for McCord and his undamaged self-esteem: "I would not think of Serving as a Deputy under a man as unreliable as McCord, and he is the man that put up all the Dirty fight agained [sic] me in Arizona, and he has (I have been told) expressed himself thoroughly againsed [sic] you on Different occasions. No Sir, I don't want a Deputy Ship under McCord. I am receiving letters from Colonel Brodie regularly every week. He is a good friend of mine and is willing to do any Thing that he can do for me."[44]

His dream of becoming U.S. marshal for Arizona had apparently been shattered, but Daniels, who "evidently attributed his fall down to the accidents of war," did not seem downcast to his friends.[45] He again devoted his energies to mining and cattle. He wrote Roosevelt in June 1902 suggesting he buy stock in the Jefferson Mining Company, of which Daniels was a director. The president respectfully declined.[46]

In 1903 Daniels was deeply involved in the development, sales, and promotion of a mine smelter he was credited with having invented. A story about its advent in the *Arizona Daily Republican* of Phoenix reads more like an advertisement written by Daniels himself than a news account:

> *Ben Daniels [is] the inventor of the new smelter which can be bought for $300. . . . This smelter will be given a practical test very soon by the mines owned by Daniels in Sonora. This property . . . is said to be very valuable property. Mr. Daniels was in Washington to see to the patents and he now has all of the papers and will have one of the smelters taken out at once to his property. The advantage of this smelter is that in the first place it is very cheap in the first cost and it can be operated at a minimum expense and does not require water. These advantages will make it invaluable to the poor man, who*

may own a good prospect and wants to work it himself. In the long run this new smelter process in a certain way will revolutionize mining. It will bring about an era of productiveness for the small high-grade propositions that are so common in this section of the mineral belt and in most cases are owned by prospectors who cannot work them. If successful, it will in a general way, make the prospector independent of the capitalist as it will place in his hands means to work his property. Such a smelter as this has been wanted for a long time.[47]

When tested at the mines the benefits of the new smelter were apparently not as propitious as had been claimed, for it was never heard of again.

A few months later, Daniels wrote Roosevelt again, this time on the letterhead of "Conrad & Daniels, Mines, Ranches and Cattle in Mexico and Arizona," advising the president that he had been elected alternate to the National Republican Convention from Arizona, and his only regret was that he had not been elected a delegate so that he could vote for Roosevelt to serve another term as president.[48] Roosevelt responded that it was a "real pleasure" to hear that his "dear comrade Daniels" was an alternate, but he also wished that Daniels was a delegate.[49]

Theodore Roosevelt was nothing if not loyal; despite the political bruising he had received over the appointment of Daniels as U.S. marshal for Arizona, the president, stubborn and tenacious as always, was still determined to do something for his friend. Shortly after the above exchange with Daniels he came up with an idea.

Chapter 10
Prison Superintendent
1904–1905

> *Governor Brodie of Arizona (late Lieutenant-Colonel of the Rough Riders) is going to appoint Ben Daniels (late one-eared hero of that organization) as warden of the Arizona Penitentiary. When I told this to John Hay he remarked (with brutal absence of feeling) that he believed the proverb ran: "Set a Rough Rider to catch a thief."*
>
> Theodore Roosevelt, June 4, 1904

HIS FAILED ATTEMPT to award the Arizona marshalship to Ben Daniels came at some political cost to President Roosevelt, but, typically, he forged ahead, ignoring the criticism, even derision, and continued to appoint other of his former comrades-in-arms to important government posts. While attending the Fourth Annual Rough Rider reunion held at San Antonio, Texas, in April 1905, he heard and laughed at a story reportedly brought to the convention by Daniels.

A former Rough Rider in New Mexico, according to the story, had written the president, saying that he had been arrested for stealing a horse and, being completely broke, needed $200 for his defense. Roosevelt sent him a check. When a few days later announcement was made that the president had appointed Rough Rider Captain W. H. H. Llewellyn to the office of U.S. Attorney for New Mexico, the accused horse thief sent the check back to the president with a note thanking him, but saying that with another Rough Rider prosecuting his case, he wouldn't need the money.¹

It was certainly true that Ben Daniels was by no means the only former Rough Rider for whom President Roosevelt actively sought a prestigious government position. One of his first appointments as president had been that of Benjamin H. Colbert, a mixed-blood Indian who had served in F Troop, whom he named in January 1902 as U.S. marshal for the southern district of Indian Territory. That year he also appointed Alexander O. Brodie, his second in command in Cuba, to the governorship of Arizona. As opportunities arose later in his presidency he appointed Frank Frantz, who had captained A Troop, governor of Oklahoma Territory, and George Curry, H Troop captain, governor of New Mexico.²

Former Rough Rider James C. Goodwin, who ran for the Arizona House of Representatives and was elected, was critical of Roosevelt's appointments and particularly his work on Daniels's behalf, saying, "I have the distinction of never holding an official position under the Roosevelt administration, and that puts me in a class by myself as far as this regiment is involved. I've held no official position and never been in jail."³

Ignoring remarks of this type, the Rough Rider governors followed the president's example by elevating other former members of the regiment to territorial positions of authority. In 1903, for instance, Governor Brodie tapped former B Troop officer Tom Rynning to lead the Arizona Rangers, when Burt Mossman, the first captain of that elite law enforcement outfit, stepped down. Other Rough Riders who wore the Arizona Ranger badge included John E. Campbell, John Foster, William W. Webb, Richard Stanton, and David Warford of B Troop; Charles McGarr of A Troop; and Oscar J. Mullen of C Troop.⁴

As president, Roosevelt was determined to provide high-placed, well-paying jobs not only for his comrades-in-arms in the Cuban conflict but for other western men of action he admired as well.

In 1901 he presented the position of collector of customs at El Paso, Texas, to western gunfighter and lawman Pat Garrett, a man he had never met but who had been long celebrated for having slain the notorious outlaw Billy the Kid.[5]

In January 1904 he invited Daniels's longtime friend Bat Masterson to the White House and offered him appointment as U.S. marshal for the Western District of Arkansas (Indian Territory), a position carrying a $4,000 annual salary and authority to name twenty-two deputies, but Bat declined, saying he did not want to leave New York City, where he had made his residence for two years. He did, however, accept appointment to the position of deputy U.S. marshal in that city, a cushy, lucrative sinecure that he could easily handle in addition to his regular work as a newspaper boxing columnist.[6]

Roosevelt in 1905 appointed Seth Bullock, veteran lawman of Deadwood, to the office of U.S. marshal for South Dakota.[7]

The following year he named lawman and celebrated wolf-catcher John R. ("Catch-'Em-Alive Jack") Abernathy, to the position of U.S. marshal for Oklahoma Territory.[8]

As early as the summer of 1902, when it became apparent that the marshal appointment for Daniels would be blocked, Roosevelt considered getting his friend a territorial position. He wrote Alexander Brodie, his appointee as governor of Arizona, asking him to offer Daniels the job of assistant superintendent at the territorial prison at Yuma. In August Brodie asked Daniels, "as a favor" to both himself and the president, to accept the appointment. Daniels, smarting over the loss of the marshal position and believing an "assistant" job beneath his capabilities, rejected the proposal out of hand.⁹

Roosevelt, still mindful of the need to do something for Daniels, waited for the uproar over the marshal appointment to subside. Then in 1904 he wrote Governor Brodie, suggesting that Daniels be given the job of penitentiary superintendent at Yuma. Brodie, no fool, knew that when a president suggests, one acts. He immediately requested the resignation of the current superintendent, W. M. Griffith, to make way for the new head man, Ben Daniels.

In a note to his close friend Senator Henry Cabot Lodge, Roosevelt bragged about his gambit: "By the way, I think it will rejoice your heart to know that Governor Brodie of Arizona (late Lieutenant-Colonel of the Rough Riders) is going to appoint Ben Daniels (late one-eared hero of that organization) as warden of the Arizona Penitentiary. When I told this to John Hay he remarked (with brutal absence of feeling) that he believed the proverb ran: 'Set a Rough Rider to catch a thief!'"¹⁰

Griffith was asked to resign in June 1904, but since Daniels required some time to wind up his financial affairs, the change did not take place until October 3, when Daniels formally took over.¹¹

The Arizona Territorial Penitentiary, located at the junction of the Colorado and Gila rivers near Yuma, was operational from 1876 until 1909. A description of it in an 1890 edition of the *Arizona Daily Republican* of Phoenix reads like it was written by a real estate promoter:

> *The Penitentiary is delightfully located on a hill overlooking the town and at a considerable elevation above it. To the north and east the Colorado leaves the base of the hill on which the Prison is located,*

and to the southeast the Gila flows into the mighty river, forming a junction just beyond the Prison grounds. . . . On the opposite bluff in California stands old Fort Yuma. . . . To the south and east is the valley of the Gila. . . . To the south and southwest is the valley of the Colorado. . . . In the sweep of the eye Pilot Knob arrests attention and marks the point where Mexico, California, and Arizona intersect. . . .

The picture is a pleasing and a satisfying one, but it also has a practical side. It is just such a place as a man trained in penology would select for a prison. Hemmed in by rivers and open valleys, escape is almost impossible. . . . The drainage is perfect and the surroundings healthful, the elevation catches refreshing and invigorating breezes. The temperature is never very high, and the nights are nearly always cool and pleasant.[12]

Anyone who has been to Yuma in the summer when temperatures sometimes reach 120 degrees and were the major reason the Arizona penitentiary was notorious throughout the Southwest as the "Hell Hole of Yuma" would scoff at that last assertion.

During the Arizona Territorial Penitentiary's thirty-four years of operation, it was headed up by sixteen wardens, or superintendents as they were called in Arizona. In addition to Ben Daniels, other notable westerners included Thomas Gates, who was stabbed severely in a foiled escape attempt in 1887; John H. Behan, the former controversial sheriff of Cochise County and political and personal foe of Wyatt Earp; William K. Meade, a former U.S. marshal for Arizona; and Tom Rynning, a former Rough Rider and captain of the Arizona Rangers.[13] Among its many infamous inmates were Barney Riggs, a well-known gunfighter who was granted a pardon after helping Superintendent Gates put down the escape attempt of 1887; Phin Clanton of the Clanton clan of Cochise County notoriety; "Buckskin Frank" Leslie, the Tombstone gunman; female stagecoach robber Pearl Hart; and desperado

Albert ("Burt") Alvord, whose controversial release from incarceration would involve Ben Daniels.

One of the first to wish Daniels good fortune when he took over at Yuma was the president. On October 17 he wrote Daniels, saying he was "mighty pleased" to hear of the appointment. "I know," he said, "you will do your work in a way that will make every one of your old friends proud of you, and none more so than . . . Your old Colonel, Theodore Roosevelt."[14]

It does not seem possible that Daniels could have entered on his new responsibility as warden of the territorial prison without musing on the irony of the situation; only twenty-five years earlier he had entered another territorial prison as a convict. Now he would be looking through the penitentiary bars from the outside instead of the inside. No other superintendent at the Arizona Territorial Penitentiary at Yuma could have felt more empathy for the inmates than did Ben Daniels, former Convict No. 88 at the Wyoming Territorial Penitentiary at Laramie.

The tenure of Daniels at the Yuma prison was uneventful and lasted only eight months, from October 3, 1904, to June 5, 1905.[15] In January 1905 he was quoted in the *Tucson Citizen* as saying "things were moving quietly at the prison," with 347 convicts currently locked up there, at a monthly cost of $14 per inmate, or a little less than fifty cents a day per capita.[16]

During the period of Daniels's service at Yuma his "Old Colonel" won reelection to the presidency. In February 1905 supporters and admirers of the president from around the nation flocked to Washington to attend the inaugural festivities, including former Rough Rider Lieutenant Colonel Alexander Brodie; Captains James McClintock and Frank Frantz; First Lieutenant George Wilcox; and enlisted men Ben Daniels and Sherman Bell. A select list of thirty members of the regiment served as Roosevelt's escort of honor in the inaugural parade and ceremony on March 4.[17]

In a full-page account headed "ROUGH RIDERS WILL HEAD ROOSEVELT'S PARADE," a correspondent for the *Atlanta Constitution* wrote of the selection of "lightning gun play artists of Arizona" and mentioned Ben Daniels, described as "once marshal of Dodge City, worst of all 'bad' towns." Writing of the heroism of the veterans of the late war, he spoke of Daniels "climbing like a schoolboy up that bullet-swept hill in front of Santiago." Struck by the diversity of the regimental veterans, some of whom were celebrated sports figures from elite eastern universities as well as western cowboy types, he wrote: "Captain Woodbury Kane of the polo and yachting sets, Private Ben Daniels, late of the penitentiary,[18] Sherman Bell, private and general and the best hated man in Colorado since he crushed the Western Federation of Miners with his iron heel, and Governor Brodie, once of West Point, but for thirty years an Arizona frontiersman, will be proud to ride beside each other at their leader's carriage."[19]

Another highlight of the inauguration parade was an assembly of Roosevelt's cowboy friends from the West who arrived in Washington with their horses and, dressed in traditional cowboy garb—big hats, neckerchiefs, chaps, high-heeled boots, and six-shooters prominently displayed—rode in the parade waving their Stetsons and twirling their lariats but judiciously refraining from firing their pistols. Among the fifty veterans of the cattle range were Seth Bullock, the Deadwood lawman; Tom Mix, later to be a top cowboy movie star; Howard Eaton, a prominent Montana rancher; and Jim Dahlman, the mayor of Omaha and a former cattle association range detective. Later the cowboys were greeted individually by the president, who stood at the north portico of the White House and shook hands with the men as they rode up with Winchesters extending from saddle scabbards and Colt six-shooters hanging from cartridge-studded belts. Roosevelt enjoyed the scene immensely, but his security people must have been appalled.[20]

Daniels presented the president with a handsome cane beautifully fashioned from a cow horn by one of the convicts in the prison.[21] A few days later the *Washington Post* commented on the stay at the Raleigh Hotel of the Arizona prison superintendent, "a big man, of typical frontier look, good-humored and unconventional. In the old days when personal encounters were frequent in Kansas he was [known] as one of the readiest men in that country and one of the most proficient shots when any affair came up that seemed to require firearms. But not long ago Mr. D. settled down into a peaceable and extremely orderly citizen and events of the past are as though they had never been."[22]

Roosevelt took the opportunity while Brodie and Daniels were in Washington to take them aside and explain that the appointment of Daniels to the Arizona prison job had only been an interim step in his ultimate goal, the successful placement of Daniels in the U.S. marshal position. He asked Brodie to pen a letter lauding Daniels's performance at Yuma, which he would use in that endeavor.

The governor complied with glowing language. He said he had found Daniels in his service as superintendent of the prison to be

honest, honorable, sober, reliable and fearless in this place of trust and responsibility; humane in his care of those in his charge, impartial in his administration and at all times absolutely in command of the situation....

I consider him to be a man of the true American type, patriotic, home loving, honest and honorable and at all times to be relied upon. He has shown himself always to be a man of dignity, whether in success or adversary.[23]

Cowboys gathered in Washington, D.C., to honor President Roosevelt at his inaugural. Seth Bullock is the tall man, front row center; Tom Mix is in the front row, third from the right. From the R. K. DeArment Collection.

Armed with this strong testimonial, Roosevelt had his secretary forward it to the attorney general, W. H. Moody, with a note: "The President wishes to appoint Mr. B. F. Daniels United States Marshal for Arizona about June next, when the present incumbent will have served four years. He directs that at that time you notify the present incumbent that the President expects his resignation and that Daniels is to be put in his place."[24]

While in the East, Daniels went to New York City and attempted to see his old Dodge City pal Bat Masterson, but missed him, as Masterson was enjoying his regular winter vacation at Hot Springs, Arkansas. When he got back Bat wrote Daniels, saying he was sorry they hadn't gotten together, and wished him success in the future. "Isn't President Roosevelt about the best ever?" he asked. "There is no red tape about that man. He thinks well of you and there is no mistake but what you will get what you want if he can give it to you. . . . I am glad you are in a good position for the time being and hope when a change is made it will be in your interest."[25]

As directed by the president, in early June U.S. Marshal Myron McCord resigned his position, effective July 1, and Daniels tendered his resignation as prison superintendent at the same time. A few days later Roosevelt announced the reappointment of Daniels to the marshal's post. Since Senate confirmation still was required, Daniels's official title was "U.S. Marshal–Designate." But Daniels forged ahead, renting a home in Phoenix, where McCord had established the marshal's office, and moving there.[26] On July 1 he took the oath of office before Judge John H. Campbell, of the First Judicial District, Territory of Arizona.[27]

Chapter 11
U.S. Marshal
1905–1909

Now the once convicted felon is lifted into an honorable office as if he had always been a man of exemplary character.
—Macon Daily Telegraph, June 25, 1905,
quoting the Boston Herald

The estimate of his character and qualifications which prompted you to appoint him marshal has been abundantly justified. He has "made good" in every way.
—Arizona Supreme Court Justice John H. Campbell

AS ONE HISTORIAN has pointed out, "the faith which Roosevelt put in Daniels, even after he had lied and embarrassed the President, is not easy to understand." But Roosevelt reasoned that if his perception of Daniels as basically an honest man, loyal and devoted to the Rough Rider regiment, was correct, then his appointee would take very seriously what the president called the "double burden" that Rough Riders accepted when they took office, an obligation "to make the best kind of record" for themselves as individuals and for the regiment as a whole.[1]

As Ben Daniels must have noticed, no advancement in his affairs ever came easily. Having at last attained the title and office of U.S. marshal he had long coveted, he still had to wait for the necessary Senate confirmation. His appointment had been made by the president on an interim basis during a period when the Senate was not in session, and, as he was soon to learn, the same red flags that had prevented his confirmation three years earlier began flying again.

When news of the appointment reached the press, newspapers politically opposed to Roosevelt leaped on it to reproach the president. Even simple news stories announcing the appointment carried a negative slant, focusing on the sordid events of Daniels's early life and ignoring his later, more approbatory career.

The headline in the *New York Times* read: "ACCUSED ROUGH RIDER WINS" with the subhead: "President to Make Him Marshal, It Is Said, Despite Jail Record."[2]

"BEN DANIELS REAPPOINTED. THE PRESIDENT MAKES EX-CONVICT U.S. MARSHAL FOR ARIZONA," ran the headline in the *Washington Post*. The paper went on to retell the story of the abortive appointment of 1902, saying that Roosevelt's excuse for withdrawing Daniels's name was that the man "had told him a falsehood," but the actual reason was that Daniels, as a convicted felon, had lost his citizenship. Now, said the paper, the president, while admitting his appointee was a "thoroughly representative of the 'bad man' type of the West," claimed that he was still a valuable man for the office, and by executive order had restored his citizenship.[3]

An editorial in the *Daily Telegraph* of Macon, Georgia, quoted "scandalized exclamations" printed in the *Boston Herald*: "The Senate not being in session, and no confirmation being required until is does meet, President Roosevelt, without a word of explanation to the country, appointed and commissioned this same Daniels to be United States marshal for Arizona! It appears that he had previously prepared the way, restoring him to citizenship by an act of executive clemency. Now the once convicted felon is lifted into an honorable office as if he had always been a man of exemplary character."

The editor of the Macon paper went on to record his own view of the affair:

The president must think that the only sure way to reform an ex-convict is to give him a government office. Perhaps he also thinks that to have been a Rough Rider is glory enough to atone for all previous sins. At any rate, "Ben" Daniels, ex-convict, now holds the post of honor which the scandalized Senate hastily took away from him three years ago. Protest is useless, for the president likes to have his own way and has ever shown a tenacity of purpose in the matter of unpopular appointments that is quite amazing. But we venture to suspect that even in Arizona there is some fear of the effect on the rising generation and the young men of this reappointment of an ex-convict to an important government office.[4]

Another Roosevelt favorite, Bat Masterson, was in Washington visiting the president in December 1905, and the president asked him to nose around the Capitol and see what he could learn about the holdup in the Senate of the appointment of their mutual pal, Ben Daniels. In a report of his findings to the president, Masterson confirmed that Senator Henry Moore Teller of Colorado was the chief stumbling block holding up the confirmation and thought it was simply "a desire on his part to take a slap at the President." Nevertheless, several congressmen were working on the "senile statesman from the Rockies" in an effort to induce him to drop his opposition. "I imagine," Bat said, "Ben is not anxious to have that penitentiary matter exploited again in the press as well as an executive session of the Senate."[5]

While Senate committees postponed consideration of his appointment, delaying for months referral of the matter

Bat Masterson as he looked when President Roosevelt asked him to check out Daniels's confirmation prospects in the Senate. The photo, dated November 24, 1904, was inscribed to E. F. Colburn, an old Dodge City friend. Courtesy of the Craig Fouts Collection.

to the full Senate, Marshal Daniels continued with his duties.[6] When he took over from Marshal McCord, he had found three other Rough Riders—David Hughes, Charles Utting, and John Foster—serving as deputies. He soon added to that list three more: Walter Gregory, Thomas Mooney, and Samuel Greenwald. Gregory had been his secretary at the Yuma prison.[7]

Early in November the marshal personally made an arrest of an Indian Territory fugitive. Acting on information that K. McKaskill, wanted for robbery in that territory, was in Globe, Arizona, Daniels went there, found his man dealing faro in a Globe saloon, and took him into custody.[8] It wasn't a particularly important collar, but it showed that the new marshal was willing to go out in the field and work as a real lawman and not just shuffle papers behind a desk. Arizonans liked that.

In the latter months of 1905 Marshal Daniels got tangled up in the bureaucratic foul-up of the Burt Alvord affair.

The story of Albert ("Burt") Alvord, a lawman who turned to outlawry, is the mirror opposite of the Daniels experience. After having served honorably as a deputy under Sheriff John Slaughter of Cochise County, Arizona, and constable of the town of Wilcox, Alvord turned to outlawry, secretly organizing a band of train robbers in 1899. The gang's holdup of a New Mexico & Arizona train in February 1900 was thwarted primarily by the prompt action and deadly shooting of noted lawman Jeff Milton. Milton mortally wounded "Three-Finger Jack" Dunlap, one of the bandits, who before he died implicated Alvord in the crime. Alvord went on the run, but was finally captured. Tried and convicted of theft of U.S. mail in December 1903, Alvord received a two-year stretch in the territorial prison at Yuma. He was one of the inmates there during the tenure of Superintendent Ben Daniels.

Since Alvord was also wanted for crimes in Mexico, Daniels, before resigning to take the marshal's position, agreed to turn him over to Mexican authorities following his release from the Yuma pen. Daniels figured that release date, based on the judge's sentence, to be October 26, 1905, and so informed the Mexicans. But his successor as prison superintendent, Jerry Millay, reduced the convict's time for good behavior and released him on October 9. Alvord promptly disappeared. The Mexican officials were irate and blamed Daniels for duplicity. An international incident appeared in the offing. Daniels was required to write a lengthy letter to the attorney general explaining his actions.[9]

When Alvord reportedly showed up at his sister's home in Los Angeles, Daniels went there personally to see about his arrest, but received no cooperation from the local police, who took the attitude that the man had been legally released from custody and was simply being harassed by the Arizona lawman, who had no extradition papers anyway. While the embarrassing standoff between the different law enforcement agencies provided some comic relief for readers of the local press, Alvord skipped town again.[10]

The matter was serious enough that the attorney general sent a special investigator to Arizona to sort the thing out and determine where the responsibility for the problem lay. After a thorough investigation lasting several months, Examiner J. D. Harris concluded that Millay "exceeded his authority and was at least guilty of gross negligence and carelessness [in] releasing the prisoner without first consulting and advising the United States Attorney and therefore conclude that he is the one who is directly chargeable with, and responsible for, the premature release of Albert Alvord," thereby exonerating Daniels of any blame.[11]

When after five months the Senate still had not confirmed the Daniels appointment, the ever-aggressive president applied pressure. He wrote a remarkable letter to Senator Clarence Don Clark of Wyoming, chairman of the Committee on Appointments, summarizing Daniels's career and listing his virtues. The letter is quite revealing of the deep respect and admiration Theodore Roosevelt held for western men of the Ben Daniels cut.

Daniels, he said, had grown to manhood under conditions "which have now as completely vanished from this country as the age of the Vikings has vanished from Europe; and Daniels and the men like him, who were the only ones who could grapple effectively with those conditions, bore no small resemblance in both their virtues and their faults to these same Vikings." At the age of eighteen Daniels was a "frontier scout and ranger [who had] fight after fight with the Indians as well as with white desperadoes." After ten years of "a turbulent life on the remote frontier of civilization . . . he finally got in with a set of men of bad character and took part in the robbery under arms of a band of horses or mules from a Government agency." The other criminals escaped, but Daniels "was captured, tried, convicted and served a term in the penitentiary. Since coming out he has served in many important positions with great credit; and both before and after the commission of the crime he displayed signal heroism in supporting the cause of law and order at the peril of his life." He spoke of his personal observance of Daniels's bravery and devotion to duty under fire in Cuba:

I speedily found that he was one of the men in whom I could place entire trust and whom I could use in the most hazardous and responsible service. A more gallant, more loyal and more trustworthy soldier never wore the United States uniform.

> *Not only was he absolutely indifferent to personal danger of any kind, but he showed excellent judgment, was a strong steadying influence on the regiment in every way....*
>
> *In battle, I repeatedly entrusted him with the performance of hazardous duty..., the leadership of the sharpshooters.*
>
> *He was always at the front in any emergency, and his coolness was absolutely unshaken..., and when the fighting was over, and the fatigue had been so great to exhaust all but the very strongest, I would employ him, although himself a sick man, in conducting on foot the carts containing the fever-stricken men whom we had to send to the fever hospitals in the rear.*

In conclusion, Roosevelt stated firmly: "I am not willing that the United States should lose the value of his proved courage and efficiency. Still less am I willing to admit that even a grave offense in a man's youth cannot be wiped out by a record such as I have given above."[12]

The president had solicited testimonials from highly placed Arizona officials and attached them to his letter to Senator Clark.

In a telegram Edward Kent, chief justice of the Arizona Supreme Court, affirmed that Daniels's record as prison warden and as marshal during the months of his service was "very good" and "satisfactory to the court." He claimed Daniels was "fearless and energetic [with a] great desire to acquit himself well in his responsible position."[13]

Joseph H. Kibbey, who earlier that year had replaced the retiring Alexander Brodie as Arizona governor, sent a wire in a similar vein.

Roosevelt also quoted the entire text of letters of commendation regarding Daniels he had received earlier, Governor Brodie's fulsome remarks the previous March, and the laudatory notes from Fred Dodge and Howell P. Myton written back in 1901 at the time of the first attempt to install Daniels in the marshal's post.[14]

Despite this all-out effort by the president on behalf of his appointee, the senators continued to drag their feet. Chairman Clark of the Appointments Committee kicked the matter over to the Judiciary Committee, and there it languished into the new year of 1906. After waiting impatiently for six weeks, Roosevelt, clearly irked by the interminable delay, in January directed a communication to the Judiciary Committee, once again recounting Daniels's history and the high regard he held for him. He demanded action.

The *New York World*, a paper not particularly friendly to the Roosevelt administration, carried the story of that letter on the front page, saying the president had "scolded" the Senate committee because it had been "a trifle slow" in approving the Daniels appointment.[15]

Roosevelt's frustration with the entire process was evident in a letter he wrote to his artist-friend Frederic Remington in February: "You know I have appointed to office in the West, and in the case of Bat Masterson, in the East, a number of the very men whose types you have permanently preserved with pencil and pen. . . . I have a good deal of difficulty to get the Senate to take the proper view about some of these men, notably Ben Daniels, who is really a first-class fellow."[16]

Despite the all-out offensive of the president to get the appointment confirmed, opposition remained strong. An Indiana doctor named D. D. Rose wrote Roosevelt in February that he had known Daniels and Bat Masterson in Dodge City, and both were murderers. Masterson had boasted, he said, of sending "twenty-six of his fellow men to their graves with their boots on." Ed Julian had been "cowardly, sneakily shot in the back by Ben. Daniels. . . . Such appointments are a blot on your otherwise brilliant administration. There are plenty of honorable, clean men who would be pleased with such appointments and would be an honor, instead of a disgrace, to our beloved country."[17]

During this period of uncertainty, while the senators procrastinated over the controversial Daniels appointment, a couple of incidents occurred that served only to embarrass the U.S. marshal–designate and his sponsor in the White House.

Marshal Daniels had practiced a common form of nepotism and appointed a nephew, a young man named Thomas E. Daniels, as one of his deputies in Arizona.[18] In November 1905 young Daniels left Globe, Arizona, for El Paso, Texas, where he and other deputies took a group of federal prisoners in charge and entrained for Indian Territory. Before arriving at his destination Thomas Daniels began "to act queerly" and was sent back. On the return trip he "became more or less violent" and had to be constrained by other officers. A telegram to Ben Daniels had advised him of the problem, and he met the train at El Paso and placed his nephew under the care of doctors. The headline in the Prescott newspaper did nothing to enhance Daniels's chances in Washington: "BEN DANIELS' NEPHEW INSANE."[19]

Another incident a few months later was a source of further embarrassment. In February 1906 U.S. Marshal Ben Daniels was arrested in Nogales, Arizona, by Sheriff Charles Fowler and charged with fraud.[20] The complainant, a man named Hans Larsen, said that Daniels a year earlier had sold him a mine for $800 to which he had no legal claim, and when Larsen demanded return of the money, Daniels refused. Daniels indignantly protested that the whole thing was a case of blackmail and an attempt by his enemies to smear him in hopes of preventing his confirmation. At a hearing a magistrate tended to agree and quickly dismissed the charges. But the story was picked up and published in the *Washington Post* and other influential papers to the delight of the president's political enemies, and although Daniels had been cleared of the allegation, those enemies added the charge to the list of crimes they said he had committed.[21] (Roosevelt may not have paid too much attention to the story, however, because on February 17, the very day it broke in the press, his daughter, Alice, was getting married in the White House.)

On February 28 Ben Daniels and his wife arrived in Phoenix on business "of an entirely private nature." When questioned by a reporter for the *Arizona Daily Republican*, Daniels said he did not care to discuss the Senate confirmation of his appointment, but was confident he would ultimately win approval. He was pleased by the discharge of the case in Santa Cruz County, which he said was only a ploy to hurt him during the Senate deliberation.[22]

Apparently impelled by the president's chiding letter, the Judiciary Committee finally sent the Daniels appointment to the Senate with a favorable recommendation. On February 16 the *Washington Post* noted that an argument on the confirmation lasted one and a half hours in an executive session of the Senate and ended in a tie vote. So the debate continued.

Typical of the press criticism Roosevelt received because of the Daniels appointment was an editorial in the *Montgomery Advertiser*:

> *The selection of Daniels for such a position as that of United States Marshal of a somewhat lawless section of the union was an act which cannot be defended. It was another of those too numerous official acts of Roosevelt where personal favoritism has been suffered to override fitness, character, or even decency. The appointment was made either without knowledge of the standing of the appointee or to*

show contempt for public opinion. We know it has been denied that Daniel [sic] was guilty of mule stealing, but the denials have failed to be convincing. The stealing of a mule, the killing of two or more men, the selling of a fake diamond mine and getting pay are among the little pecadillos [sic] charged to his account. If Roosevelt did not know of these charges when he made the appointment he was guilty of negligence in not inquiring into the character of a man to whom he was giving a responsible position. The Senators were better informed and have so far refused to confirm the appointment.

It may be asked why the President did not withdraw the nomination when he learned of these grave charges and of the Senate's dissatisfaction? Well, all who know anything of Roosevelt know that he has a horror of admitting himself in the wrong. He has shown this quality of stubbornness on so many occasions that nobody expects him to take the back track, even though he may know that he is committing an error. After hearing the charges and objections against Daniels it would have been both manly and proper to admit that he was deceived. There would have been no lowering of Presidential dignity in so doing and no reflection on his integrity. As it is, he has seriously embarrassed the Senate and even if that body should swallow its scruples and confirm the appointment, it will have little effect on the sentiment of the country. That sentiment is decidedly unfavorable.[23]

Not all the press coverage was negative, however. Out in Arizona many newspaper editors defended the president and his controversial appointee. Under the headline "GOOD WORDS FOR BEN DANIELS," the *Tucson Post* opined:

Ben Daniels is a good citizen and a capable official and those who know him have the utmost confidence in his integrity. Men who do not know Mr. Daniels personally will be able to gain from the blackmailing schemes, to which his enemies are resorting, some idea of the nature of the fight which is being conducted against his confirmation by the United States senate. The president knows his man and is standing by him in this fight and it is to be hoped that Daniels will be confirmed at an early date. The interest which a Santa Cruz county official showed in the charge brought there against Mr. Daniels don't [sic] look well on its face.[24]

The *Prescott Morning Courier* chimed in, saying: "The United States Senate is holding up the nomination of Ben Daniels because of something Ben is said to have done in early youth. Should St. Peter apply the same rule to United States senators when they appear for admission to the pearly gates, there will be no United States senators in heaven—no, not a one."[25]

But perhaps the most powerful defense of Daniels was published that month by L. C. Hughes, editor of the *Arizona Daily Star*, former governor of the territory, and a longtime defender of Daniels:

Ben F. Daniels was appointed United States Marshal for Arizona about eight months ago. During his service the people and the Department of Justice have had the opportunity of observing the character of the man as a public servant. . . . He has and is making a superb United States Marshal in every particular. This fact will not be gainsaid by any responsible citizen of Arizona. . . .

The question is being asked throughout Arizona by those who know him and of his public service: "Why don't [sic] the United States Senate confirm Ben Daniels as United States Marshal?"

The Star declared and challenges contradiction of the fact that no man has filled the office of U.S. Marshal during the last thirty-five years in Arizona more efficiently and with stricter integrity, with more satisfaction to the people, the courts and the Department of Justice than has Ben F. Daniels during the last eight months.

We speak from personal knowledge for the editor of the Star had known every U.S. Marshal of Arizona and his public record during that period of time and hence we speak from knowledge of the fact and not from hearsay. . . .

> When the safety, the honor of our common country was challenged; when the Maine went down in foreign waters; when the world looked on to witness the spirit of America's sons, the same Ben F. Daniels whose name is now before you was among the first to tender his services in defense of our common country—the flag and its honor. . . .
>
> Is this not accepted as the rule in every country under every government—that he who may have violated the law can offer no more higher or acceptable atonement than tendering his life to defend the laws and country in time of peril?[26]

Finally, on April 25, almost ten months after Daniels had assumed office, the opposition to the Daniels appointment collapsed, and the Senate confirmed his appointment without a dissenting vote.[27] The editor of the *Arizona Weekly Republican*, while applauding the news, credited much of the campaign's success to the work of Sidney Bieber, former fire marshal of Washington, D.C., who had spent a year in Arizona and had become closely acquainted with Daniels. No doubt Bieber's friendship with Speaker of the House Joseph G. Cannon also contributed.[28]

The *Washington Post* remarked dryly that the senators finally decided that since Daniels "stole a government mule and rode it several hundred miles, he had been sufficiently punished."[29]

After all those agonizing months of debate and delay, Ben Daniels, out in Arizona, could heave a huge sigh of relief and remove the "designate" appendage from his title; he was at last a U.S. marshal with no strings attached. He wrote a letter of appreciation to the president, thanking him for his steadfast support. Roosevelt's reply was short, but reaffirmed the boundless faith he had in his old Rough Rider comrade: "That is a bully letter of yours, and I appreciate it. You are one of the men I swear by, and I was bound to fight for you with every ounce of strength there was in me."[30]

In another letter Roosevelt said he took pride in his appointments and singled Ben Daniels out as one of his best. He had placed in office "thoroughly fearless, honest and intelligent" officials, "marshals like Ben Daniels in Arizona—and in short, a great variety of men who, in different positions, are all doing their duty and more than their duty with a hearty zeal. . . . When I look at the men I have named and their like I feel we have got a pretty good country with pretty good men in it."[31]

In a long editorial the *Albuquerque Journal* reviewed the lengthy history of the Daniels appointment and the president's battle with the Senate to secure confirmation, saying the story was "as interesting as a novel." The determining factor, the writer believed, was Roosevelt's letter to Senator Clark extolling Daniels and his adventurous life in the frontier West:

Those were the ecstatic times when the celebrated Wild Bill was at the zenith of his fame in and around the old Santa Fe trail and kept order only by being the deadest shot in town. Bat Masterson and Ben Daniels were hardly such terrors with a gun as Wild Bill, and their fame has come to them in later and more effete civilization, but it is to be cheerfully conceded that they did their share in the conquest of the west from the "bad men" whom the Civil War let loose upon the great plains. . . .

Like some of the most distinguished frontier heroes, Daniels served the cause of law and order at times most brilliantly, but like them, too, he had his lapses. Even Wild Bill was no saint, and Bat Masterson was never in the habit of saying his prayers. . . .

The President's appeal to the Senate in favor of Comrade Daniels evidently had the desired effect. One very prominent senator remarked when the case was under consideration, "Although I am not a champion of this administration, I heartily endorse the position

When the U.S. Senate finally confirmed his appointment in 1906, U.S. Marshal Ben Daniels celebrated by posing for these two portraits, sending one to his old friend Bill Tilghman in Oklahoma. As usual when photographed, he was careful to conceal his damaged right ear. *At left*, courtesy of the Kansas State Historical Society; *at right*, courtesy of the Arizona Historical Society.

taken by the President when he says, 'I am not willing to admit that even a grave offense in a man's youth can not be wiped out by a record such as I have given above, and we must take for granted that senators generally took the same view of the subject, for as is known, the vote was unanimous in favor of confirming the nomination of Benjamin Franklin Daniels to be marshal of Arizona.'" And why not? Hasn't the same senate voted many a time in favor of the confirmation of men guilty of much more serious offenses than that of swiping a mule?[32]

Amid all this newspaper give and take about his controversial appointment, Ben Daniels continued to do the job he had been given. He appointed a number of deputies—during his tenure in office he would commission a total of forty-three. Among these were some notable Arizona Rangers: Lieutenant John Foster, Sergeant Arthur A. Hopkins, and Privates Leonard S. Page and Charles E. McGaw, giving these officers arrest authority for federal offenses as well as territorial crimes. He also issued deputy marshal papers to his old friend Fred Dodge, the Wells Fargo detective, who was on a case in Arizona.[33]

In June Daniels had a rather exciting experience. He had entrained for San Francisco with twenty illegal immigrant Chinese his deputies had rounded up. While he was having his breakfast in the dining car the train derailed. He was unhurt, but the car with his deputies and the Chinese turned completely over, and a fire broke out. In the excitement one of the immigrants escaped but was later recaptured. After several hours a relief train arrived to take the officers and the deportees on to their destination. "Arrests for being unlawfully in the United States are frequent on the border and the marshal has nearly a second carload for shipment," noted the *Arizona Daily Republican*.[34]

On hearing reports that certain Arizona merchants were selling arms to rampaging Yaqui Indians in Mexico, Roosevelt in July directed Marshal Daniels to put a stop to it. Daniels acted immediately, deputizing fifty special officers and stationing them along the border near Nogales to interdict arms shipments being smuggled into Mexico. On the 23rd of the month Acting Attorney General W. M. Hoyt cautioned the president about this action, questioning it on two grounds, its cost and its doubtful legality. "The per diem expense of each of these men will be about $6," he said, "and therefore the per diem expense of the posse will be $300." Additionally, he pointed out that laws prohibiting sales of weapons to Indians applied only to Indians within this country and not to those in a foreign land. "The purchase of arms and ammunition generally and the smuggling of them into Mexico . . . is an illicit transaction morally, rather than an illegal transaction."[35]

After conferring with the president about the matter, Hoyt directed Daniels to disband most of his special deputies as quickly as possible, but to retain two who were to be deployed along the border "to act in co-operation with Mexican customs authorities in preventing sales of arms to Yaqui Indians." Daniels dismissed his "specials" at once, as directed, but refrained from assigning two to work with the Mexican officials. His response to Acting Attorney General Hoyt indicates his sense that this scenario could lead to serious international difficulties that might reflect adversely on his performance as marshal and provide additional fodder for those critics of the president and his newly installed appointee. "I would prefer not to appoint any deputies," he said, "if they are to have any communication with the Mexican authorities, for the reason that I am desirous of not having anything happen which might result in censure to my administration of the Marshal's office, which might occur if these suggestions were carried out."[36]

The matter was resolved without any further difficulty, but only a few weeks later Daniels was struck an entirely unexpected severe personal blow. His wife, Laura, had gone to Blue Springs, Missouri, early in August to visit her mother. On the 23rd Daniels entrained from Tucson to meet her at Emporia, Kansas,[37] where she was stopping with her sister-in-law, Mrs. E. L. Copple, and accompanying her the rest of the way back home. But while at Emporia Laura fell ill and died quite

The gravestone of Annie Laura Daniels, Ben's first wife, at Blue Springs, Missouri. At the top of the stone is an open book with the inscription, "Dear Wife." From the Jack DeMattos Collection.

suddenly. Forty-seven years old, she had been married to Ben for nineteen years. Ben took her body back to Blue Springs for burial with her family.[38]

Alone now, with his wife gone and no children, Ben Daniels devoted his energies to his law enforcement work. He did have an enjoyable respite in the spring of 1907 when he went to Washington to visit with his friend and benefactor, President Roosevelt.

On March 20 Roosevelt invited him to a luncheon to honor the Right Honorable James Bryce, the British ambassador. Ben Daniels, the roughhewn western frontiersman, sat down and dined with the president, the ambassador, and a host of dignitaries, including Secretary of State Elihu Root; Secretary of War (and soon to be president) William Howard Taft; Secretary of the Treasury George B. Cortelyou; Secretary of the Interior James R. Garfield; Assistant Secretary of State Robert Bacon; Commissioner of Labor Charles P. Neill; the Right Reverend Ethelbert Talbert, Episcopalian missionary bishop of Wyoming and Idaho; and Edward H. Butler, publisher of the *Buffalo Evening News*.[39]

A few days later Daniels was back in the White House again, this time with companions with whom he surely felt more comfortable: Bat Masterson, who had been invited down from New York City, and William H. ("Bull") Andrews, delegate from the territory of New Mexico. According to press reports, when they arrived the president immediately dropped what he was doing and greeted them warmly. After a chat with the three westerners he took them out on the grounds and introduced them to Theodore Jr., who was playing tennis. There was no indication that any of the visitors joined Junior on the court.[40]

While in Washington Daniels stayed at the Raleigh Hotel, where Masterson always put up when in the capital. The two old friends must have spent many a pleasant hour cutting up old touches about Dodge City and its characters in the early days.[41]

On April 10 Ben Daniels, Bat Masterson, and Bull Andrews were invited back to the White House again. A wire service dispatch took note of the visit by the three under the head: "MEETING OF GUN FIGHTERS."

It was lucky that nobody "started anything" at the White House this forenoon. Had trouble started it is pretty certain that it would have been ended at the morgue for the unwise originators. "Bat" Masterson, "Ben" Daniels and "Bull" Andrews all happened to drop in to see the president about the same time. Both "Bat" and "Ben" have notches on their guns. "Bull" is not supposed to have ever shot daylight through any of his brethren, but he has been in some tight places down in the lively southwest and it is not recorded that he ever showed the white feather. He is at present delegate to congress from New Mexico, but gained his nickname and political training in Pennsylvania. Masterson is just now a deputy marshal over in New York but is known and respected for his deeds throughout the border states. When it comes to getting out a shooting iron and getting it out quick few are believed to excel Marshal Masterson. Ben Daniels is United States marshal of Arizona and one of the most indefatigable crook-chasers that the department of justice has upon its payroll.[42]

All was not White House visitations, sightseeing excursions, and reminiscences with old friends at the bar of the Raleigh for Marshal Ben Daniels while in Washington. On April 12 he penned a long, detailed report for the attorney general about the smuggling of arms across the border to Yaqui Indians in Mexico, a problem still complained about by the Mexican government. His investigation had shown, Daniels said, that although some weapons and ammunition were crossing the border, Americans were not engaged in anything illegal, and the blame lay with the Mexican government itself, which was issuing permits to both Americans and Mexicans to take guns and ammunition across the border as long as the duty was paid. This was going on despite the claim of the Mexican government that strict orders had been issued prohibiting firearms and ammunition entering Mexico. As long as this state of affairs continued, he said, "it would be useless for the United States to try to help them to stop the smuggling, and especially so until they show some inclination in that direction themselves."[43]

Returning to Arizona, Daniels became involved in the controversy over the burning statehood question for that territory and neighboring New Mexico. President Roosevelt favored admission of the two territories as a single state, a plan called "jointure." This idea was unpopular in both territories, and many residents fought against it vigorously. Ben Daniels, ever loyal to his "Old Colonel," made no secret of his support for the plan. As one historian has noted, "the citizens of the territory regarded him as more important as the local voice of President Theodore Roosevelt than as the federal lawman of Arizona."[44] When Secretary of the Interior James R. Garfield and Postmaster Frank H. Hitchcock came west to test the political waters for the "jointure" idea,[45] Daniels accompanied them to the Grand Canyon, where a "jointure consultation" was held. "What did Garfield tell Ben?" was the big question in newspapers of both territories. The tight-lipped Daniels told the reporters nothing.[46]

He did, however, report immediately to his friend, sponsor, and big boss in Washington, Theodore Roosevelt. While careful to have his official correspondence, like the letter to the attorney general quoted above, typed by a secretary well versed in spelling and grammar, when writing to his "Old Colonel" Daniels often wrote in longhand with spelling,

U.S. Marshal Ben Daniels, with his distinctive paunch, in Tombstone, Arizona, 1906. Courtesy of the Arizona Historical Society.

grammar, and generous use of capitals indications of his meager education. "I saw Secretary Garfield, also Mr. Hitchcock," he wrote.

Now I want to tell you, through Friendship, *that if you appoint a Joint Statehood man for Governor of this Territory, I feel quite Shure that we can Send a Deleation from this Territory to the National Convention, instructed for you or any one whom you may name.*

But on the other hand, if you appoint one of the Party who fought Joint Statehood, last Election, I would be pretty Shure that the Deligation would go from here, for Some one Other than yourself or any one whom you may name.

They will promise you any Thing in order to mislead you. They can not be dependid upon, I am warning you fir your own good, Sturgis is not to be trusted, by you any more than the rest, and they are all againsed me because I am your Friend *I mean the antie Joint Statehood outfit.*[47]

The deportation of illegal Asian aliens continued to occupy much of Marshal Daniels's time. Between January 1903 and August 1907 U.S. marshals escorted nine hundred Chinese and three hundred other Asian nationals to San Francisco for deportation.[48] There was no letup in the following years—the *Tucson Citizen* noted in March 1908: "United States Marshal Ben Daniels will leave here Saturday evening with a party of Chinamen who have been ordered deported"[49]—and the deportation would continue until the Mexican Revolution disrupted the flow of Asians across the border after 1911.[50]

The year 1908 was an eventful time in the personal life of Ben Daniels. In May he was made a thirty-second degree Mason.[51] On July 15 he remarried, taking as his wife thirty-nine-year-old Annie Evalina Stakebake Seayrs, also recently widowed.[52]

Annie, a native of Indiana, was first married to Hampton Seayrs, who died in 1907. Educated as a schoolteacher, she would in later years become a highly regarded figure for her educational and social work in Arizona and would be a great asset to Ben's political ambitions.

Meanwhile, across the continent in Washington, D.C., Theodore Roosevelt, who had chosen not to seek another term in the White House, was paving the way for his handpicked successor, William Howard Taft. In a note to Daniels five days before the national election he exuded his usual optimism and confidence in success; "We shall carry Taft thru with a jump!"[53] He was correct; on November 3 Taft handily defeated the Democratic candidate, William Jennings Bryan.

Before leaving office, Roosevelt did his best to ensure that President Taft would continue in office those appointees he had worked so diligently to get into important positions, particularly Ben Daniels. Letters of commendation were solicited and received from prominent Arizonans John H. Campbell, associate justice of the Arizona Supreme Court, and C. M. Reynolds, a leading attorney of Bisbee, Arizona.

Justice Campbell wrote: "From one who has closely observed his official conduct, the manner in which he has conducted the affairs of his office . . . it affords me the great pleasure to assure you that the estimate of his character and qualifications which prompted you to appoint him marshal has been abundantly justified. He has 'made good' in every way."[54]

The plaudits were echoed by Reynolds: "I consider him one of the most conscientious and efficient officials it has ever been my pleasure to know. . . . He is as square a man as I have ever met. I consider this one of the best appointments you have made."[55]

In February 1909 Daniels took the long train ride to Washington, D.C., to visit once again with Roosevelt before the Taft inaugural. Bat Masterson was also there, and the two old friends met at the Raleigh. They were walking down Pennsylvania Avenue, discussing old times, when they ran into three other friends from the West—Jack Abernathy, Chris Madsen, and Bill Tilghman.

Abernathy, who had gained Roosevelt's attention by catching wolves with his bare hands, had been rewarded with appointment as U.S. marshal for Oklahoma. Madsen, who had been a quartermaster sergeant in the Rough Rider regiment, had gone to Washington to lobby Roosevelt for a U.S. marshal appointment in Indian Territory. However, since Madsen had never gone to Cuba and accompanied him in the charge up San Juan Hill, the president opted for another Rough Rider, Benjamin Colbert, to fill that post, and Madsen had to settle for a deputy marshal position under Colbert. Tilghman, a staunch Democrat, had never sought or received a Roosevelt appointment, but traveled on his well-earned reputation as a lawman of long experience and always found a job in local law enforcement or as a deputy U.S. marshal.[56]

The Oklahomans were in town to promote some Wild West motion pictures Tilghman had produced. After viewing the films at the White House, the president invited the three to an upcoming army and navy reception, the last formal function of his administration. Daniels and Masterson knew all about that reception, having been invited to attend also. While talking the matter over they discovered that the Oklahoma lawmen had concluded that since the reception was to honor the military, guns would be in evidence. They had polished up their six-shooters and, in consideration of the dignity of the affair, purchased string ties to match their flannel shirts.

Daniels and Masterson quickly remonstrated with their friends, saying that the reception would be a highly formal affair. "You fellows will sure have to shuck them duds; it's against the rules of the game, and you couldn't get in," said Bat. "Nothing less than a clawhammer coat and a stovepipe hat goes in this country."

The Oklahomans "turned pale at the thought," and at this juncture Abernathy decided he would pass on the whole idea, but Tilghman and Madsen plunged on. "Neither had ever worn a dress suit in his life, [but] were overpowered by the persuasion of Masterson and Daniels, and led to a shop where the use of such apparel could be enjoyed upon payment of a small fee." Bat and Ben "laughed until tears streamed down their cheeks" at the sight of their Oklahoma friends in their finery.

Madsen had the most trouble with his shirt, the sides of the front flaring up from beneath his vest like a tent wall in a cow camp on a windy night. He asked for a tent stake, but there was none handy. Tilghman's distress was most acute after he had choked himself into a "standup collar"—the first he ever wore. He had seen bad results from "chokings" at Dodge City when vigilantes were on the warpath, and the remembrance made him gasp for breath.[57]

Bat Masterson had borrowed a tuxedo from a friend for the event, but after beholding Tilghman and Madsen in their soup-and-fish he decided to bow out. That evening he sent a telegram to his friend: "I ain't going to any reception. Am heading east."[58]

Ben Daniels was of like mind. He boarded a train and headed west for Arizona.

Chapter 12
The Final Years
1909–1923

> *Mr. Daniels embodies the true spirit of the west—a spirit of alertness, enterprise, coolness and courage—and no taint of dishonor has ever marred his adventures or shadowed his good name. He is today one of the most respected and esteemed men of Tucson, honored in business circles and very popular among his many friends.*
> —James H. McClintock

BEN DANIELS HAD NO REASON to believe William Howard Taft's accession to the presidency would endanger his tenure as U.S. marshal for Arizona. After all, Taft was a Republican, the head of the party for which Daniels had labored and served as a convention delegate. Theodore Roosevelt, Daniels's sponsor, had personally selected Taft as his successor. And then there were those highly complimentary endorsements of Daniels's work written by prominent Arizonans in his file at the Justice Department. He could not have been aware that Roosevelt was also actively lobbying President Taft to reappoint him as marshal. In a memo to the president, Roosevelt named eleven federal appointees who, he said, had "been staunch adherents of Mr. Taft under stress of adverse assault." Ben Daniels was the only Arizonan on the list.[1]

But President Taft was listening to other powerful figures in the Republican Party, men like Hovel Smith, chairman of the party's 1908 campaign. In a letter to Ralph Cameron, Republican representative to Congress from Arizona, Smith urged the removal of Daniels. "I have heard rumors," he said, "that President Roosevelt had requested President Taft to reappoint Mr. Ben Daniels U.S. Marshal. Mr. Daniels will undoubtedly fulfill the duties of the office in a creditable manner, but the fact is he is a Democrat, did not take any interest in the campaign last Fall and did not contribute any amount of money which should be forthcoming from him, and I do not feel he is entitled to consideration at the hands of the Republican Party at all."[2]

Daniels and other Roosevelt appointees would soon learn that President Taft did not share his predecessor's admiration for former Rough Riders and western frontier characters and began replacing them one after another. Daniels's turn came in August 1909 when he was called to Washington and Attorney General George W. Wickersham requested his resignation and informed him that he would be replaced by Charles A. Overlock.

Daniels knew Overlock well. A native of Maine, Overlock had opened a butcher shop in Tombstone in 1882 and invested in cattle ranches. In 1900 he and others organized the town of Douglas near the site of a Phelps-Dodge Company smelter, and the venture made them wealthy. Overlock later became mayor of Douglas.[3]

Daniels also had an audience with President Taft, who, as a sort of concession for removing him from his U.S. marshal job, offered him another position, special agent, or chief of police, at the Menomonee Indian Reservation in Wisconsin.[4] He would be well paid, with a salary of $2,500 a year and a $3 per diem expense account for traveling.[5] Daniels accepted the offer, and, after settling up his affairs in Arizona, he and his wife moved to Wisconsin.

In a letter to his friend and former deputy D. N. Willets, written in October 1909, he seemed pleased with the country and his new assignment:

I am located here with my tribe, and it's a pretty nice place. With the exception of a few days it has been very pleasant weather here. We had about four inches of snow just after I arrived here, but it melted in a few days.

We have a saw mill at this place with a capacity of 200,000 feet of lumber per day. We have an electric light plant, and all of the officials' houses are heated by steam, and they are nice, modern dwellings, two stories high. The house in which I reside has seven rooms, with hot and cold water. We have also here a big, three-story hotel with about 100 rooms, for the benefit of the mill hands, but it is not large enough to accommodate all of them, as we have about 450 men working at the mill.

The government has spent about $900,000 at this place building the mill and the eight different logging camps, which in themselves look like young cities, together with about 200 logging teams and their equipments, and miles of logging roads, which are about thirty feet wide and hued right out of the pine forests and made as level as a floor.

The sum of $9,000 has been spent here for dynamite alone, with which to blow out the stumps of trees.

The town is located on the Wisconsin & Northern Railroad and on the Wolf river. The railroad is only about forty miles long.

The streams here are very numerous and the water is clear as crystal. Speckled trout is the only kind of fish found in them, however, and the boys go out every Sunday and catch from ten to fifty, and they are splendid eating. There are a few deer and some bear and lots of partridges, which resemble prairie chickens. I imagine that the whisky tastes about the same here as it does in Arizona, as the Indians seem to like it as well here as they did there.[6]

However, a letter written by James A. Carroll, officer in charge at the reservation, on October 14, 1909, to Commissioner of Indian Affairs Robert G. Valentine indicates Daniels was unhappy with his new job from the start:

Ben Daniels arrived here last Sunday. He approved of the suggestion I made . . . that a commissioner should be stationed here—and at my suggestion he has gone to Milwaukee to consult the judge and ascertain if such an appointment can be made. Daniels was not pleased with the prospect when he came; said he had been deceived and that he intended to go to Washington. I trust I have succeeded in convincing him of the great responsibility that devolved upon him, of the dignity of his position, of the confidence the office reposed on him, and its willingness to lend him every assistance.[7]

Daniels gave it a try. But he had too long held positions of responsibility with no one looking over his shoulder, reporting to higher authority at distant offices in the territorial or national capital, to adjust easily to an on-site boss. In May 1910, after seven months on the job, he tendered his resignation and announced he was returning to Arizona. His explanation set forth in a special dispatch from Sewano, Wisconsin, to the *Milwaukee Journal* and reprinted in several Arizona papers contained more than a hint of bitterness: "I understood that I was to have full charge of the reservation and took the position," he said. "Later I found that I was under Agent Wilson of the reservation of Keshena. I felt that my contract with the government had been broken, and I have now resigned."[8]

Daniels's disinterest in the Wisconsin job could well be ascribed to his continuing activity in mining ventures in the Southwest. While still employed at the Menomonee Indian Reservation, he and his wife, together with a friend named J. J. Tremaine, had signed articles of incorporation at Tucson for the "Elephant Head Mining, Milling and Development Company." On February 9, 1910, the business was incorporated by the three with a $1 million initial stock offering of two hundred thousand shares at $5 each. Its aims and purposes were far-reaching and ambitious:

To own, acquire, lease, hold, sell or otherwise acquire and dispose of water rights, irrigating canals; to locate town sites, and buy, sell or otherwise acquire town sites and in anyways hypothecate said town sites and town lots; to buy, sell, own, operate and erect electric light and power plants and gas works, and deal in all the products of the same; to but and sell all kinds of merchandise and to own and operate stores for dealing in the same; to manufacture, buy, sell and in any manner deal in all kinds of machinery and mining appliances and implements and all kinds of patents covering the same, and to erect, own, and otherwise acquire all buildings necessary to the proper establishment of such factories or iron works and for the carrying on of the business incident to such manufactories; to manufacture, purchase, own, construct, sell, and maintain any and all kinds of works for smelting, reducing, developing and working all kinds of ores and minerals, and to buy and sell all kinds of patents covering the same; to locate all kinds of mineral and oil lands, and to obtain title to the same from the United States or any other country in which the same may be located; to buy, sell and develop and operate mines and mining properties of every character and kind; to build, buy, or otherwise acquire and maintain railroads, canals, tramways, or any other means of transportation from the Company's works or property to any public highway, river, or other constructed line of railway; and generally to conduct any business afforded . . . in the said Territory of Arizona, or in any other state or territory of the United States of America, or in the Republic of Mexico, or in any foreign country.[9]

Far-reaching and ambitious indeed, but this project, like Daniels's smelter, evidently never got beyond the planning (and dreaming) stage.

Daniels returned to Tucson, but made it a point to be in Denver, Colorado, in August to greet the man he still referred to as his "Old Colonel," although Theodore Roosevelt was six years younger than himself. Roosevelt was on a speaking tour covering some five thousand miles and sixteen states. When the popular ex-president stepped off his private railroad car at the Denver depot a throng led by Colorado governor John F. Shafroth at the head of a reception committee surged forward to greet him. As Roosevelt was shaking the governor's hand he spotted a familiar face in the crowd and, according to an account in the *Denver Post*, "dropped the hand of the chief executive of Colorado to throw both arms about a man he addressed familiarly as 'Ben.' . . . 'Excuse me a minute,' said Roosevelt to Gov. Shafroth, 'but this is Ben Daniels and I haven't seen him for years. He went with the Arizona boys and there's none better than he.'"

With Daniels was "old Fred Dodge of Tombstone . . . , Chief of Detectives for Wells Fargo and company, and an intimate friend of Teddy." A *Post* photographer snapped a picture of "Dodge walking slightly ahead of Roosevelt and the ex-President, with a big smile showing [and] his teeth much in evidence . . . , reaching out with his hand to grasp the old Arizonan by the shoulder." Later Roosevelt made it a point to get together with Daniels and Dodge, and the three old friends reminisced for hours.[10]

Several months later, Roosevelt, still on the campaign trail, was scheduled to visit Arizona. Daniels, in a letter he dictated to his wife, importuned him to make a stop in Tucson. "Now, Colonel," he said, "I am not very popular with the Politicians and Office Holders of Arizona, all on account of their not being able to handle me as they saw fit while I was Marshal of the Territory under you, but I want to show them that I am just as popular with my old Colonel today as when I was

In 1910 the *Denver Post* published this photograph of the arrival of President Theodore Roosevelt in Denver. Among the dignitaries greeting him were Ben Daniels, in the derby hat to the president's left, and Fred Dodge, in the white hat to his right. Courtesy of the Huntington Library.

Marshal of this Territory under him while he was President of the United States." He signed the letter, "From your Old Friend and Comrade, B. F. Daniels."[11]

Roosevelt replied that his itinerary regretfully did not allow for a stop in Tucson, but he hoped to see Ben and his wife while in Arizona. He congratulated Annie Daniels on her "admirable handwriting" and said he wished he wrote as well so he would not have to use the typewriter as much.[12]

In March 1911 Roosevelt came back to Arizona for the formal dedication of the great dam on the Salt River that had been named for him. He was honored at a Rough Rider luncheon in Phoenix that was attended by more than thirty veterans of the old regiment, including Ben Daniels of Tucson, J. L. B. Alexander of Phoenix, Sam Greenwald of Florence, James McClintock of Phoenix, Thomas Mooney of Florence, Charles Utting of Yuma, Tom Rynning of Florence, Richard Stanton of Yuma, and George Wilcox of Phoenix.[13]

By 1911 the performance of Taft, his personally selected successor in the White House, had disappointed Roosevelt greatly. His displeasure escalated into open hostility as the months went by. The last ties between the two were severed on Roosevelt's fifty-third birthday, October 27, 1911, the day the Taft administration brought suit against U.S. Steel, charging, among other things, that Roosevelt had been misled during the panic of 1907 when he allowed U.S. Steel to violate the antitrust laws by purchasing the Tennessee Coal and Iron Company.

Roosevelt, cut to the quick, responded with an article in *Outlook* magazine castigating Taft and his administration. There was clearly a schism within the Republican Party, with the "Old Guard" supporting Taft, while a more progressive element urged Roosevelt to challenge the sitting president for leadership of the party at the convention scheduled to be held in Chicago in June 1912. Both Ben Daniels and Bat Masterson, strong Roosevelt supporters, were delegates to that convention,[14] but their efforts on his behalf failed when the majority of the delegates chose Taft as their candidate to face Woodrow Wilson, the Democratic challenger, in the general election. Avid Roosevelt supporters, including Masterson and Daniels, would angrily contend that the voting at the convention had been rigged by bribery or other means. Masterson wrote in his New York newspaper column that in Chicago he had witnessed "cold-blooded burglary" in which the better man had been defeated by foul tactics.[15] Daniels, in a letter to Roosevelt, would charge that "thieves" stole seventy-eight committed Roosevelt delegates, enough to ensure Taft's nomination.[16] Roosevelt did not publicly subscribe to these allegations, but, headstrong and resolute as always, he refused to accept the party's candidate or platform and took leadership of a third party to compete for the presidency. This new political faction was known officially as the Progressive Party, but, following a Roosevelt remark that he was as "strong as a Bull Moose," was commonly called the "Bull Moose Party." At a convention, also held in Chicago and attended by Ben Daniels as a delegate, Roosevelt loyalists unanimously and enthusiastically nominated him for president.

There is a story that Ben Daniels bet $500 that Roosevelt would be nominated in Chicago. The Republicans nominated Taft, and he appeared to have lost his wager, but when the Progressives met and made Roosevelt their candidate, Daniels claimed he had won. His betting opponent adamantly disputed this. The parties to the wager had deposited $500 each in an Arizona bank, and the winner was to collect $1,000. When the matter could not be resolved to everyone's satisfaction, there was no recourse to the courts, since gambling had been ruled illegal in Arizona in 1907 and gambling contracts became unenforceable. The original bet was returned to each man.[17]

While on the campaign trail, Roosevelt was beginning a speech in Milwaukee on October 14, 1912, when a deranged man shot him. With the courage and determination that made him so admired by his supporters, Teddy finished his fifty-minute address with a bullet buried four inches in his chest. He recovered but lost the election when he had to remain in bed on doctors' orders for the critical two-week period just before the voting.

The Roosevelt defeat was a hard blow for avid supporters like Ben Daniels, but Daniels, while pursuing his mining interests, continued to profess allegiance to the Progressive Party. He made an effort to return to public service in 1914, running for sheriff of Pima County, Arizona, on the Progressive ticket against the Republican and Democratic candidates.

The *Tucson Citizen* announced his candidacy in July. "Mr. Daniels," it said, "is at present engaged in mining in the Santa Rita mountains where he has a promising property."[18]

As election day neared letters of endorsement from Daniels's friends began appearing in the Tucson paper. A letter from New York City dated October 13, and headed "Bat Masterson Says," was reproduced as a quarter-page advertisement. In it Bat recounts (with some inaccuracies) his friend's extensive law enforcement experience and the long relationship he and Ben had enjoyed. (But of course he made no mention of the fact he had once arrested Daniels and turned him over to the federal court as a common horse thief.)

The Pima County Progressive Party in nominating Ben Daniels as its candidate for Sheriff could not possible have made a better selection. I have known Mr. Daniels for more than forty years; in fact we hunted buffalo on the same range in Southwestern Kansas in the early seventies.

I was instrumental, in a way, in having him appointed city marshal of Dodge City. Kansas, in 1884. My reason for supporting Daniels for the position was that I knew him. I was satisfied that he would make good and as it required a man of excellent judgment, unwavering courage and ability to act promptly and decisively when circumstances required such action. I did not hesitate to recommend Ben Daniels for the place. And I wish to say further that he fulfilled every obligation the position imposed upon him by discharging his duties faithfully and efficiently.

I knew him later as Deputy Sheriff of Bent County, Colorado, Deputy Marshal of Cripple Creek and Marshal of Guthrie, Okla., all of which positions he filled with honor to himself and fidelity to the public.

When Ben was appointed Marshal of Dodge City, I remember having cautioned him against being too reckless with regard to his personal safety, telling him that if he did not at all times exercise the utmost care and vigilance he would not last six months. I felt at the time that I knew whereof I was speaking, as I had had a brother murdered while serving as City Marshal of the town. Also, I had had four years experience as sheriff of the county. The fact that Ben is still alive is ample proof that he knew his way through and that he was equal to the task confronting him.

If experience, courage, and rare good judgment are to be reckoned as necessary qualifications in order for a man to be an efficient sheriff, Ben Daniels is without doubt one of the best equipped men in Pima County for the office.[19]

A few days later another large ad lauding the Progressive candidate appeared in the *Citizen*. It was in the form of a letter from a man named J. E. Dickson, who described himself as "just an old-timer who has knocked about the West ever since it was brand new, and I hope . . . can claim credit for making the West what it is today." Dickson said his motivation for writing was to do "a good turn for a man who has done so many good turns for others in his life." He went on to tell of the part Daniels played in helping victims of the smallpox plague that struck hunters on the Texas buffalo range back in the 1870s. He said he hadn't seen Daniels again until coming to Tucson a few years earlier when he ran into the man who was then U.S. marshal for Arizona.

Time and his high place had not changed him a bit. He was the same old Ben with a ready welcome and glad to do anything to help a man that needed help. . . . Now I am a Democrat and the Texas high-proof variety and have voted the Democratic ticket all my life, but when a man like Ben Daniels is running for office it makes no difference to me what ticket he runs on—I'm for him strong. And I hope that on election day every Western man and woman in this country will take advantage of the opportunity to do a good turn for a man who has done so many good turns for others, and vote for Ben Daniels, Progressive candidate for sheriff.[20]

But Daniels, who had been one of the staunchest followers of Roosevelt and the Progressives in Arizona, found that loyalty a distinct disadvantage now, when the Progressive movement was fading in popularity. Despite the strong personal endorsements of his frontier friends, Daniels was defeated in the election for Pima County sheriff, finishing a "bad third," as he admitted in a letter to Roosevelt. "The Democrats," he said

won everything in the State on account of the Republican Split. The Republicans made a desperate effort to draw all of the Progressives back into the Republican ranks and succeeded with a great many weak-kneed ones but, especially those who understood the proceedings of the last Republican Convention in Chicago did not feel like going back to join the thieves who stole those seventy-eight delegates at the Convention in order to nominate Mr. Taft instead of you.

Well, Colonel, I shall not say anything more about my defeat for it was of very little consequence compared to your defeat for the Presidency. . . .

Enough said on politics; I am more interested in you personally. Colonel, does the wound you received in Milwaukee bother you any now, and have you fully recovered from the fever you contracted on your Southern Expedition?

My own health is as good as I could ask for, but my financial affairs are so embarrassing on account of the [World] War that I have about reached the limit; however I shall have to make the best of it until money matters loosen up.[21]

Within a year of the assassination attempt, Roosevelt was off on a South American exploration trip. He returned on May 19, 1914, a very sick man. In the Brazilian wilderness he had contracted jungle fever, lost thirty-five pounds, and almost died. He would never regain his old vitality.

As was his habit, Roosevelt answered promptly, assuring his friend that he still carried the Milwaukee bullet in his body, but it did not bother him in the least, and he had completely recovered from the jungle fever. He expressed concern about Daniels's financial problems, but reminded him that "everyone is suffering at present."[22]

Although the times were tough for everyone, Roosevelt once again made an effort to aid Daniels. He dropped a note to Charles Campbell Greenway, another former Rough Rider, who was currently active in the mining business in Arizona, asking him if he could do something on Daniels's behalf.

Greenway in 1914 was midway into a fabulous career. After graduation from Yale, where he studied engineering and gained national fame as an athlete, he enlisted as a private in the Rough Rider regiment, but Colonel Roosevelt, recognizing his leadership abilities, quickly promoted him to second, and then first lieutenant, and awarded him a Silver Star for his bravery at the Battle of San Juan Hill. After the war Greenway devoted his remarkable energies to mining exploration and development. In the years 1904 to 1910 he was primarily responsible for the opening up of the iron ore mines of the Mesabi Range in the wilds of northern Minnesota. He moved to Arizona in 1910 to take over management of the copper mines owned by the Calumet and Arizona Company at Bisbee. A year later he oversaw the construction of a $3 million copper processing plant at the town of Ajo. Successful in all his operations, he became a millionaire before the age of forty.[23]

Always a strong supporter of Theodore Roosevelt, Greenway was one of the foremost leaders of the Progressive Party in Arizona. It took little urging on the part of the ex-president to convince him to find a place in his mining operation for Ben Daniels, a fellow Rough Rider and a committed Progressive Party advocate.

In addition to Greenway, leaders of the Progressive movement in Arizona were Alexander Brodie, John L. B. Alexander, George Wilcox, Dwight N. Heard, and Ben Daniels. All but Heard had been Rough Riders, and Daniels was the only one who had not been an officer. Brodie, Alexander, Wilcox, and Daniels held appointments under Roosevelt, and all but Brodie were dismissed by the Taft administration.[24] No doubt bitterness toward the Republican Party over those political firings contributed to the zeal with which Daniels, Alexander, and Wilcox embraced the new Progressive movement, but staunch loyalty to Roosevelt was the prime motivation. The remarkable political rise of Roosevelt had dramatically changed the lives of all these men, particularly Daniels and Brodie, who, having proved themselves in combat, were rewarded with high positions in Arizona. As one writer noted, "Brodie and Daniels were more than transformed; they had been reborn. These men were possibly the most useful to President Roosevelt. For these reborn public officials the angel they felt over their shoulder was Roosevelt. They were deeply in his debt."[25]

Roosevelt's suggestion to Greenway that he do something to help Daniels produced immediate results as evidenced by a flurry of communications—telegrams and letters—flying back and forth between Daniels and Roosevelt as 1914 ended and 1915 began. Daniels wired Roosevelt on December 30 from

Warren, Arizona, saying he had secured a permanent job, and in a letter written on the stationary of Bisbee's Copper Queen Hotel the same day thanked his friend for his intercession. "Your writing to Jack Greenway," he said, "caused me to get a good position under him [and] he also fixed me out with what immediate help I wanted financially. It will be a permanent position as long as I give satisfaction, which I will try to do as in every other position I have held during my life." The very next day Roosevelt acknowledged Daniels's telegram with the reassurance: "You are one of the men I shall always stand by as a matter of course."[26]

Within five days Roosevelt had been updated on the situation by the receipt of communications from both Daniels and Greenway and on January 4, 1915, sent Daniels a congratulatory letter: "I am awfully pleased at the news you give me. It's fine! I have received a line from John Greenway in the matter. Good luck to you and do let me know how things are."[27]

So it was that, for the fourth time in fourteen years, Theodore Roosevelt had come to the aid of his friend Ben Daniels at a time when it counted most. Unfortunately, Daniels's Arizona benefactor, John Greenway, would soon go off to fight in World War I, and Daniels would once again be in need of steady employment.[28]

The presidential election year of 1916 brought many Progressives, including Roosevelt and Daniels, back into the Republican fold. Roosevelt toured the nation, campaigning for the Republican nominee, Charles Evans Hughes. In October he was in Arizona, and Daniels had an opportunity to see his old friend and benefactor once more. A wire service dispatch from Phoenix said that the still popular ex-president met many old friends at the depot, including Ben Daniels, "another half-eared gent of belligerent proclivities who lost part of his aural appendage when he got between another man's molars as they happened to come together."²⁹

Daniels was himself in the midst of a political campaign, running again for the office of Pima County sheriff, this time on the Republican ticket. Shortly after returning from Phoenix he suffered a severe ankle sprain and was not able to get out and campaign in the critical final days before the election. The *Tucson Citizen*, in reporting his accident, took the opportunity to speak out on his behalf, however, saying: "Ben Daniels has been an officer most of his life and Pima County needs a trained officer as sheriff at this time, when four deputies of the present sheriff have been sentenced to the penitentiary and the public does not know what protection means."³⁰ In its official endorsement the paper praised Daniels as being "well qualified, both by long experience as a peace officer and by personal character."³¹

An advertisement in the paper characterized Daniels as a "born officer" with a "remarkable record" who was well "qualified by experience" for the position of county sheriff. It summarized his life, "fraught with many adventures and dangerous phases," as a cowboy and trail-driver; buffalo hunter; peace officer in Kansas, Colorado, and Oklahoma; Rough Rider; Wells Fargo guard; prison superintendent; and U.S. marshal.³² No mention was made, of course, of his record as a horse thief and penitentiary convict.

Like the Republican presidential candidate Charles Evans Hughes, who failed in his effort to oust the White House incumbent, Democrat Woodrow Wilson, Daniels was defeated.

He then looked elsewhere for a political job.

In 1909 the notorious prison at Yuma had been closed and the prisoners moved to a new facility at Florence, which, after

Arizona finally attained statehood three years later, became the state penitentiary. Daniels coveted the job of warden at the new institution, but knew his experience would not be enough to get him the job; he needed political pull. After the disastrous election he wrote Roosevelt, advising of his second defeat for sheriff and, as had become his custom, asked a favor: "Well, Colonel, I got defeated for Sheriff but . . . we elected our Governor, Tom Campbell. I have already put in an application for the appointment of Superintendent of the Penitentiary, but I suppose he will be obligated to some one else who will want some friend to have that office. I thought I might get a recommendation from Governor Brodie if I can get his address."[33]

Roosevelt responded, saying he was "awfully sorry" to hear of Daniels's defeat. He did not provide an address for Brodie, but did enclose his own personal letter of recommendation for Daniels's use in lobbying Governor Campbell, something Daniels undoubtedly sought in the first place.[34]

Despite the help of his "Old Colonel," Daniels was unsuccessful in his bid to again administer the Arizona prison, and returned to his mining activities in the Santa Rita Mountains.

The United States declared war on Germany on April 6, 1917, and entered the "war to end all wars," as it was called. A few days later Ben Daniels was the recipient of a job offer, one he hardly could have expected. "The Papago Indians in the vicinity of Tucson have announced their desire to raise a regiment to be tendered to the service of the government in the war against Germany," the *Citizen* reported. "They have picked Ben Daniels, former United States marshal, as a commander and have urged him to communicate with the war department in Washington."[35] Needless to say, Daniels, at the age of sixty-four, passed on this job opportunity.

Ben Daniels at the age of sixty-five could still work his mining property in 1918. Courtesy of the Arizona Historical Society.

Daniels also passed on a third try for the sheriff's job in the election of 1918, probably because of the popularity of the Democratic incumbent, J. T. ("Rye") Miles, who handily won reelection.

Two months later, on January 6, 1919, Ben Daniels, as well as millions across the nation, was shocked by the tragic news that Theodore Roosevelt had died at the age of sixty. Daniels mourned for the loss of the man whom he so admired and who had done so much to advance his career.

In 1920 Ben threw his hat in the ring again and for the third time tried to gain the Pima County shrievalty.

Vying for the Republican nomination for sheriff was a formidable opponent, D. C. Hamer, a former city detective

The last known photograph of Theodore Roosevelt, taken shortly before his death on January 6, 1919. Barely visible on his left arm is a black mourning band honoring his son, Quentin, killed in a World War I aerial battle six months earlier. Courtesy of the National Archives.

and special agent for the Southern Pacific Railroad, who had come to Tucson from Mexico and Texas and had gained some fame by downing a federal prisoner who escaped from a deputy marshal in a revolver duel, and averting an impending cattle war.[36] Tucson and Pima County were not that distant from the old frontier in 1920, and folks still respected that kind of lawman. Hamer announced early in March that he was going for the nomination on the Republican ticket, and for several months it looked like he would run unopposed. It wasn't until July that Daniels, who reportedly had been toying with the idea of running for the office of Tucson chief of police, jumped in to oppose him for the nomination. He may well have been influenced by a catfight he saw developing on the Democratic side. Rye Miles, the incumbent sheriff, was being challenged for the nomination by Wilfred Sullinger, his former chief deputy, with whom he had had a falling-out. When Tucson chief of police Frank Bailey made sounds like he might get into the nomination race, it looked like the Democratic nomination might develop into a three-cornered battle with an attendant fallout beneficial to the Republican candidate.[37]

Daniels managed to overcome the opposition mounted by Hamer to gain the Republican nomination. And then in the general election he finally won, at the age of sixty-eight, a two-year term as Pima County sheriff.

It is ironic that the first newspaper acclaim received by the new sheriff, a convicted horse thief in the horseback nineteenth century, was for his skill in capturing auto thieves in the automobile-dominated twentieth century. "New Sheriff's Force Makes Record Getting Stolen Autos," was a headline in the *Tucson Citizen* of January 3, 1921.

Automobiles also were the bone of contention between Sheriff Daniels and the newly elected board of supervisors. On taking office Daniels discovered that there was no county-owned automobile for his usage. His predecessor, Rye Miles, had been provided an allowance of $125 a month for the use of his own car. Daniels requested the same consideration, but the board, in an economy move, voted to expend $75 a month for the use of a vehicle from the Blue Bar Taxi Company of Tucson when needed by the sheriff. Daniels stormed out of the meeting in a huff, and the *Citizen* headline read: "Ben Daniels to Be Known as Taxi Sheriff as Supervisors Finally Decide He Doesn't Need to Walk."[38]

Finding the fight between the sheriff and the supervisory board quite amusing, the newspaper continued the story in a later issue:

Can Sheriff Ben Daniels run with sufficient speed to overtake burglars and auto thieves on foot? Would he be able to accomplish, hailing back to the frontier days of Tucson, the duties of his modern office on horseback? Would it not add to the picturesqueness and value to tourists of our wild western city should Uncle Ben and his corps of deputies be prepared with faithful nags with or without the Blue Bar? How romantic would be the sight of Ben tearing down Congress street after an auto, firing his pistol in the air or galloping frantically up North Stone street after a fleeing "Cad" eight?

Who will prophesy whether Ben will overtake lawbreakers mounted on four wheels, on foot, on horseback, in his own car, which the board of supervisors refuses to maintain for him, or whether he will ring 77 [telephone Blue Bar Taxi Company] when law violators assail Tucson?[39]

When he needed to serve a summons in an outlying district, almost a hundred miles from Tucson, Daniels had called the taxi company, and Shad Bowyer, proprietor of the concern, showed up with "a shining new [Ford] flivver," which he had purchased for the personal use of the sheriff. "Ben, on arrival of the brilliant flivver, swore by all that was holy that he would walk the entire distance before he would subject himself to the disquietude and injury to his disposition resultant from the trip in Shad's new purchase." Bowyer responded that his contract with the county required him to furnish no car heavier than a Ford, and Daniels and his deputies might walk or ride in the flivver as they chose.[40] The paper carried no more information regarding the dispute, but it was apparently resolved to everyone's satisfaction.

Automobiles provided more newsprint for the sheriff a few months later when he opened a drive to apprehend motorists driving without licenses and using one set of license plates on multiple vehicles.[41]

A more dramatic event involving the sheriff's office took place in March 1921 when Charles Fletcher, alias Oklahoma Charley, and Frank Allen, inmates of the county jail awaiting trial on a charge of robbing a taxi driver, pulled a pistol on the jailer and made their escape. Sheriff Daniels sent out wanted bulletins, and officers in Albuquerque, New Mexico, nabbed the pair. Daniels went there and brought them back, along with Pearl Butler, a woman believed to be responsible for smuggling the pistol into the jail.[42]

In June Sheriff Daniels caused a little dustup when he announced the firing of ten deputies. The *Arizona Daily Star*, a Tucson paper politically opposed to Daniels and the Republican Party, criticized the dismissals, but the *Citizen* came to his defense, saying those fired were "the class of deputy sheriffs known traditionally as 'gun toters,' and of little actual value to the sheriff. . . . The type of deputies to whom the new order refers are those carrying commissions with the privilege of carrying a gun but not actively performing any sheriff's office duties."[43]

Arguments over automobiles, licenses, and deputy firings were all pretty routine, nonchallenging stuff for a man of action like Ben Daniels, and it wasn't until he had been in office more than a year that he had an opportunity to demonstrate what a real peace officer could do.

On May 15, 1922, an attempted holdup of the Golden State Limited of the Chicago, Rock Island & Pacific Railroad in Pima County, about twenty miles west of Tucson, was thwarted by Harry Stewart, an intrepid express messenger, who routed the gang of eight with accurate rifle fire, killing one of the bandits and wounding another.[44] Sheriff Daniels, quickly on the scene, took up the trail of the robbers, and arrested suspects George C. Winkler and his son, George Jr.[45] A Tucson old-timer named Harry J. Blacklidge recalled forty-four years later how

Ben mounted his trusty horse and went out there. He prowled around for a half-hour, then called his men together and took off. He tracked the gang to an old and deserted mine in the Tucson Mountains and captured the whole bunch. I never thought Ben got the credit due for that job. The newspapers treated it just as an ordinary piece of lawman's job. Ben was on the job at daylight, cut sign until he figured just what happened, took their trail, and "cotched 'em." Personally, I think it was a darned good piece of work.[46]

A couple of months later Daniels led an extensive manhunt for a pair of vicious killers.

A gang of Mexican desperadoes armed with rifles and pistols a year earlier had raided the post office and store of a couple in Ruby, Arizona, a tiny community in the Oro Blanco mining district of Santa Cruz County.[47] They looted the store and brutally murdered Postmaster Frank J. Pearson and his wife, Myrtle. One of the gang, Manuel Martinez, shot Myrtle Pearson through the head and knocked out her teeth, just to get the gold crowns in her mouth. Elizabeth Purcell, Myrtle's sister, suffered a gunshot wound to the hand and powder burns, but survived. The gang escaped across the border into Mexico. Arizona authorities, appalled by the atrocious crime, offered a $5,000 reward for each of the murderers, dead or alive.[48]

In April 1922 Oliver Parmer, a former Arizona Ranger who was working the case, got a break when an attempt to peddle Myrtle Pearson's gold teeth led him to Placido Silva, believed to be one of the gang. He arrested Silva and turned him over to Sheriff Daniels in Tucson for safekeeping. Following up on another tip, Parmer located Manuel Martinez and took him into custody. Under intense grilling, Martinez confessed to taking part in the raid and murdering Myrtle Pearson for her gold teeth. The two accused were rushed to trial and convicted of murder. Silva got off with a life term, but Martinez was sentenced to hang on August 18, 1922.[49]

Sheriff George J. White and his deputy, Leonard Smith, with their two prisoners, set out in an automobile on July 13, 1922, for the state penitentiary at Florence. Sheriff White drove, Deputy Smith sat beside him in the front seat, Martinez and Silva, shackled, were in the back. At a point in the road near Continental, some eighteen miles south of Tucson, the prisoners suddenly attacked the officers, striking White over the head with a heavy tool they had found under the rear seat. The car careened wildly and crashed. Martinez and Silva escaped into the night, leaving the officers bleeding and near death in the car. Sheriff White died within moments from the vicious blow to the head, and Smith, critically injured, lingered a few days before expiring on July 17.[50]

Since the auto crash and prisoner escape had happened in Pima County, Sheriff Daniels took charge of the massive manhunt that was launched for the murderers. Over the next five days seven hundred men—officers from Pima and surrounding counties and civilian volunteers—participated in "perhaps the most extensive manhunt in the history of the entire Southwest."⁵¹

Shortly before noon on Tuesday, July 18, a posse led by former Santa Cruz County Sheriff Harry J. Saxon of Nogales came upon the fugitives, "lying among rocks . . . , exhausted and hardly able to move," about two miles from Amadoville.⁵²

They were transported to Florence, where Martinez, after several stays of execution, was finally hanged on August 10, 1923.⁵³

The story of the chase for the murderers of the Pearsons and the Santa Cruz County lawmen received extensive press coverage through dispatches by the national news services, but the important role played by Sheriff Ben Daniels in the hunt got little attention. It was not until fourteen years later, when Oliver Parmer told the complete story in a pulp detective magazine, that Daniels's contribution was properly recognized.⁵⁴ And, by that time, Ben Daniels was long since dead and buried.

Later in 1922 Daniels was defeated in the Republican primary in his bid for reelection. Tom Mills, a much younger man, got the party's nod for the sheriff's job. Considered too old to be an effective lawman, Daniels was now relegated to the status of elder adviser. "Very much to the credit of that old war-horse of law enforcement, Sheriff Daniels is giving valuable assistance to Mills," commented the *Citizen*.⁵⁵ Despite Daniels's help, however, Mills was defeated in the November race for sheriff by Walter W. Bailey.

That same month, two days before his seventieth birthday, Daniels filed for a veteran's pension. His application stated that he was suffering from groin rupture, rheumatism, and heart trouble.⁵⁶

Six months later, on April 20, 1923, while seated in his car outside the office of his doctor, he was suddenly stricken. A

Seventy-year-old Ben Daniels in his last known photograph, taken shortly before his death in 1923. Courtesy of the Arizona Historical Society.

Time has taken its toll on Ben Daniels's black marble tombstone in Evergreen Cemetery, Tucson, Arizona. From the Jack DeMattos Collection.

passerby assisted him into the doctor's office, where he was given emergency treatment for a stroke and then rushed to a hospital. Summoned to his side, Annie Daniels was with him when he passed on. She had the body removed to the Parker-Grimshaw Undertaking Parlors to be prepared for burial. On Monday, April 22, funeral services were conducted at the Daniels home, 628 North Ninth Avenue, and the Scottish

Rite Cathedral, and Daniels was interred in the Masonic plot at Tucson's Evergreen Cemetery. A large black marble headstone marks the grave.[57]

Little note was taken in the press of the passing of the man who, two decades earlier, had elicited a great deal of interest when a president had fought so hard for him. A few Arizona newspapers reported his death. The *Arizona Daily Star* of Tucson provided an abbreviated account of his career, concentrating on his Spanish-American War service and his later years in Arizona.[58] The *Tombstone Epitaph*, saying that he was "known to all the older residents of the southern part of Arizona," gave him two short paragraphs.[59]

No paper, of course, mentioned his early transgressions or the remarkable redemption that so distinguished the life of Ben Daniels.

Afterword

THREE MONTHS AFTER Ben's death Annie Daniels applied for a widow's pension.[1] Surviving her husband by twenty-three years, she continued to devote her life to children, teaching in the Tucson public schools and serving as the first president of the Arizona Children's Home. Elected to the office of Pima County school superintendent in 1924, she served three consecutive two-year terms. She followed her husband's lead and remained active in the Republican Party until her death on March 23, 1946.[2]

She had lived to see her husband honored by the naming of the Spanish-American War veterans' encampment at Tucson "Camp Ben Daniels."[3] But actually this was about the only public recognition Ben Daniels ever received after a long and eventful life, and a career that was incredible for its dramatic turns.

Once the inmate of a territorial penitentiary, he had become the warden of another territorial prison. He had gone from horse thievery to being an honored guest in the White House and a particular protégé of the president, and from being a wanted outlaw to the highest federal law enforcement officer in Arizona. It was a remarkable story.

Ben Daniels stole horses and mules and served a little more than three years for his offense. Some, having heard that horse thieves were universally despised and often summarily hanged for their crimes in the West, may wonder why his punishment was not more severe. Ben Daniels shot and killed another man in cold blood, pumping three bullets into his body after he was on the ground. Many believed it was his gun that killed an inoffensive citizen in a street battle. And yet he was acquitted for the first killing and not even tried for the second. When his misdeeds became common knowledge, many highly respected men spoke out on his behalf and promoted and supported him for important government positions.

To understand the incongruity of this history it is necessary to understand the thinking of late-nineteenth-century westerners and what has come to be called the Code of the West.

Judgments are often made, according to the old expression, according to "whose ox is gored." So in the early West, when it came to horse thievery, it made a great deal of difference whose horse was stolen. Most men living on the western frontier were, to a great extent, completely dependent on a horse or mule for the ability to work and get around. To steal a man's mount was considered a theft of his very means of survival. Therefore thieves who stole horses and mules from ordinary folks in the West *were* considered the lowest form of human vermin and, according to that unwritten Code, were often harshly punished, and sometimes lynched.

But the theft of animals belonging to other groups—Indians, for instance—was viewed from an entirely different perspective. Such thievery was widely condoned and even applauded, for the Indian, to most frontiersmen, was his natural enemy and to deprive an Indian of his livelihood and sustenance—that is, to kill his buffalo and steal his horses—were acts deemed forgivable and even commendable. Thus daring young frontiersmen like Bat Masterson and Bill Tilghman, who stole Indian horses and bragged about it in Dodge City and other raw new settlements, were hailed as heroes.

Frontiersmen cherished their personal freedom, and many of them looked with a certain disdain on the federal government, seen by them as a possible threat to that freedom, so the theft of government stock, the crime for which Daniels was convicted, was not considered a serious offense. That is why professional horse thieves who professed to confine their thievery to Indian ponies and U.S. government mounts, men like "Dutch Henry" Born, managed successful operations for some time without raising public outcry.

The Code of the West came into play most notably with regard to the crime of murder. American law had long recognized the necessity of gradation of judgment when one man killed another, based upon circumstances and motivation. The right of self-protection when attacked was a legal defense, but the Code carried this concept one step further. Since little or no law enforcement was present in the new western settlements, each man was responsible for his own protection. Therefore the mere threat on a man's life, voiced in public, was considered just grounds for the threatened individual to kill his enemy at the first opportunity. The murder of Ed Julian by Ben Daniels fell into this classification. Each had publicly threatened the life of the other, and each knew, or should have known, that from that time on, death might come at any time without warning. Although by 1886 Dodge City and Ford County, Kansas, had an established law enforcement and court system in place, jury members could be still be found who retained enough of the mind-set of the Code to acquit a man who killed another under these circumstances.

Although he was an easterner born and bred, Theodore Roosevelt ranched in the West and briefly served there in a law enforcement role. He understood the Code and the men who honored it, men like Ben Daniels. To Roosevelt, it was much more important in judging the character of a man like Daniels to remember the bravery he had displayed in running up San Juan Hill into the deadly fire of Spanish sharpshooters than the fact that he had once served prison time for stealing government mules or killed a man who had threatened his life. When learning of Daniels's early offenses, Roosevelt expressed disappointment, not because of the commission of the transgressions, but because Daniels's failure to advise him of his past life subjected the president to embarrassing ridicule.

It is noteworthy that Roosevelt, despite his displeasure with his friend on that point and the political cost to him personally, continued to push for Daniels's ascendancy to the position he coveted and finally was successful.

In bestowing positions of responsibility on former Rough Riders, including Ben Daniels, President Roosevelt stressed what he called the "double burden" they were called upon to carry. In addition to performing honorably to reflect credit upon themselves as individuals, he said, they were also to remember that as veterans of the renowned Rough Rider regiment, they must maintain the honor of that unit they all loved. One historian of the regiment has stated it well: "No Rough Riders felt this double burden more than Ben Daniels. Roosevelt had risked his personal reputation a second time for Daniels after the lawman had once betrayed his confidence. Daniels met the challenge splendidly and the record he made suggests the redemptive power of the faith of one human being in another."[4]

Notes

Chapter 1. Twice at the Door of Death

1. Perhaps in gunfighter history the story of Joe Horner most closely approximates Ben Daniels's strange saga. After escaping from a Texas prison where he had been sent for bank and stagecoach robbery, Horner adopted the name Frank Canton and began a lengthy career in law enforcement in Wyoming, Oklahoma, and Alaska, ending up as the highly respected adjutant general of the new state of Oklahoma (DeArment, *Alias Frank Canton*).

2. *Tucson (Arizona) Citizen*, August 30, 1916.

3. U.S. Census, Rutland, LaSalle County, Illinois, 1850, 1860. The children were sons Edward, Jonathan, Aaron, and Benjamin, and daughters Menewa, Elizabeth, Ruth, Judith, and Maria.

4. He was listed on the 1850 U.S. Census at "The Middle Fork of the American River" in California, while his family was enumerated back in LaSalle County, Illinois. Aaron evidently made some money in California; the 1860 census showed he had real estate and personal assets totaling over of $11,000, a substantial figure for the period.

5. McClintock, *Arizona*, 798. McClintock, an intimate friend of Daniels, presumably got this story directly from him.

6. Both sisters were enumerated with Ben in the 1860 U.S. Census for Rutland, LaSalle County, Illinois.

7. The stepbrothers were Edward, born in 1849; Henry, 1852; Albert, 1856; George, 1858. The half-sisters and brother were May, 1861; Flora, 1864; and Stephen, 1867 (U.S. Census, LaSalle County, Illinois, 1860; Franklin County, Kansas, 1870).

8. McClintock, *Arizona*, 799.

9. Wormwood to Roosevelt, February 10, 1902.

10. *Tucson (Arizona) Citizen*, August 30, 1916; February 9, 1929.

11. In endorsing Daniels for a political office many years later, Bat Masterson would write: "I have known Mr. Daniels for more than forty years; in fact we hunted buffalo on the same range in Southwestern Kansas in the early seventies" (*Tucson [Arizona] Citizen*, October 30, 1914).

12. McClintock, *Arizona*, 799.

13. Actually, he was twenty-five.

14. McClintock, *Arizona*, 799; *Arizona Daily Star* (Tucson), May 17, 1906; *Tucson (Arizona) Citizen*, February 9, 1929; Shirley, *Guardian of the Law*, 142; Bartholomew, *Biographical Album of Western Gunfighters*.

15. Tyler, *New Handbook of Texas*, 5:452.

16. The Comanche was called "Nigger Horse" by his contemporaries (see Cook, *Border and the Buffalo*, passim), but in a politically correct world the name of this long-dead Indian has become "Black Horse."

17. One of the Indian band was Herman Lehmann, a white captive who would be wounded in the battle with the buffalo hunters (Tyler, *New Handbook of Texas*, 6:1116–17).

18. Among the camps raided were those of Pat Garrett, later to become a celebrated New Mexico sheriff, and Willis Skelton Glenn, whose memoirs provide much information about this episode (Tyler, *New Handbook of Texas*, 6:1116–17).

19. In his chronicle Skelton Glenn listed the name of Ben Daniels as one of those he remembered as participating in the punitive expedition (Strickland, "Recollections of W. S. Glenn," 64). Other frontier notables in the party were Jim White (called "the Boss Hunter" by his peers), "Whiskey Jim" Greathouse, "Smokey Hill" Thompson, "Six-Shooter Bill" Hillman, "Wild Bill" Kress, John Cook, and Frank Collinson. Cook and Collinson would later write accounts of the expedition (Cook, *Border and the Buffalo*, 263–329; Collinson, *Life in the Saddle*, 101–106).

20. *Dodge City Times*, May 26, 1877.

21. Ibid.

22. Tyler, *New Handbook of Texas*, 6:1116–17.

23. Ibid., 4:1028–29.

24. Ibid.

25. *Tucson (Arizona) Citizen*, October 24, 1914.

Chapter 2. Convict

1. H. P. Myton, an early resident and prominent citizen of Dodge City, wrote in 1901 that he remembered Daniels in the town as early as 1878 (Myton, "To Whom It May Concern," December 14, 1901).

2. Brooks and two of his confederates were lynched near Wellington, Kansas, in July 1874.

3. For information on Martin, see DeArment, "'Hurricane Bill' Martin."

4. *Dodge City Times*, September 13, 1879, quoting the *Larned (Kansas) Chromoscope*, which said that Daniels was "supposed to be the partner of the infamous Dutch Henry."

5. Walker, "Born and Leuch," 46; Thrapp, *Encyclopedia of Frontier Biography*, 1:139–40; Dary, *More True Tales of Old-Time Kansas*, 80.

6. Tilghman, *Marshal of the Last Frontier*, 79; Shirley, *Guardian of the Law*, 38.

7. Walker, "Born and Leuch," 47

8. Ibid.; Thrapp, *Encyclopedia of Frontier Biography*, 1:140; *Denver Field and Farm*, December 21, 1872.

9. Baker and Harrison, *Adobe Walls*, 76; Dary, *More True Tales of Old-Time Kansas*, 82; Shirley, *Guardian of the Law*, 66. Historians have disagreed with regard to the participants in this memorable battle, and Born has been one of those in dispute. There were many "Dutch Henrys" on the frontier—anyone named Henry with a German accent immediately acquired the nickname it seems—and the man involved in the Adobe Walls fight does not appear to have been the well-known horse thief.

10. *Ellsworth (Kansas) Reporter*, June 18, 1874.

11. As characterized by the editor of Dodge City's *Ford County Globe* (Haywood, *Cowtown Lawyers*, 83).

12. Thrapp, *Encyclopedia of Frontier Biography*, 1:140.

13. *Indianapolis Sentinel*, September 5, 1876. "Slapping Jack" was probably "Slap Jack Bill," a notorious desperado.

14. Thrapp, *Encyclopedia of Frontier Biography*, 1:140.

15. *Dodge City Times*, June 1, 1878.

16. Ibid., January 7, 1879.

17. Ibid., January 11, 1879.

18. Haywood, *Cowtown Lawyers*, 83.

19. *Topeka (Kansas) Commonwealth*, March 4, 1879.

20. *Denver Tribune*, March 1, 1879.

21. Thrapp, *Encyclopedia of Frontier Biography*, 1:140; Walker, "Born and Leuch," 47.

22. *San Francisco Bulletin*, July 24, 1879.

23. *Philadelphia Inquirer*, August 7, 1879.

24. *Dodge City Times*, September 13, 1879, quoting the *Larned (Kansas) Chronoscope*.

25. *Cheyenne Daily Leader*, February 10, 1902.

26. *Larned (Kansas) Optic*, September 12, 26, 1879; *Dodge City Times*, September 13, 1879, quoting the *Larned (Kansas) Chronoscope*.

27. *Larned (Kansas) Optic*, September 12, 1879.

28. National Archives.

29. *Larned (Kansas) Optic*, September 12, 1879.

30. It is interesting that "Dutch Henry" Born's outlaw career began at Fort Lyon, and, according to this charge, Daniel's did also.

31. *Larned (Kansas) Optic*, September 26, 1879. According to the paper, Thomas S. Jones of Dodge City, "one of the brightest and sharpest attorneys in this judicial district," defended Daniels and "gave United States district attorney Hallowell such a tussle as he seldom has to encounter in this part of the country." Before moving to Dodge City to practice law, Jones, from Cottonwood Falls, Kansas, had twice been elected mayor of that town and in 1874 won a surprise victory over a politician of statewide prominence, Samuel N. Wood, for a seat in the state legislature (Haywood, *Cowtown Lawyers*, 171).

32. *Cheyenne Daily Leader*, November 20, 21, 23, 1879; *Cheyenne Daily Sun*, November 21, 1879; *Laramie Sentinel*, November 21, 22, 1879.

33. *Laramie Sentinel*, December 6, 1879.

34. Ibid., November 30, 1879; *Cheyenne Daily Leader*, February 10, 1902.

35. Frye, *Atlas of Wyoming Outlaws*, 64.

36. *Laramie Sentinel*, April 22, 1880; Frye, *Atlas of Wyoming Outlaws*, 29, 62, 63, 64, 67. Taylor, Blair, and Condon were later apprehended and returned to prison; Wilbert and Hamilton were never recaptured.

37. U.S. Census, Laramie County, Wyoming, 1880. The jail, presided over by Sheriff George W. Draper, held twenty-three prisoners—twenty-one men and two women. Ben Daniels's occupation was given as "laborer."

38. *Cheyenne Daily Leader*, June 11, 1880; Frye, *Atlas of Wyoming Outlaws*, 64. Deputy U.S. Marshal W. R. Schnitger was the officer who again escorted Daniels to Cheyenne for his second trial and back to the Laramie penitentiary (*Cheyenne Daily Leader*, February 10, 1902).

39. Secrest, "Fighting Man!" 9; Frye, *Atlas of Wyoming Outlaws*, 77.

40. Roosevelt, *Rough Riders*, 25–26.

41. *Lincoln (Nebraska) Daily Star*, October 22, 1916.

42. Secrest, "Fighting Man!" 11.

43. Curtius to Roosevelt, February 6, 1902. Equally fallacious was a newspaper story that in the late 1890s Daniels "made it warm for 'Black Jack,' the famous New Mexican bandit, who was the terror of the Southwest for many years. One of 'Black Jack's' men clopped off a piece of Daniels' ear with a pistol bullet, but the bandit himself paid the forfeit of death for his temerity in facing the Dodge City gun fighter" (*Dallas Morning News*, August 17, 1903). Aside from the fact that the lobe of Daniels's ear was missing long before the heyday of the New Mexico bandit called "Black Jack," Daniels was never involved in the hunt for this desperado.

44. U.S. Census, Osage County, Coffey County, Kansas, 1880.

45. Frye, *Atlas of Wyoming Outlaws*, 77.

Chapter 3. Dodge City Lawman

1. Miller and Snell, *Why the West Was Wild*, 126, 643–44. In his recent *Encyclopedia of Western Lawmen and Outlaws* (101–102), Jay Robert Nash makes the erroneous assertion that Ben Daniels was a deputy sheriff in Arizona in the early 1880s and that in January 1884 he "tracked down William Delaney, a lethal desperado who was one of the killers responsible for the Bisbee, Ariz., Massacre. . . . Delaney fled to

Sonora, Mexico . . . , where Daniels tracked him down and arrested him on Jan. 5, 1884." Nash has confused Benjamin F. Daniels with William A. ("Bill") Daniels, a deputy sheriff of Cochise County, Arizona, who, on New Year's Day, 1884, arrested "Big Dan" Dowd, one of the Bisbee robbers, in Chihuahua, Mexico, and later took custody of Delaney, captured by Mexican officers in Sonora, and smuggled him back to Arizona in a boxcar (Miller, *Arizona*, 222; Chisholm, *Brewery Gulch*, 39).

2. On July 10, 1884, he was paid $25 for ten days' service (*Dodge City Democrat*, July 12, 1884).

3. Shirley, *Guardian of the Law*, 143.

4. From the testimony of eyewitness M. E. Robinson in the *Kansas Cowboy* (Dodge City), July 12, 1884.

5. Ibid.; *Ford County Globe* (Dodge City), July 8, 1884; *Globe Live Stock Journal* (Dodge City), July 15, 1884; Young, *Dodge City*, 135.

6. *Ford County Globe* (Dodge City), July 8, 1884.

7. Daniels's salary was the same as Tilghman's except that $25 a month was added to Tilghman's pay for collecting services rendered (Miller and Snell, *Why the West Was Wild*, 127). Many years later, in a testimonial to Ben Daniels's integrity, Bat Masterson claimed that he was "instrumental, in a way, in "having [Daniels] appointed city marshal of Dodge City, Kansas, in 1884" (*Tucson [Arizona] Citizen*, October 30, 1914). Masterson, who was in Dodge that month for the big Fourth of July festivities and witnessed the killing of his friend Tom Nixon, may well have recommended Daniels's promotion, but Bill Tilghman was mainly responsible for the appointment.

8. Tilghman, *Marshal of the Last Frontier*, 164–65.

9. Ibid. Mrs. Tilghman's story is of dubious veracity, as no contemporary newspaper corroborates it. Robert M. Wright, an intimate of all the parties in the affair, does not mention it in his Dodge City history, nor does Bill Tilghman in his extensive journals.

10. This was probably gambler Walter Hart, who had been mentioned in the *Dodge City Democrat* only two weeks earlier: "Bat Masterson and Walter Hart won $2,500 at the Newton races" (July 19, 1884).

11. *Dodge City Democrat*, August 9, 1884.

12. *Kansas Cowboy* (Dodge City), August 9, 1884.

13. *Dodge City Democrat*, August 16, 1884.

14. *Kansas Cowboy* (Dodge City), May 16, 1885.

15. *Dodge City Democrat*, August 15, 1885.
16. Schmidt, *Ashes of My Campfire*, 52; *Colorado Transcript* (Golden), February 12, 1902.
17. *Dodge City Democrat*, June 6, 1885.
18. Wright, *Dodge City*, 309.
19. McClintock, *Arizona*, 797–98.
20. Ibid.
21. Haywood, *Merchant Prince of Dodge City*, 140–41.
22. *Dodge City Democrat*, January 23, 1886.
23. Silva, *Wyatt Earp*, 1:252–53.
24. *Ford County Globe* (Dodge City), March 9, 1886.
25. *Globe Live Stock Journal* (Dodge City), April 13, 1886; *Dodge City Democrat*, January 31, 1902.

Chapter 4. The Killing of Ed Julian

1. *Dodge City Democrat*, November 15, 1884.
2. Schmidt, *Ashes of My Campfire*, 51; *Wichita (Kansas) Sunday Eagle Magazine*, January 31, 1926. Pat Sughrue's powder-blackened face helped people distinguish him from his identical twin, Mike, also a career Kansas lawman.
3. Schmidt, *Ashes of My Campfire*, 51.
4. *Colorado Transcript* (Golden), February 12, 1902.
5. Schmidt, *Ashes of My Campfire*, 52.
6. *Wichita (Kansas) Sunday Eagle Magazine*, January 31, 1926.
7. *Globe Live Stock Journal* (Dodge City), April 20, 1886.
8. Haywood, *Cowtown Lawyers*, 165.
9. The same week as the trial began Daniels sold his saloon, renamed the Eldorado, to a man named Haines (*Globe Live Stock Journal* [Dodge City], November 16, 1886).
10. *Wichita (Kansas) Sunday Eagle Magazine*, January 31, 1926.
11. *Globe Live Stock Journal* (Dodge City), November 23, 1886.
12. Ibid.; *Dodge City Democrat*, November 20, 1886.
13. Haywood, *Cowtown Lawyers*, 187.
14. *Kansas City Journal*, January 25, 1902, reprinted in *Dodge City Democrat*, January 31, 1902. Two years later Senator Burton would be facing serious charges about his own integrity. Indicted on numerous fraud charges, he would be convicted and sentenced to prison in 1907

(*Fort Worth [Texas] Telegram*, April 4, 1904; *Grand Forks [North Dakota] Herald*, October 20, 1906).

15. *Dodge City Democrat*, January 31, 1902.

Chapter 5. The Daniels-Vaden Affair

1. Alexander, *Lawmen, Outlaws and S.O.Bs.*, 167. A Vaden family member in a recent monograph of his life has viewed Vaden's character more sympathetically, concluding that "John Vaden may have had his faults, [but] he was not the desperado he has previously been made out to be" (Page, *Badges, Bullets and Blood*, 23).

2. Page, *Badges, Bullets and Blood*, 3–4; Alexander, *Lawmen, Outlaws and S.O.Bs.*, 167; Hunter, "Some Tragedies I Have Witnessed," 189.

3. *San Angelo (Texas) Standard*, October 12, 1912.

4. Loomis, *Texas Ranchman*, 13.

5. *San Angelo (Texas) Standard*, October 12, 1912.

6. Page, *Badges, Bullets and Blood*, 6–9.

7. *San Angelo (Texas) Standard*, October 12, 1912.

8. Page, *Badges, Bullets and Blood*, 10.

9. Loomis, *Texas Ranchman*, 13.

10. Ibid., 15.

11. Ibid., 73.

12. *Fort Worth (Texas) Gazette*, August 7, 1886.

13. Ibid. Hill was city marshal of Abilene, Texas, at this time and also held a lawman's position in Ballinger (Alexander, *Lawmen, Outlaws and S.O.Bs.*, 160–72).

14. Alexander, *Lawmen, Outlaws and S.O.Bs.*, 170; Zachry, *Buffalo Gap Historic Village*, 103.

15. Page, *Badges, Bullets and Blood*, 4–6; *San Angelo (Texas) Standard*, October 12, 1912; Tise, *Texas County Sheriffs*, 371.

16. Page, *Badges, Bullets and Blood*, 19; *San Angelo (Texas) Standard Times*, October 8, 1886.

17. *San Angelo (Texas) Standard*, October 12, 1912.

18. Ibid.

19. Ibid.

20. Ibid.

21. *San Angelo (Texas) Standard Times*, October 8, 1886.

22. Hunter, "Some Tragedies I Have Witnessed," 190. John Loomis, Vaden's one-time employer, was not present at the shooting, but told the story as he had heard it. Vaden, he said, had ripped off all of Daniels's clothes with his long-handled steel hook. Daniels "managed to get some other clothes, went home, got his gun, came back and found Vadon [*sic*] in a saloon. He shot him down as Vadon turned to face him" (Loomis, *Texas Ranchman*, 73).

23. *San Angelo (Texas) Standard*, October 12, 1912.

24. Page, *Badges, Bullets and Blood*, 21.

25. Ibid., 22; *San Angelo (Texas) Standard Times*, October 8, 1886; *San Angelo (Texas) Standard*, October 12, 1912; Hunter, "Some Tragedies I Have Witnessed," 190. John Loomis said erroneously that Daniels was tried and acquitted (*Texas Ranchman*, 73).

26. *San Angelo (Texas) Standard*, October 12, 1912.

27. Hunter, "Some Tragedies I Have Witnessed," 190.

28. In *The Biographical Album of Western Gunfighters*, a seminal gunfighter volume published in 1958, author Ed Bartholomew made the connection. Bill Secrest, the first to recount the remarkable career of Ben Daniels from penitentiary to presidential pet in his 1969 article, "Fighting Man!" included the Vaden killing as part of the story. Jack DeMattos, coauthor of this volume, in 1979 took Daniels as one of his subjects in his long-running magazine series on prominent gunfighters and included the Vaden killing ("Gunfighters of the Real West: Ben Daniels," 50–52). Writing of Daniels's career in his biography of Bill Tilghman published in 1988, eminent western historian Glenn Shirley, without mentioning the Vaden shooting, affirmed that Daniels worked as a bartender at Fort McKavett in 1886, thus giving credibility to the story (*Guardian of the Law*, 168). Jay Robert Nash, in his sketch of Daniels in a 1989 encyclopedia, credited him with the Vaden killing (*Encyclopedia of Western Lawmen and Outlaws*, 101). In her 1997 monograph of John W. Vaden, Anita Vaden Page affirmed positively that the famous lawman of Kansas, Colorado, and Arizona, Ben Daniels, was the man who killed her relative (*Badges, Bullets and Blood*, 16–25). In their sketch of the life of the one-time buffalo hunter and later noted lawman Ben Daniels, the authors of a multivolume encyclopedia of buffalo hunters published in 2003 mentioned the slaying of Vaden at his hands (Gilbert, Remiger,

and Cunningham, *Encyclopedia of Buffalo Hunters and Skinners*, vol. 1, *A–D*, 164).

29. *Dodge City Democrat*, July 12, August 9, 1884; Miller and Snell, *Why the West Was Wild*, 126.

30. *Dodge City Democrat*, November 15, 20, 1886; Haywood, *Cowtown Lawyers*, 164–65.

31. Page, *Badges, Bullets and Blood*, 15.

32. Ibid., 19. J. W. Mears served as sheriff of Menard County, Texas, from November 1884 to November 1886 (Tise, *Texas County Sheriffs*, 371).

33. Page, *Badges, Bullets and Blood*. A month later both the sheriff and his deputy were among several men arrested and charged with "unlawful gaming." The case against Sheriff Russell was quickly dismissed on the grounds of insufficient evidence, and the other cases were continued and evidently also dropped later (ibid).

Chapter 6. Lawman of Lamar and the Battle of Cimarron

1. Betz, *Prowers County History*, 216.

2. Ibid., 64–65, quoting Bent County pioneer George Baxter. In another passage (242) this writer states that Jim Talbot "was actually W. M. (alias 'Mysterious Dave') Matthers [sic], another of the gun-for-hire Dodge City bunch and one of the buffalo hunters involved in the defense of Adobe Walls with Bat Masterson in 1874," an assertion containing several inaccuracies. Talbot was not "Mysterious Dave" Mather, and neither he nor Mather were participants in the Adobe Walls battle.

3. Ibid.; *Cripple Creek (Colorado) Morning Times*, May 17, 1898.

4. Tennyson, "Locksley Hall," 1842, in *Poems*.

5. Secrest, "Fighting Man!" 42. Annie Laura, born December 6, 1858, was the daughter of John Ware (1822–1901) and Belle Ware (1826–93) (Hickman, *History of Jackson County*, 494–96).

6. Quoted in Betz, *Prowers County History*, 217. Bent County was in the process of being divided during this period, with the eastern section, including Lamar, under organization as Prowers County. But at this time Lamar was still in Bent County, and as a Bent County officer, Daniels continued to make his home in Lamar. Ben Daniels was also reported to be the first elected sheriff of Scott County in western Kansas in 1886 (*Annals of Kansas, 1886 to 1925*, 1:12), but in fact this was

another man; J. T. Daniels served as sheriff from August to November 1886 (O'Brien to DeArment, January 11, 2007).

   7. Secrest, "Fighting Man!" 42.
   8. Betz, *Prowers County History*, 217.
   9. Ibid.
   10. Ibid., 219.
   11. Ibid., 216.
   12. Ibid., 216–17. The three papers were weeklies: the *Register*, the *Leader*, and the *Sparks*.
   13. Ibid., quoting Robert Christy, *Three Score and Ten*.
   14. George Bolds, quoted in Horan, *Across the Cimarron*, 289.
   15. *Gray County Echo* (Cimarron, Kansas), October 27, 1887.
   16. Quoted in Lynch, "War for the Gray County Seat," 12.
   17. Bat Masterson identified these fellows, whom he characterized as "all professional killers," in a letter to the editor of the *Advocate* of Lamar, Colorado, later reprinted in the *Montezuma (Kansas) Chief* of November 18, 1887, and the *Ingalls (Kansas) Union* of November 26, 1887.
   18. Shirley, *Guardian of the Law*, 178.
   19. *Cimarron (Kansas) Jacksonian*, January 18, 1889.
   20. *Dodge City Times*, January 17, 1889.
   21. *Atchison (Kansas) Daily Globe*, January 14, 1889.
   22. Secrest, "Fighting Man!" 44. Riley also claimed Daniels was a mercenary who was paid $1,500 for the raid on Cimarron and that he played a major role in most of the other Kansas county seat fights.
   23. *Atlanta Constitution*, January 26, 1889, reporting a dispatch from Wichita by way of Chicago. In this story "desperado" Daniels (called "Ed" erroneously) killed English "in cold blood."
   24. Ibid.; *Atchison (Kansas) Daily Globe*, January 14, 1889; *Trenton (New Jersey) Times*, January 14, 1889; *Mitchell (South Dakota) Daily Republican*, January 15, 1889; *Ingalls (Kansas) Union*, January 17, 1889.
   25. *Cimarron (Kansas) Jacksonian*, January 18, 1889.
   26. *Atlanta Constitution*, January 26, 1889.
   27. Horan, *Across the Cimarron*, 272–73.
   28. *Cimarron (Kansas) Jacksonian*, January 18, 1889.
   29. Bill Tilghman's wife, Zoe, in her biography of her husband, said that he had been struck in the calf of his leg by a bullet, "the only time he

was ever touched by gunfire" (Tilghman, *Marshal of the Last Frontier*, 275), but in its account of the battle the *Dodge City Times* (January 17, 1889) said Tilghman only suffered a sprained ankle.

30. Horan, *Across the Cimarron*, 274–75.

31. Newspapers throughout the country carrying the story of the "Battle of Cimarron" included the *Atchison (Kansas) Daily Globe* of January 14, 1889; the *Trenton (New Jersey) Times* of January 14, 1889; the *Topeka (Kansas) Capital-Commonwealth* of January 15, 1889; and the *Atlanta Constitution* of January 26, 1889. Of course the local papers —the *Ingalls Union* of January 17, 1889; the *Dodge City Times* of January 17, 1889; and the two Cimarron papers, the *Jacksonian* of January 18, 1889, and the *New West-Echo* of January 17, 1889—carried highly prejudiced accounts.

32. *State of Kansas v. N. F. Watson, et al.*

33. *Cimarron (Kansas) Jacksonian*, June 28, 1889.

34. Ibid., July 5, 1889.

35. Ibid., July 12, 1889.

36. *State of Kansas v. N. F. Watson, et al.*

37. Quoted in Secrest, "Fighting Man!" 44.

Chapter 7. Cripple Creek

1. *Tucson (Arizona) Citizen*, October 30, 1914.

2. Ibid., August 30, 1916.

3. Quoted in Secrest, "Fighting Man!" 44.

4. Guthrie city records for 1889.

5. A man named Volney Hoggett, who later made a fortune during the Nevada mining boom of the early years of the twentieth century, told a reporter for a Reno paper that as the "first mayor of Guthrie" he made Ben Daniels "an all around bad man of the west, a running mate of Bat Masterson," his chief of police (*Reno Evening Gazette*, February 15, 1907). Actually, Hoggett ran for mayor in Guthrie's first election, but was defeated and Daniels was never "chief of police" (Thoburn, "Frank H. Greer," 276).

6. All three served as deputy U.S. marshals during the turbulent outlaw years of Oklahoma Territory. Jim Masterson died of "galloping consumption" at Guthrie in March 1895. Bill Tilghman, at the age of seventy, was still wearing a badge when he was shot to death

at Cromwell, Oklahoma, in October, 1924. Neal Brown died in 1926, shortly before his eighty-second birthday (Browning, *Violence Was No Stranger*).

7. Like the "Ben Daniels" who killed John Vaden back in 1886, the gambler and saloon man named Ben Daniels who got a lot of local press coverage in North Dakota in the 1890s when he ran a "blind pig" saloon in violation of the prohibition laws was not "our" Ben Daniels (*Grand Forks [North Dakota] Daily Herald*, September–October 1893; December 14, 1894; April 17, 1898; *Bismarck [North Dakota] Daily Tribune*, September 27, 1893; *Duluth [Minnesota] News Tribune*, October 24, 1893).

8. *Cheyenne Daily Leader*, February 10, 1902.

9. Feitz, *Myers Avenue*, 5.

10. *Idaho Daily Statesman* (Boise), August 23, 1894.

11. Holbrook, *Rocky Mountain Revolution*, 74. The Cripple Creek strike was the first test of a fledgling labor union, the Western Federation of Miners (WFM). In the decade to come the WFM would be led by William Dudley ("Big Bill") Haywood Jr., a dedicated Marxist who at his death was buried with full Communist honors in the Kremlin. Under Haywood's leadership, assisted by Charles H. Moyer and Charles A. Pettibone, the WFM would become widely known for its hard-fought labor wars and especially for the use of assassins like the notorious Harry Orchard (Robertson and Harris, *Soapy Smith*, 144; Lukas, *Big Trouble*).

12. Rastall, "Labor History of the Cripple Creek District," 23.

13. *Leadville (Colorado) Daily and Evening Chronicle*, August 15, 1894.

14. *Dallas Morning News*, August 17, 1903.

15. *Minneapolis Journal*, July 31, 1895.

16. Holbrook, *Rocky Mountain Revolution*, 75.

17. Ibid., 75–76.

18. Ibid.; *Castle Rock (Colorado) Journal*, March 28, 1894.

19. *Albuquerque Morning Democrat*, May 26, 1894.

20. *Idaho Daily Statesman* (Boise), May 30, 1894.

21. *Albuquerque Morning Democrat*, May 30, 1894.

22. *Bismarck (North Dakota) Daily Tribune*, June 7, 1894.

23. *Albuquerque Morning Democrat*, May 26, 1894.

24. Ibid., June 5, 1894.

25. Ibid.
26. Collier and Westrate, *Reign of Soapy Smith*, 164–77.
27. Holbrook, *Rocky Mountain Revolution*, 77.
28. Ibid., 77–78.
29. Ibid., 78–79.
30. Ibid., 79–80.
31. Ibid.
32. One bulletin stated that "over 300 shots were fired but no one was killed" (*Albuquerque Morning Democrat*, June 8, 1894), which does not say much for the marksmanship of the combatants.
33. The strikers had no cannon, as was widely reported, but they did have a formidable array of improvised weaponry. They "had mined the hill with dynamite charges connected with electric wires to explode at the press of a button. Every miner had in a vest pocket five dynamite cartridges the size of pencils, fitted with percussion caps." They had "a tremendous bow gun capable of throwing missiles a quarter of a mile with fine accuracy; the missiles were beer bottles filled with explosive and capped to go off on impact" (Holbrook, *Rocky Mountain Revolution*, 81).
34. *Dallas Morning News*, August 17, 1903.
35. Holbrook, *Rocky Mountain Revolution*, 81.
36. Ibid., 82. Junius Johnson settled in Little Rock, Arkansas. At the outbreak of the Spanish-American War he was appointed colonel of an Arkansas regiment, but died before embarking for Cuba. Jack Smith, the ex-convict, was arrested by officers in Gunnison, Colorado, in February 1895 while gambling in the Bank saloon. He had reportedly received a five-year sentence after shooting a man in the thigh, but escaped, and a large reward was offered for his capture. He told his captors he feared being lynched if returned to Colorado Springs (*Colorado Transcript* [Golden], February 13, 1895). He did return to the Cripple Creek district, however, and was shot to death several years later at Altman (Holbrook, *Rocky Mountain Revolution*, 83).
37. *Santa Fe Daily New Mexican*, June 11, 1894; *Albuquerque Morning Democrat*, June 12, 1894. Once again the marksmanship of both contingents comes into question. Perhaps neither the miners nor the mercenaries really wanted to kill anybody.
38. *Greeley (Colorado) Tribune*, June 7, 1894.

39. *Boulder (Colorado) Daily Camera*, June 9, 1894.
40. Ibid., June 11, 1894.
41. *Kansas City Star*, June 23, 1894. Tarsney was a man with high political connections beyond Colorado. He had brothers who were U.S. congressmen from Missouri and Michigan (*Aberdeen [South Dakota] Daily News*, June 25, 1894).
42. *Boulder (Colorado) Daily Camera*, August 7, 1894.
43. *Idaho Daily Statesman* (Boise), August 21, 1894.
44. *Sioux City (Iowa) Journal*, March 27, 1895; *Castle Rock (Colorado) Journal*, April 17, 1895; *Greeley (Colorado) Tribune*, May 23, 1895.
45. *Boulder (Colorado) Daily Camera*, July 25, 1895; *Minneapolis Journal*, July 31, 1895.
46. DeArment, *Knights of the Green Cloth*, 212; *Omaha (Nebraska) World Herald*, December 25, 1895; *Cripple Creek (Colorado) Morning Times*, July 26, 1899.
47. *Cripple Creek (Colorado) Morning Times*, October 19, 1899.
48. *Omaha (Nebraska) World Herald*, August 23, 1901.
49. Ibid.
50. *Philadelphia Inquirer*, August 23, 1901; *Charlotte (North Carolina) Daily Observer*, August 23, 1901; *Fort Worth (Texas) Morning Resister*, August 26, 1901; *Tucson (Arizona) Daily Citizen*, November 9, 1901; *Omaha (Nebraska) World Herald*, November 9, 1901; *Colorado Transcript* (Golden), August 28, November 13, 1901.
51. *Cripple Creek (Colorado) Morning Times*, December 10, 1897, April 1, 1898.
52. Ibid., December 8, 1897.
53. Ibid., December 11, 1897.
54. *Cripple Creek (Colorado) Prospector*, December 11, 1897. It is curious that one of those calling for Daniels's suspension pending investigation of the charges was Sherman M. Bell, a detective and deputy reporting to Daniels (*Cripple Creek [Colorado] Morning Times*, December 8, 1897). Before many months passed the two would be serving together as Rough Riders in Cuba.

Chapter 8. Rough Rider

1. "The First United States Volunteer Cavalry . . . was the official title of the regiment," wrote Roosevelt, "but for some reason or other the

public promptly christened us the 'Rough Riders.' At first we fought against the use of the term, but to no purpose; and when finally the Generals of Division and Brigade began to write in formal communications about our regiment as the 'Rough Riders,' we adopted the term ourselves" (Roosevelt, *Rough Riders*, 10–11).

2. Wagoner, *Arizona Territory*, 396, 399.
3. Thrapp, *Encyclopedia of Frontier Biography*, 2:892–93.
4. *Cripple Creek (Colorado) Morning Times*, May 17, 1898.
5. B. F. Daniels Military Record, National Archives.
6. *Colorado Springs (Colorado) Daily Gazette*, January 1, 1899. The paper said Bainter and Underwood were left at Tampa, Florida, to care for the regimental horses, but the other Colorado men were in the fight at San Juan and throughout the Santiago campaign. The regiment's mustering out rolls showed Abraham Bainter of Colorado Springs was a corporal in Troop I, and Clarence Underwood of Colorado Springs was a trumpeter in Troop H. Also in Troop H was Private Charles Wilson of Boulder. Colorado Springs resident Private Walter S. Cash of Troop K received a slight arm wound on July 1, 1898, shot by a Mauser rifle. Daniels, Bell, and Devereaux were all assigned to Troop K (Regimental Muster Rolls, in Roosevelt, *Rough Riders*).
7. *Tucson (Arizona) Citizen*, February 9, 1929.
8. Roosevelt, *Rough Riders*, 25–26.
9. *Idaho Daily Statesman* (Boise), July 13, 1913, reprinted from "His Own Story of His Life—the Western Spirit," by Theodore Roosevelt, in the *Outlook*, Roosevelt's magazine.
10. Roosevelt, *Rough Riders*, 22–30.
11. Ibid., 17.
12. Ibid., 58. Roosevelt himself carried into battle a .38 Colt army and navy revolver recovered from the sunken battleship *Maine*.
13. McClintock, *Arizona*, 797–99.
14. Roosevelt, *Rough Riders*, 42.
15. McRill, "Story of an Oklahoma Cowboy." Sherman Bell was a flamboyant headline-grabbing type who after the war became manager of David H. Moffat's extensive mining operations in the Cripple Creek District, and then rose to the position of adjutant general of Colorado under Governor J. H. Peabody. In 1904 he played a prominent role in another Cripple Creek strike called by the WFM. Newspapermen loved

him for his outrageous comments about the hated miners' union. Asked what he intended to do when he led a force of seven hundred National Guardsmen into Cripple Creek, he replied: "I came here to do up this damned anarchistic federation." He said his "orders were to wipe 'em off the face of the earth." He said he would tell his men, "Kill 'em—when one of 'em pokes his head up, slug it—shoot 'em down—exterminate 'em." When union leader William Haywood spoke of habeas corpus proceedings, Bell blurted: "Habeas corpus be damned! We'll give 'em post-mortems!" He was such a thorn in the side of the union bosses that in 1905 their hired assassin, Harry Orchard, tried unsuccessfully to murder him. Bell later appeared on the vaudeville stage in a melodrama called *Ding Dong Bell*, a rendition of his Colorado exploits (Holbrook, *Rocky Mountain Revolution*, 91, 106, 179, 239; Lukas, *Big Trouble*, 225, 375; Jameson, *All That Glitters*, 45, 203–209).

16. Roosevelt, *Rough Riders*, 17.

17. *Des Moines (Iowa) Capital*, February 11, 1902.

18. Feess, *Theodore Roosevelt's Arizona Boys*, 26.

19. *Philadelphia Inquirer*, August 3, 1898.

20. B. F. Daniels Military Record, National Archives.

21. According to the *Kansas City World*, Laura was living at 1301 McGee Street in Kansas City, Missouri.

22. Devereaux was struck in the left wrist by a bullet in the fight at San Juan Hill. It looked for a time that amputation would be necessary, but his hand was saved (*Cripple Creek [Colorado] Morning Times*, October 19, 1898).

23. *Cripple Creek (Colorado) Morning Times*, July 31, 1898.

24. Ibid.

25. Feess, *Theodore Roosevelt's Arizona Boys*, 26, 29.

26. Lorant, *Life and Times of Theodore Roosevelt*, 328.

27. B. F. Daniels Military Record, National Archives; Secrest, "Fighting Man!" 47. Westerners like Daniels were each given an additional $200 to cover expenses for their trip home (Feess, *Theodore Roosevelt's Arizona Boys*, 29).

Chapter 9. The Marshalship Quest and the Spectral Past

1. Dodge to Roosevelt, December 18, 1901.

2. *Cripple Creek (Colorado) Morning Times*, May 17, 1899.

3. Ibid., May 20, 1899.

4. Secrest, "Fighting Man!" 47; U.S. Census, Nogales, Santa Cruz County, Arizona Territory, 1900.

5. Roosevelt to Daniels, March 29, 1899. The letter was addressed to 2100 Summit Street, Kansas City, Missouri, where Daniels was still living at the time.

6. Roosevelt to Daniels, November 22, 1900.

7. Daniels to Roosevelt, March 9, 1901.

8. Daniels to Roosevelt, October 20, 1901.

9. Myton, "To Whom It May Concern," December 14, 1901.

10. Dodge to Roosevelt, December 18, 1901.

11. Quoted in Feess, *Theodore Roosevelt's Arizona Boys*, 54–55.

12. Cortelyou to Knox, December 5, 1901.

13. *El Paso (Texas) Herald*, January 7, 1902.

14. Ibid.

15. *Tucson (Arizona) Citizen*, January 9, 1902.

16. Rowland to Roosevelt, January 14, 1902.

17. Robinson to Roosevelt, January 14, 1902.

18. Stoddard to Roosevelt, January 14, 1902.

19. *Tucson (Arizona) Citizen*, January 27, 1902, quoting the *Washington Post*.

20. Roosevelt to Daniels, February 1, 1902.

21. Washington dispatch reported in the *Durango (Colorado) Democrat*, February 6, 1902.

22. *Atlanta Constitution*, February 7, 1902.

23. Ibid.; *Marion (Ohio) Daily Star*, February 6, 1902.

24. *Cheyenne Daily Leader*, February 10, 1902.

25. DeMattos, "Daniels and Roosevelt," 45.

26. Curtius to Roosevelt, February 6, 1902.

27. *Prescott (Arizona) Morning Courier*, January 13, 1902, quoting the *Arizona Star*.

28. Remington to Roosevelt, February 16, 1902.

29. Roosevelt to Daniels, February 17, 1902.

30. Roosevelt to Daniels, February 22, 1902.

31. Daniels to Roosevelt, March 4, 1902.

32. *Arizona Daily Republican* (Phoenix), January 23, 1902.

33. *Atlanta Constitution*, February 7, 1902.

34. *Colorado Transcript* (Golden), February 26, 1902; *Castle Rock (Colorado) Journal*, February 28, 1902.

35. *Colorado Transcript* (Golden), February 12, 1902, reprinting an article in the *Denver Republican*. There is at least one inaccuracy in the Bloom account. He said that *after* killing Julian, Daniels was in a gunfight "and had a piece shot out of his right ear. Whether he killed the other fellow or not I can't remember." Of course we know from the Wyoming prison records that Daniels was missing the lobe of his ear years before the Julian affair.

36. *Atlanta Constitution*, February 13, 1902

37. Ibid., February 12, 1902.

38. Ibid., February 16, 1902.

39. Ibid., March 10, 1902.

40. Ibid., March 17, 1902.

41. Ibid., March 28, 1902.

42. *Fort Worth (Texas) Register*, March 9, 1902.

43. Roosevelt to Mrs. Daniels, March 15, 1902.

44. Daniels to Roosevelt, March 23, 1902. According to the *Tucson (Arizona) Citizen* of February 13, 1902, James McClintock, former Rough Rider and friend of Roosevelt and Daniels, aspired for the marshal job when Daniels's bid fell through, but Roosevelt surprised many when, on March 18, 1902, he reappointed McCord to the office, although McCord reportedly had spoken "disrespectfully" about the president during the controversy over the Daniels appointment (Ball, *United States Marshals*, 216).

45. *Tucson (Arizona) Citizen*, February 13, 1902. In addition to his own problems, in April 1902 he received the disquieting news that Horace H. Allen, a close friend and gambling partner during his Colorado period, had shot and killed his inamorata, Mollie Conrad, at Tucson, and then turned the gun on himself. Allen was about thirty-six years old, said the Tucson paper. "He had been a gambler all his life where he met Ben Daniels and there formed a close friendship with him. When Daniels was last in Tucson, he went to see his old friend and for a long time they talked over the old days in Colorado. Allen was a tall, nice looking man. He had a scar on his face by which one could easily identify him. He had a cool eye and was known as a bad man. It is said that he had been in many a fight with Ben Daniels in Colorado. Allen had eight

marks on his body from bullet wounds, the result of a few of the many fights in which he had been engaged.... Allen was one of the most expert faro dealers in the country. He always carried the gun with which he committed the desperate deed (ibid., April 14, 1902).

46. Daniels to Roosevelt, June 18, 1902; Roosevelt to Daniels, June 22, 1902.

47. *Arizona Daily Republican* (Phoenix), January 8, 1904.

48. Daniels to Roosevelt, April 12, 1904. Accompanying Daniels as a delegate to the convention was Governor Alexander Brodie (*Arizona Daily Republican* [Phoenix], March 9, 1904). The election of Daniels as an alternate rather than a delegate was probably due to the suspicion on the part of some old-line Arizona Republicans that Daniels was a Democrat in spirit and that his loyalty to Roosevelt was personal, not political (Ball, *United States Marshals*, 236).

49. Roosevelt to Daniels, April 18, 1904.

Chapter 10. Prison Superintendent

1. *Prescott (Arizona) Morning Courier*, April 22, 1905.

2. When appointed, Frantz was the youngest governor in the country. Brodie was a lifelong Republican, but Frantz and Curry were both Democrats (Feess, *Theodore Roosevelt's Arizona Boys*, 175). Their appointments showed that Roosevelt placed greater value on Rough Rider relationship than party loyalty.

3. Feess, *Theodore Roosevelt's Arizona Boys*, 93.

4. Herner, *Arizona Rough Riders*, 222. When Rynning resigned in 1907 to become superintendent of the new Arizona territorial prison at Florence, he was replaced by Harry Wheeler, his Ranger lieutenant, who had been in the U.S. Army during the Spanish-American War, but not in Roosevelt's regiment (ibid.; O'Neal, *Captain Harry Wheeler*, 18–20).

5. Metz, *Pat Garrett*, 243; DeMattos, *Garrett and Roosevelt*, passim.

6. DeArment, *Broadway Bat*, 63–65; DeMattos, *Masterson and Roosevelt*, passim.

7. Bullock was reappointed by Roosevelt's successor, President William Howard Taft, and served until 1910 (Thrapp, *Encyclopedia of*

Frontier Biography, 1:190; White, *Index of U.S. Marshals*, 11; Kellar, *Seth Bullock*).

8. White, *Index of U.S. Marshals*, 1.

9. Feess, *Theodore Roosevelt's Arizona Boys*, 72. Two other former Rough Riders, Wesley A. Hill and ex-Arizona Ranger Richard Stanton, were not so proud and eagerly sought the appointment (ibid).

10. Roosevelt to Lodge, June 4, 1904.

11. *Arizona Daily Republican* (Phoenix), September 27, 1904; Jeffrey, *Adobe and Iron*, 55.

12. *Arizona Daily Republican* (Phoenix), August 24, 1890.

13. Jeffrey, *Adobe and Iron*, 51–55. Former Rough Riders serving at the prison during Daniels's tenure were Walter T. Gregory, treasurer and secretary, and Cliff Middleton, a guard (Herner, *Arizona Rough Riders*, 221).

14. Roosevelt to Daniels, October 17, 1904.

15. Jeffrey, *Adobe and Iron*, 55.

16. *Tucson (Arizona) Citizen*, January 25, 1905.

17. *Philadelphia Inquirer*, March 2, 1905; Feess, *Theodore Roosevelt's Arizona Boys*, 96.

18. The writer was perhaps intentionally ambiguous here as to which side of the penitentiary bars were referenced.

19. *Atlanta Constitution*, February 26, 1905. Readers of western history might be interested in knowing that the lengthy piece was written by William MacLeod Raine, later a prolific author of western books and articles, both factual and fictional.

20. DeArment, "Omaha's Cowboy Mayor," 24.

21. *Atlanta Constitution*, March 2, 1905. Daniels presented a similar cane to William Loeb, the president's personal secretary (ibid.).

22. *Washington Post*, March 7, 1905.

23. Brodie to Roosevelt, March 8, 1905.

24. Loeb to Moody, March 10, 1905.

25. Masterson to Daniels, April 18, 1905, quoted in DeMattos, "Between Pals," 10–11.

26. *Washington Post*, June 15, 1905; *Tucson (Arizona) Citizen*, June 29, 1905.

27. National Archives.

Chapter 11. U.S. Marshal

1. Feess, *Theodore Roosevelt's Arizona Boys*, 99–100.
2. *New York Times*, June 15, 1905.
3. *Washington Post*, June 15, 1905.
4. *Macon (Georgia) Daily Telegraph*, June 25, 1905.
5. Masterson to Roosevelt, December 7, 1905.
6. Among the deputy marshals serving under him were Sam Greenwald, who had so favorably acquitted himself as a member of the Rough Riders that Colonel Roosevelt promoted him from private to lieutenant (Herner, *Arizona Rough Riders*, 160), and former Rough Riders Charles Utting and John Foster (ibid., 221). Foster later was an outstanding officer in the Arizona Rangers.
7. Feess, *Theodore Roosevelt's Arizona Boys*, 101.
8. *Arizona Daily Republican* (Phoenix), November 5, 1905.
9. Daniels to Moody, November 30, 1905.
10. Chaput, *Odyssey of Burt Alvord*, 120–22.
11. Harris to Moody, April 30, 1906.
12. Roosevelt to Clark, December 8, 1905.
13. Kent to Roosevelt, December 8, 1905.
14. Brodie to Roosevelt, March 8, 1905; Dodge to Roosevelt, December 18, 1901; Myton to Roosevelt, December 14, 1901.
15. *New York World*, January 20, 1906.
16. Roosevelt to Remington, February 20, 1906.
17. Quoted in DeMattos, *Masterson and Roosevelt*, 56–57.
18. Thomas E. Daniels was presumably the son of one of Ben's stepbrothers or his half-brother.
19. *Prescott (Arizona) Morning Courier*, November 15, 1905.
20. A public examiner investigating county officials' misconduct about this time found that Sheriff Fowler had performed tax-assessing duties in a "careless manner" (Ball, *Desert Lawmen*, 287).
21. *Washington Post*, February 17, 20, 1906; *Daily Nevada State Journal* (Reno), February 17, 1906.
22. *Arizona Daily Republican* (Phoenix), March 1, 1906.
23. *Montgomery (Alabama) Advertiser*, February 24, 1906.
24. *Prescott (Arizona) Morning Courier*, March 1, 1906, quoting the *Tucson Post*.
25. Ibid., March 5, 1906.

26. March 1906 issue of the *Arizona Daily Star* (Tucson), quoted in Secrest, "Fighting Man!" 51.

27. Land to Secrest, March 23, 1964; *Journal of the Executive Proceedings of the Senate*, vol. 36, 59th Congress, 1st Session.

28. Ball, *United States Marshals*, 217.

29. *Washington Post*, April 27, 1906.

30. Roosevelt to Daniels, July 14, 1906.

31. Quoted in Feess, *Theodore Roosevelt's Arizona Boys*, 119.

32. *Arizona Daily Star* (Tucson), May 17, 1906, quoting the *Albuquerque Journal*.

33. Arizona Marshal Web site: www.genealogy-quest.com/collections/armars.html; Miller, *Arizona Rangers*, 241–43. Another of Daniels's deputy appointments went to George Bravin, a Cochise County constable and jailer who had been overpowered and wounded by outlaw Billy Stiles in breaking Burt Alvord out of the Tombstone calaboose in 1900 (Chaput, *Odyssey of Burt Alvord*, 82–83). Alvord later ended up in the Yuma prison, and the controversy over his release caused Daniels some difficulty.

34. *Arizona Daily Republican* (Phoenix), June 13, 1906.

35. Hoyt to Roosevelt, July 23, 1906.

36. Daniels to Hoyt, July 28, 1906.

37. Emporia was the home of famed editor William Allen White, a close friend of Theodore Roosevelt, who six years later would join Roosevelt in forming the Progressive Party.

38. *Tucson (Arizona) Citizen*, August 27, 1906; *Emporia (Kansas) Gazette*, August 27, 1906; *Arizona Daily Republican* (Phoenix), August 29, 1906. Only a few months before Laura's death an ad for a nostrum called "Nature's Rheumatism Remedy" had appeared in an Arizona paper with an endorsement by "Ben Daniels, U.S. Marshal of Arizona." It said the medicine had "cured my wife when all others had failed" (*Arizona Daily Republican* [Phoenix], March 4, 1906).

39. *Washington Post*, March 21, 1907.

40. Ibid., March 26, 1907; *Columbus (Georgia) Enquirer-Sun*, March 29, 1907.

41. *Washington Post*, April 3, 1907.

42. *Olympia (Washington) Morning Olympian*, April 11, 1907.

43. Daniels to Attorney General, April 12, 1907.

44. Ball, *United States Marshals*, 234.

45. James R. Garfield was the third child of James A. Garfield, president of the United States. He was only fifteen when his father died on September 19, 1881, from the effect of an assassin's bullet.

46. *Albuquerque Journal*, August 15, 1907, quoting the *Tucson (Arizona) Citizen*.

47. Daniels to Roosevelt, August 16, 1907.

48. Ball, *United States Marshals*, 234.

49. *Tucson (Arizona) Citizen*, March 9, 1908.

50. Ball, *United States Marshals*, 234.

51. *Tucson (Arizona) Citizen*, May 5, 1908.

52. Marriage Certificate, Pima County, Arizona: Benjamin F. Daniels and Eva Stakebake Seayrs, July 15, 1908.

53. Roosevelt to Daniels, October 29, 1908.

54. Campbell to Roosevelt, January 30, 1909. William Loeb, Roosevelt's private secretary, attached a note to the letter: "The President desires the accompanying letter of Judge Campbell to be kept with the papers in Marshal Daniels' record. The President believes Daniels to be one of the best Marshals we have had in the country" (Loeb to Bonaparte, February 10, 1909).

55. Reynolds to Roosevelt, February 27, 1909.

56. Samuelson, *Shoot from the Lip*, 86–87; Shirley, *Guardian of the Law*, passim. Tilghman, Madsen, and Heck Thomas, another renowned deputy marshal of the Indian and Oklahoma territories, would be celebrated as the "Three Guardsmen" of Oklahoma.

57. This amusing account was in a March 14, 1909, unidentified newspaper clipping quoted in Shirley, *Guardian of the Law*, 332.

58. "Bat Shows White Feather"; *Washington Post*, January 13, 1910.

Chapter 12. The Final Years

1. Quoted in Feess, *Theodore Roosevelt's Arizona Boys*, 132.

2. Ibid., 132–33.

3. Ball, *United States Marshals*, 217–18.

4. The reservation had been established by the treaty of May 12, 1854, in which the Menomonee relinquished all claim to lands granted

them under previous treaties and were assigned a reservation of 432 square miles on the Wolf River.

    5. *Tucson (Arizona) Citizen*, October 29, 1909. The average yearly income for a working man at the time was $500 a year.

    6. Ibid.

    7. Carroll to Valentine, October 14, 1909.

    8. *Tucson (Arizona) Citizen*, May 26, 1910; *Tombstone (Arizona) Epitaph*, June 5, 1910.

    9. Articles of Incorporation of the Elephant Head Mining, Milling and Development Company.

    10. *Tombstone (Arizona) Prospector*, September 2, 1910, quoting the *Denver Post*.

    11. Daniels to Roosevelt, January 26, 1911.

    12. Roosevelt to Daniels, January 31, 1911.

    13. Feess, *Theodore Roosevelt's Arizona Boys*, 142–43.

    14. *Colorado Springs (Colorado) Daily Gazette*, July 30, 1912; DeArment, *Broadway Bat*, 148.

    15. *New York Morning Telegraph*, June 25, 1912.

    16. Daniels to Roosevelt, November 15, 1914.

    17. Feess, *Theodore Roosevelt's Arizona Boys*, 148–49.

    18. *Tucson (Arizona) Citizen*, July 20, 1914.

    19. Ibid., October 30, 1914. In his zeal to extol his friend, Masterson made several misstatements. Daniels was never city marshal of Dodge City or Guthrie, and Bat served one two-year term as Ford County sheriff.

    20. Ibid., October 24, 1914.

    21. Daniels to Roosevelt, November 15, 1914.

    22. Roosevelt to Daniels, November 30, 1914.

    23. *Tucson (Arizona) Citizen*, February 14, 1917; Boese, "John C. Greenway"; "Story of John Campbell Greenway and Ajo."

    24. Feess, *Theodore Roosevelt's Arizona Boys*, 13. J. L. B. Alexander was a prominent Phoenix attorney and Democrat who had captained C Troop of the Rough Rider regiment and had been district attorney for Arizona during Daniels's term as U.S. marshal (Wagoner, *Arizona Territory*, 344–45, 502). In 1905 George Heard, a Phoenix banker, led a delegation of Arizonans to Washington to protest the pro-

posed union of Arizona and New Mexico for admission as a single state (ibid., 433). George B. Wilcox was a lieutenant in McClintock's B Troop who later was a minor official in Greenway's copper mining company (Roosevelt, *Rough Riders*; Byrkit, *Forging the Copper Collar*, 188).

25. Feess, *Theodore Roosevelt's Arizona Boys*, 11. "Other Rough Riders active in the Progressive campaign of 1912 included Richard Salmon, who had been turned down by the Republican Party in his bid to replace Daniels as marshal, and Charles Utting, a former deputy under Daniels" (ibid., 179).

26. Daniels to Roosevelt (wire), December 30, 1914; Daniels to Roosevelt (letter), December 30, 1914; Roosevelt to Daniels, December 31, 1914.

27. Roosevelt to Daniels, January 4, 1915.

28. Greenway served a year as regent of the University of Arizona before accepting a commission as major in the U.S. Army and leaving to fight in World War I. He remained in the army after the war and rose to the rank of brigadier general. He was only fifty-four when he died in 1926. In the rotunda of the Capitol at Washington, D.C., next to a bust of Daniel Webster, stands a large bronze of Greenway in his army uniform. It was wrought by Gutzon Borglum, the sculptor who immortalized Theodore Roosevelt on Mount Rushmore. Today a major thoroughfare and a high school in Phoenix bear his name (Boese, "John C. Greenway; "Lady at Large").

29. *Lincoln (Nebraska) Daily Star*, October 22, 1916.

30. *Tucson (Arizona) Citizen*, November 6, 1916.

31. Ibid., November 1, 1916. The Pima County sheriff at this time was Albert W. Forbes, who served one two-year term, 1915–16 (Eppinga, *Arizona Sheriffs*, 179).

32. *Tucson (Arizona) Citizen*, August 30, 1916.

33. Daniels to Roosevelt, November 25, 1916.

34. Roosevelt to Daniels, December 4, 1916.

35. *Tucson (Arizona) Citizen*, April 9, 1917.

36. Ibid., July 22, 1920.

37. Ibid., March 15, 28, 1920.

38. Ibid., January 4, 1921.

39. Ibid., January 6, 1921.

40. Ibid.

41. Ibid., May 13, 1921.

42. Ibid., March 21, 1921.

43. Ibid., June 30, 1921.

44. *Kansas City Star*, May 15, 1922; *Philadelphia Inquirer*, May 16, 1922.

45. *Nevada State Journal*, May 30, 1922.

46. Blacklidge to Secrest, November 11, 1966. Actually, Blacklidge's memory was a little faulty, as Daniels did not track the outlaws on his "trusty horse" but followed them by automobile, for this was 1922 and not 1892, after all.

47. The postmaster's job at Ruby was highly dangerous during this period, according to press reports. The Pearsons had come from Texas only a year earlier to replace the previous postmaster, who, together with another victim, had been murdered by bandits (*Fort Worth [Texas] Star-Telegram*, August 27, 1921).

48. *Fort Worth (Texas) Star-Telegram*, August 27, 1921; *Duluth (Minnesota) News Tribune*, August 27, 28, 1921; *Idaho Daily Statesman* (Boise), August 28, 1921; Parmer and O'Donnell, "How We Trapped the Deadly Border Bandits," 19.

49. Parmer and O'Donnell, "How We Trapped the Deadly Border Bandits," 73.

50. *Bellingham (Washington) Herald*, July 14, 1922; *Fort Worth (Texas) Star-Telegram*, July 14, 1922; *Albuquerque Morning Journal*, July 15, 1922; *Idaho Daily Statesman* (Boise), July 15, 19, 1922; *Olympia (Washington) Morning Olympian*, July 15, 1922.

51. Parmer and O'Donnell, "How We Trapped the Deadly Border Bandits," 74. For the first time Daniels saw an airplane used in the search, a dramatic example of how the new century differed from the last (ibid., 75).

52. *Idaho Daily Statesman* (Boise), July 19, 1922.

53. Parmer and O'Donnell, "How We Trapped the Deadly Border Bandits," 75.

54. Ibid.

55. *Tucson (Arizona) Citizen*, October 15, 1922.

56. Declaration for Pension, Benjamin Daniels, November 2, 1922. For reasons known only to himself, Daniels incorrectly gave his birth year as 1854 and his age as sixty-eight on this application. Perhaps

he had shaved a couple of years off his age when wooing Annie, seventeen years his junior.

57. *Arizona Daily Star* (Tucson), April 21, 1923; Browning, *Violence Was No Stranger*, 69. The official cause of death, according to the death certificate, was "acute dilatation of the heart."

58. *Arizona Daily Star* (Tucson), April 21, 1923.

59. *Tombstone (Arizona) Epitaph*, April 24, 1923.

Afterword

1. Annie E. Daniels's Declaration for Widow's Pension, filed July 16, 1923.

2. *Tucson (Arizona) Citizen*, March 25, 1946.

3. Ibid., February 9, 1929.

4. Feess, *Theodore Roosevelt's Arizona Boys*, 176.

Bibliography

Abbreviations for Collections, Libraries, and Records Holdings
AHS   Arizona Historical Society
RKDC Robert K. DeArment Collection
JDC   Jack DeMattos Collection
NARS National Archives and Records Service
WBSC William B. Secrest Collection
WLHU Widener Library, Harvard University

Government Documents

Affidavit of Charles H. Pogue and Ophelia Pogue regarding marriages of Ben Daniels, September 18, 1923, Pima County, Arizona

Certificate of Death, Benjamin Franklin Daniels, Pima County, Arizona, April 23, 1923

Declaration for Pension, War with Spain, Philippine Insurrection and China Relief Expedition, Benjamin Daniels, Pima County, Arizona, November 2, 1922

Declaration for Widow's Pension, War with Spain, Philippine Insurrection and China Relief Expedition, Mrs. Annie E. Daniels, Pima County, Arizona, July 16, 1923

Guthrie, Oklahoma, City Records for 1889

Journal of the Executive Proceedings of the Senate, Vol. 36, 59th Congress, 1st Session

Marriage Certificate, Pima County, Arizona: Benjamin F. Daniels and Eva Stakebake Seayrs, July 15, 1908

Marriage License, Pima County, Arizona: Benjamin F. Daniels and Evelina Seayrs, July 14, 1908

National Archives, Central Plains Region

U.S. Census

Arizona: Santa Cruz County, 1900
California: "The Middle Fork of the American River," 1850
Illinois: LaSalle County, 1850, 1860
Kansas: Coffee County, 1880; Franklin County, 1870; Osage County, 1880
Wyoming: Laramie County, 1880

Court and Prison Records

Kansas: *State of Kansas v. N. F. Watson, et al.*

Manuscripts

DeMattos, Jack. "Daniels and Roosevelt" (JDC).
Rastall, Benjamin McKie. "The Labor History of the Cripple Creek District: A Study in Industrial Evolution." Ph.D. diss., University of Wisconsin, 1906.

Letters, Telegrams, and Unpublished Documents

Charles Belson to Theodore Roosevelt, February 19, 1902 (NARS)
Harry J. Blacklidge to William Secrest, November 11, 1966 (WBSC)
W. S. Boynton to Theodore Roosevelt, February 19, 1902 (NARS)
Alexander O. Brodie to Theodore Roosevelt, March 8, 1905 (NARS)
John H. Campbell to Theodore Roosevelt, January 30, 1909 (NARS)
James A. Carroll to Robert G. Valentine, October 14, 1909 (Report in the matter of investigation of the Indian Bureau, 62nd Congress, 3rd Session) (NARS)
Certification of citizens of Nogales, Arizona, regarding qualifications of Ben Daniels (NARS)
George B. Cortelyou to P. C. Knox, December 5, 1901 (NARS)

Augustus Curtius to Theodore Roosevelt, February 6, 1902 (NARS)
B. F. Daniels to Attorney General, April 12, 1907 (NARS)
B. F. Daniels to W. M. Hoyt, July 28, 1906 (NARS)
B. F. Daniels to William H. Moody, July 1, November 30, 1905; July 28, 1906 (NARS)
B. F. Daniels to Theodore Roosevelt, March 9, 1901; March 4, 23, June 18, 1902; April 12, 1904; August 16, 1907; January 26, 1911; November 15, December 30, 1914 (wire); December 30, 1914 (letter); November 25, 1916; February 16, 1918 (WLHU)
B. F. Daniels to Theodore Roosevelt, October 20, 1901; February 25, 1902 (NARS)
Mr. and Mrs B. F. Daniels to Theodore Roosevelt, June 14, 1918 (WLHU)
Daniels Family Bible (Boot Hill Museum, Dodge City, Kansas)
S. W. Drachman to Theodore Roosevelt, February 18, 1902 (NARS)
Fred Dodge to Theodore Roosevelt, December 18, 1901 (NARS)
J. D. Harris to William H. Moody, April 30, 1906 (NARS)
W. M. Hoyt to Theodore Roosevelt, July 23, 1906 (NARS)
L. C. Hughes to Theodore Roosevelt, February 17, 1902 (NARS)
Edward Kent to Theodore Roosevelt, December 8, 1905 (NARS)
Joseph H. Kibbey to Theodore Roosevelt, December 8, 1905 (NARS)
Robert H. Land to William Secrest, March 23, 1964 (WBSC)
William Loeb to Charles J. Bonaparte, February 10, 1909 (NARS)
William Loeb to William H. Moody, March 10, June 13, 1905 (NARS)
W. B. Masterson to B. F. Daniels, April 18, 1905 (WLHU)
W. B. Masterson to Theodore Roosevelt, December 7, 1905 (WLHU)
H. P. Myton, "To Whom It May Concern," December 14, 1901 (NARS)
Frederic Remington to Theodore Roosevelt, February 16, 1902 (WLHU)
C. M. Reynolds to Theodore Roosevelt, February 27, 1909 (NARS)
Charles B. Riley to Theodore Roosevelt, February 24, 1902 (NARS)

C. H. Robinson to Theodore Roosevelt, January 14, 1902 (NARS)

Theodore Roosevelt to Don Clark, December 8, 1905 (WLHU)

Theodore Roosevelt to B. F. Daniels, March 29, 1899; November 22, 1900; February 1, 16, 17, 22, June 22, 1902; April 18, October 17, 1904; July 14, 1906; September 29, 1907; October 29, November 11, 1908; January 31, 1911; February 29, 1912; November 30, December 31, 1914; January 4, 1915; December 4, 1916; February 28, 1918 (WLHU)

Theodore Roosevelt to Mr. and Mrs. B. F. Daniels, June 24, 1918 (WLHU)

Theodore Roosevelt to Mrs. B. F. Daniels, March 15, 1902 (WLHU)

Theodore Roosevelt to William H. Moody, March 10, June 13, 1905 (NARS)

Theodore Roosevelt to Frederic Remington, February 20, 1906 (WLHU)

D. D. Rose to Theodore Roosevelt, February 25, 1905 (NARS)

R. A. Rowland to Theodore Roosevelt, January 14, 1902 (NARS)

H. N. Seigfreid to Theodore Roosevelt, February 17, 1902 (NARS)

Isaac T. Stoddard to Theodore Roosevelt, January 14, 1902 (NARS)

Thomas S. Wilson to Theodore Roosevelt, February 18, 1902 (NARS)

Sam W. Wormwood to Theodore Roosevelt, February 10, 1902 (NARS)

Newspapers

Aberdeen (South Dakota) Daily News, June 25, 1894

Albuquerque Morning Democrat, May 26, 30, June 5, 8, 12, 1894; August 15, 1907

Albuquerque Morning Journal, August 15, 1907; July 15, 21, 1922

Arizona Daily Star (Tucson), May 17, 1906; April 21, 1923

Arizona Daily Republican (Phoenix), August 24, 1890; January 23, 1902; January 8, March 9, September 27, 1904; November 5, 1905; February 17, March 1, 4, June 13, August 29, 1906

Arizona Republican-Herald (Phoenix), January 18, 1900

Atchison (Kansas) Daily Globe, January 14, 1889
Atlanta (Georgia) Constitution, January 26, 1889; February 7, 12, 13, 16, March 10, 17, 28, 1902; February 26, March 2, 1905
Bellingham (Washington) Herald, July 14, 1922
Bismarck (North Dakota) Daily Tribune, September 26, 27, 1893; June 7, 1894; July 25, 1895
Boulder (Colorado) Daily Camera, June 9, 11, August 7, 1894; July 25, 1895
Castle Rock (Colorado) Journal, March 28, June 13, 1894; April 17, 1895; February 28, 1902
Charlotte (North Carolina) Daily Observer, August 23, 1901
Cheyenne Daily Leader, March 2, November 20, 21, 23, 1879; June 11, 1880; February 5, 10, 15, March 5, 1902
Cheyenne Daily Sun, November 21, 1879
Chicago Daily Inter Ocean, July 1, 1881
Cimarron (Kansas) Jacksonian, January 18, June 28, July 5, 12, 1889
Cimarron (Kansas) New West Echo, January 17, 1889
Colorado Springs (Colorado) Daily Gazette, January 1, 1899; July 30, 1912
Colorado Transcript (Golden), February 13, 1895; August 28, November 13, 1901; February 26, 1902
Columbus (Georgia) Enquirer-Sun, March 29, 1907
Cripple Creek (Colorado) Morning Times, December 8, 11, 1897; July 31, October 19, 1898; May 17, 20, July 26, October 19, 1899
Cripple Creek (Colorado) Prospector, December 11, 1897
Daily Nevada State Journal (Reno), February 17, 1906; August 14, 1909; May 30, 1922
Dallas Morning News, August 17, 1903
Denver Field and Farm, December 21, 1872
Denver Tribune, March 1, 1879
Des Moines (Iowa) Capital, February 11, 1902
Dodge City Democrat, July 12, 19, August 9, 16, November 15, 1884; June 6, August 15, 1885; January 23, November 15, 20, 1886

Dodge City Times, May 26, June 2, 1877; June 1, 1878; January 4, 7, 11, 14, 25, June 7, 11, September 13, 1879; January 17, 1889

Duluth (Minnesota) News Tribune, October 24, 1893; August 27, 28, 1921

Durango (Colorado) Democrat, February 6, 1902

Ellsworth (Kansas) Reporter, June 18, 1874

El Paso (Texas) Herald, January 7, 1902

Emporia (Kansas) Gazette, August 27, 1906

Ford County Globe (Dodge City), July 8, 1884; March 9, 1886

Fort Worth (Texas) Gazette, August 7, 1886

Fort Worth (Texas) Morning Register, August 26, 1901; February 6, March 9, 1902

Fort Worth (Texas) Star-Telegram, August 27, 1921; July 14, 1922

Globe Live Stock Journal (Dodge City), July 15, 1884; April 13, 20, November 16, 23, 1886

Grand Forks (North Dakota) Daily Herald, September–October, 1893; December 14, 1894; April 17, 1898; October 20, 1906

Gray County Echo (Cimarron, Kansas), October 27, 1887

Greeley (Colorado) Tribune, June 7, July 5, 1894; May 23, 1895

Idaho Daily Statesman (Boise), May 30, June 7, August 21, 23, 1894; November 14, 1896; July 13, 1913; August 28, 1921; July 15, 19, 1922

Indianapolis Sentinel, September 5, 1876

Ingalls (Kansas) Union, November 26, 1887; January 17, 1889

Kansas City Star, June 23, 1894; May 15, 1922

Kansas Cowboy (Dodge City), July 12, August 9, 1884; May 16, 1885

Laramie (Wyoming) Sentinel, November 21, 22, 30, December 6, 1879; April 22, 1880

Larned (Kansas) Optic, September 12, 26, 1879

Leadville (Colorado) Daily and Evening Chronicle, August 15, 1894

Lincoln (Nebraska) Daily Star, October 22, 1916

Macon (Georgia) Daily Telegraph, June 25, 1905;, April 4, 1907

Marion (Ohio) Daily Star, February 6, 1902
Minneapolis Journal, July 31, 1895
Mitchell (South Dakota) Daily Republican, January 15, 1889
Montezuma (Kansas) Chief, November 18, 1887
Montgomery (Alabama) Advertiser, February 24, 1906
Nevada State Journal (Reno), May 30, 1922
New York Morning Times, June 25, 1912
New York Times, June 15, 1905
New York World, January 20, 1906
Olympia (Washington) Morning Olympian, August 8, 1894; April 11, 1907; July 15, 1922
Omaha (Nebraska) World Herald, December 25, 1895; August 23, November 9, 1901; March 29, 1904
Philadelphia Inquirer, August 7, 1879; August 3, 1898; August 23, 1901; March 2, 1905; May 16, 1922
Prescott (Arizona) Morning Courier, January 13, 1902; April 22, November 15, 1905; March 1, 5, 1906
Reno Evening Gazette, February 15, 1907
San Angelo (Texas) Standard, October 12, 1912
San Angelo (Texas) Standard Times, October 8, 1886
San Francisco Bulletin, July 24, 1879
Santa Fe New Mexican, June 11, 1894
Sioux City (Iowa) Journal, March 27, 1895
Tombstone (Arizona) Epitaph, June 5, 1910; April 24, 1923
Tombstone (Arizona) Prospector, September 2, 1910
Topeka (Kansas) Capital-Commonwealth, January 15, 1889
Topeka (Kansas) Commonwealth, March 4, 1879
Trenton (New Jersey) Times, January 14, 1889
Tucson (Arizona) Daily Citizen, November 9, 1901; January 9, 27, February 13, 15, April 14, 1902; September 28, 1904; January 24, June 29, 1905; January 24, February 2, August 27, 1906; August 12, 1907; March 9, May 5, 1908; October 27, 29, 1909;

May 26, 1910; July 20, October 24, 30, 1914; August 30, September 11, November 1, 6, 1916; February 14, April 9, 1917; March 15, 22, 28, July 21, 1920; January 3, 4, 6, March 21, May 13, June 30, 1921; October 15, 1922; February 9, 1929; March 25, 1946

Washington Post, March 7, June 15, 1905; February 16, 17, 20, April 27, August 27, 1906; March 21, 26, April 3, 1907; January 13, 1910

Wichita (Kansas) Sunday Eagle Magazine, January 31, 1926

Miscellaneous

Articles of Incorporation of the Elephant Head Mining, Milling and Development Company (AHS)

Books and Pamphlets

Alexander, Bob. *Lawmen, Outlaws and S.O.Bs.* Silver City, N.Mex.: High-Lonesome Books, 2007.

Annals of Kansas, 1886 to 1925. Vol. 1.

Baker, T. Lindsey, and Billy R. Harrison. *Adobe Walls: The History and Archeology of the 1874 Trading Post.* College Station: Texas A&M University Press, 1986.

Ball, Larry D. *Desert Lawmen: The High Sheriffs of New Mexico and Arizona, 1846–1912.* Albuquerque: University of New Mexico Press, 1992.

———. *The United States Marshals of New Mexico and Arizona Territories, 1846–1912.* Albuquerque: University of New Mexico Press, 1978.

Bartholomew, Ed. *The Biographical Album of Western Gunfighters.* Houston: Frontier Press of Texas, 1958.

Betz, Ava. *A Prowers County History.* Lamar, Colo.: Prowers County Historical Society, 1986.

Brent, William, and Milarde Brent. *The Hell Hole: The Yuma Prison Story.* Yuma, Ariz.: Southwest Printers, 1962.

Browning, James A. *Violence Was No Stranger: A Guide to the Grave Sites of Famous Westerners.* Stillwater, Okla.: Barbed Wire Press, 1993.

Byrkit, James W. *Forging the Copper Collar: Arizona's Labor-Management War 1901–1921.* Tucson: University of Arizona Press, 1982.

Chaput, Don. *The Odyssey of Burt Alvord: Lawman, Train Robber, Fugitive.* Tucson, Ariz.: Westernlore Press, 2000.

Chisholm, Joe. *Brewery Gulch: Frontier Days of Old Arizona—Last Outpost of the Great Southwest.* San Antonio, Tex.: Naylor, 1949.

Collier, William Ross, and Edwin Victor Westrate. *The Reign of Soapy Smith: Monarch of Misrule in the Last Days of the Old West and the Klondike Gold Rush.* Garden City, N.Y.: Sun Dial Press, 1935.

Collinson, Frank. *Life in the Saddle.* Norman: University of Oklahoma Press, 1963.

Cook, John R. *The Border and the Buffalo: An Untold Story of the Southwest Plains.* Chicago: Lakeside Press, 1938.

Dary, David. *More True Tales of Old-Time Kansas.* Lawrence: University Press of Kansas, 1987.

DeArment, Robert K. *Alias Frank Canton.* Norman: University of Oklahoma Press, 1996.

——. *Ballots and Bullets: The Bloody County Seat Wars of Kansas.* Norman: University of Oklahoma Press, 2006.

——. *Broadway Bat: Gunfighter in Gotham: The New York City Years of Bat Masterson.* Honolulu: Talei Publishers, 2005.

——. *Knights of the Green Cloth: The Saga of the Frontier Gamblers.* Norman: University of Oklahoma Press, 1982.

DeMattos, Jack. *Garrett and Roosevelt.* College Station, Tex.: Creative Publishing, 1988.

——. *Masterson and Roosevelt.* College Station, Tex.: Creative Publishing, 1984.

Eppinga, Jane. *Arizona Sheriffs: Badges and Bad Men.* Tucson, Ariz.: Rio Nuevo, 2006.

Feess, Marty F. *Theodore Roosevelt's Arizona Boys: Cowboys and Politics in the Old West.* New York: Writers Club Press, 2001.

Feitz, Leland. *Cripple Creek! A Quick History of the World's Greatest Gold Camp.* Colorado Springs, Colo.: Little London Press, 1967.

———. *Myers Avenue: A Quick History of Cripple Creek's Red-Light District.* Colorado Springs, Colo.: Little London Press, 1967.

Frye, Elnora L. *Atlas of Wyoming Outlaws at the Territorial Penitentiary.* Laramie, Wyo.: Jelm Mountain, 1990.

Gilbert, Miles, Leo Reminger, and Sharon Cunningham. *Encyclopedia of Buffalo Hunters and Skinners.* Vol. 1, A–D. Union City, Tenn.: Pioneer Press, 2003.

Haywood, C. Robert. *Cowtown Lawyers: Dodge City and Its Attorneys, 1878–1886.* Norman: University of Oklahoma Press, 1988.

———. *The Merchant Prince of Dodge City: The Life and Times of Robert M. Wright.* Norman: University of Oklahoma Press, 1998.

Herner, Charles. *The Arizona Rough Riders.* Tucson: University of Arizona Press, 1970.

Hickman, W. Z. *History of Jackson County, Missouri.* Topeka, Kans.: Historical Publishing, 1920.

Holbrook, Stewart H. *The Rocky Mountain Revolution.* New York: Henry Holt, 1956.

Horan, James D. *Across the Cimarron.* New York: Crown, 1956.

Jameson, Elizabeth. *All That Glitters: Class, Conflict, and Community in Cripple Creek.* Urbana: University of Illinois Press, 1998.

Jeffrey, John Mason. *Adobe and Iron: The Story of the Arizona Territorial Prison at Yuma.* La Jolla, Calif.: Prospect Avenue Press, 1969.

Keithley, Ralph. *Buckey O'Neill*. Caldwell, Idaho: Caxton Printers, 1949.

Kellar, Kenneth C. *Seth Bullock: Frontier Marshal*. Aberdeen, S.Dak.: North Plains Press, 1972.

Lorant, Stefan. *The Life and Times of Theodore Roosevelt*. Garden City, N.Y.: Doubleday, 1959.

Loomis, John A. *Texas Ranchman: The Memoirs of John A. Loomis*. Chadron, Neb.: Fur Press, 1982.

Lukas, J. Anthony. *Big Trouble: A Murder in a Small Western Town Sets Off a Struggle for the Soul of America*. New York: Simon and Schuster, 1997.

Marshall, Edward, and Richard F. Outcault. *The Story of the Rough Riders, 1st U.S. Volunteer Cavalry*. New York: G. W. Dillingham, 1899.

McClintock, James H. *Arizona, Prehistoric—Aboriginal—Pioneer—Modern: The Nation's Youngest Commonwealth within a Land of Ancient Culture*. Chicago: S. J. Clarke, 1916.

Metz, Leon C. *Pat Garrett: The Story of a Western Lawman*. Norman: University of Oklahoma Press, 1974.

Miller, Joseph. *Arizona: The Last Frontier*. New York: Hastings House, 1956.

———. *The Arizona Rangers*. New York: Hastings House, 1972.

Miller, Nyle H., and Joseph W. Snell. *Why the West Was Wild: A Contemporary Look at the Antics of Some Highly Publicized Kansas Cowtown Personalities*. Topeka: Kansas State Historical Society, 1963.

Morison, Elting E. *The Letters of Theodore Roosevelt*. 8 vols. Cambridge, Mass.: Harvard University Press, 1951–54.

Nash, Jay Robert. *Encyclopedia of Western Lawmen and Outlaws*. New York: Paragon House, 1992.

O'Neal, Bill. *Captain Harry Wheeler, Arizona Lawmen*. Austin, Tex.: Eakin Press, 2003.

Page, Anita Vaden. *Badges, Bullets and Blood*. Silver City, N.Mex.: n.p., 1997.

Rawlings, Isaac D. *The Rise and Fall of Disease in Illinois*. 2 vols. Springfield, Ill.: State Department of Public Health, 1927.

Robertson, Frank G., and Beth Kay Harris. *Soapy Smith: King of the Frontier Con Men*. New York: Hastings House, 1961.

Roosevelt, Theodore. *The Rough Riders*. New York: Charles Scribner's Sons, 1899.

Samuelson, Nancy B. *Shoot from the Lip: The Lives, Legends and Lies of the Three Guardsmen of Oklahoma and U.S. Marshal Nix*. Eastford, Conn.: Shooting Star Press, 1998.

Schmidt, Heinie. *Ashes of My Campfire: Historical Anecdotes of Old Dodge City as Told and Retold*. Dodge City, Kans.: Dodge City, Kansas, Journal, 1952.

Shirley, Glenn. *Guardian of the Law: The Life and Times of William Matthew Tilghman (1854–1924)*. Austin, Tex.: Eakin Press, 1988.

Silva, Lee A. *Wyatt Earp: A Biography of the Legend*. Vol. 1, *The Cowtown Years*. Santa Ana, Calif.: Graphic Publications, 2002.

Tennyson, Alfred. *Poems*. Boston: William D. Ticknor, 1842.

Thrapp, Dan L. *Encyclopedia of Frontier Biography*. 4 vols. Glendale, Calif.: Arthur H. Clark, 1988–94.

Tilghman, Zoe Agnes. *Marshal of the Last Frontier: Life and Service of William Matthew (Bill) Tilghman for 50 Years One of the Greatest Peace Officers of the West*. Glendale, Calif.: Arthur H. Clark, 1964.

Tise, Sammy. *Texas County Sheriffs*, Albuquerque, N.Mex.: Oakwood Publishing, 1989.

Tyler, Ron, ed. *The New Handbook of Texas*. Austin: Texas State Historical Society, 1996.

Wagoner, Jay J. *Arizona Territory, 1863–1912*. Tucson: University of Arizona Press, 1970.

White, Virgil D. *Index of U.S. Marshals, 1789–1960*. Waynesboro, Tenn.: National Historical Publishing, 1988.

Wright, Robert M. *Dodge City, the Cowboy Capital, and the Great Southwest in the Days of the Wild Indian, the Cowboy, Dance Halls, Gambling Halls, and Bad Men*. Wichita, Kans.: Wichita Eagle Press, 1913.

Young, Frederic R. *Dodge City: Up through a Century in Story and Pictures*. Dodge City, Kans.: Boot Hill Museum, 1972.

Zachry, Juanita Daniel. *Buffalo Gap Historic Village*. Austin, Tex.: Nortex Press, 1992.

Articles

"Bat Shows White Feather." *Santa Fe Magazine*, March 1909.

Boese, Donald L. "John C. Greenway." http://www.hascahistorical.com/greenway.html.

DeArment, R. K. " 'Hurricane Bill' Martin, Horse Thief." *True West*, June 1991.

———. "The Killing of John W. Vaden by a Man Named Ben Daniels." *Journal, Wild West History Association* (February 2008).

———. "Omaha's Cowboy Mayor." *True West*, March 1995.

DeMattos, Jack. "Between Pals: A Missive Between Presidential Gunfighters." *Quarterly of the National Association for Outlaw and Lawman History* (July–September 1993).

———. "Gunfighters of the Real West: Ben Daniels." *Real West*, September 1979.

Hunter, J. Marvin. "Some Tragedies I Have Witnessed." *Frontier Times*, January 1941.

Hunter, John Warren Hunter. "Killing of John Vaden at Ft. McKavett." *San Angelo Standard*, October 12, 1912, reprinted in *Frontier Times*, November 1924.

"Lady at Large." *Time*, August 21, 1933.

Lynch, Brendan M. "War for the Gray County Seat." http://www.hppr.org/seatwar/.

McRill, Leslie A. "The Story of an Oklahoma Cowboy, William McGinty and His Wife." *Chronicles of Oklahoma* 34, no. 4 (Winter 1956–57).

Parmer, Oliver, and Kathleen O'Donnell. "How We Trapped the Deadly Border Bandits." *Startling Detective Adventures*, March 1936.

Secrest, William B. "Fighting Man." *Frontier Times*, May 1969.

"The Story of John Campbell Greenway and Ajo." *Ajo Copper News*. http://www.cunews.info/greenwat.html.

Strickland, Rex W., ed. "The Recollections of W. S. Glenn, Buffalo Hunter." *Panhandle-Plains Historical Review* 22 (1949).

Thoburn, Joseph B. "Frank H. Greer." *Chronicles of Oklahoma*, September 1936.

Walker, Wayne T. "Born and Leuch: The Two Dutch Henrys." *Real West*, October 1983.

Index

Abbott, A. J., 65
Abernathy, John R. ("Catch-'Em-Alive Jack"), 126, 158, 159
Abilene, Tex., 200n13
Adams, Charles, 72
Ady, L. L., 38
Ajo, Ariz., 174
Albuquerque, N.Mex., 182
Alexander, John L. B., 168, 174, 217n24
Allen (Cripple Creek Fire Chief), 80
Allen, Frank, 182
Allen, Horace H., 211n45
Allensworth, William H. ("Billy"), 60, 62, 63
Altman, Colo., 73, 75, 206n36
Alvord, Burt, 129, 138–39, 215n33
Amadoville, Ariz., 185
Andrews, William H. ("Bull"), 153, 154
Angus, William, 116
Arizona Children's Home, 189
Arizona counties: Cochise, 198; Pima, 180, 183, 184, 189, 218n31; Santa Cruz, 144, 146, 183, 185
Arizona House of Representatives, 125
Arizona Rangers, 89, 125, 128, 150, 184, 213n9, 214n6

Arizona Supreme Court, 134, 141, 158
Army camps: Ben Daniels, 189; Carlin, 16; Wikoff, 100; Wood, 90

Bacon, Robert, 153
Bailey, Frank, 180
Bailey, Walter W., 185
Bainter, Alonzo, 86, 208n6
Ballard, Charles L., 89
Ballinger, Tex., 43
Barrett, S. H., 30
Battle Mountain, 73
Battles: Adobe Walls, 13, 14, 195n9, 202n2; Cimarron, 60–63, 65, 204n29, 204n31; Las Guasimas, 84, 91, 109, 173; San Juan Hill, 95, 96, 97, 103, 105, 120, 159, 173, 192, 209n22; Santiago siege, 95, 103, 130, 208n6; Yellow House Canyon, 6–7
Baxter, George, 202n2
Bedell, Mike, 11
Behan, John H., 128
Bell, Hamilton, 63
Bell, Sherman, 86, 91, 92, 93, 105, 129, 130, 207n54, 208n15
Belson, Charles, quoted, 34
Benedict, George W., 57
Bickerstaff, Ben, 41, 42, 45
Bieber, Sidney, 147

235

236 INDEX

"Billy the Kid," 126
Bisbee, Ariz., 158, 173, 197n1
Black Horse (Comanche chieftain), 5, 7, 194n16
"Black Jack" (bandit), 197n43
Blacklidge, Harry J., 183
Blair, Myron M. ("Buffalo Sam"), 19, 197n36
Bliss, A. J. ("Jack"), 61
Bloom, Jacob C. ("Jakey"), 29–30, 80, 119, 211n15; quoted, 35–36
Blue Springs, Mo., 53, 151, 152, 153
Bolds, George, 60, 61, 62, 63
Borglum, Gutzon, 218n28
Born, "Dutch Henry," 10–16, *12*, 191, 195n9
Born, Jake, 13
Bornan, Frank, 44
Bowers, M. F. ("Frank"), 66, 70–78
Bowyer, Shad, 181, 182
Boynton, W. S., 75
Bravin, George, 215n33
Brice, Harry, 63
Bridges, Jack, 23
Brodie, Alexander O., 83, 84, 89, 112, 122, 124, 125, 126, 127, 129, 130, 131, 141, 174, 177, 212n48, 212n2
Brooks, "Buffalo Bill," 11
Brooks, Edward D. ("Ed"), 60, 62, 64
Brooks, E. J., 75
Brown, Neal, 9, 10–11, 23, 57, 59, 62, 63, 65, 66, 67, 205n6
Bryan, William Jennings, 158
Bryce, James, 163
"Buck" (buffalo hunter), 8
Buffalo, N.Y., 107
Buffalo City, Kans. *See* Dodge City
Bull Hill, 73, 74, 75
Bullock, Seth, 126, 130, *132*, 212n7

Burton, Joseph R., 39, 199n14
Butler, Edward H., 153
Butler, Pearl, 182

Calderwood, John, 73, 74, 76
Cameron, Ralph, 162
Campbell, John E., 125
Campbell, John H., 133; quoted, 134, 158
Campbell, Tom, 177
Canada, 3
Cannon, Joseph G., 147
Canton, Frank, 193n1
Capitol, Washington, D.C., 218n28
Carr, Joseph A., 90
Carroll (prosecutor), 17
Carroll, James A., 164
Cash, Walter, 86, 208n6
"Cherokee Bill" (Rough Rider), 88, 113, 115
Cheyenne, Wyo., 16, 17, 19, 67
Chicago, Ill., 72, 168, 169, 172
Chihuahua, Mexico, 198
Chisholm Trail, 11
Choate, K. B. ("Bing"), 26
Chouteau, A. S., 27–28
Christy, Charles, 13
Christy, Sheriff, 10
Churches: Baptist, 88; Methodist, 20, 88; Methodist Episcopal, 109; Presbyterian, 78
Cimarron, Kans., 116, 120, 203n22
Civil War, 34, 42, 148
Clanton, Phin, 128
Clark, Ben, 11
Clark, Don, 140, 141, 142, 148
Code of the West, 36, 39, 190, 191
Colbert, Benjamin H., 125, 159
Collier, I. J., 33
Colorado College, 74
Colorado Counties: Bent, 202n6; El Paso, 66, 70, 76; Prowers, 202n6

INDEX

Colorado Springs, Colo., 67, 74, 86, 90, 206n36
Colt revolver, 85, 90, 131, 208n12
Companies: Blue Bar Taxi, 181; Calumet and Arizona, 173; Conrad & Daniels, 123; Jefferson Mining, 122; Phelps-Dodge, 162; Tennessee Coal and Iron, 168; Tucson Electric, 116; Wells, Fargo, 102, 107, 150, 166, 176
Condon, Charles ("Kid"), 19, 197n36
Conrad, Mollie, 211n45
Continental, Ariz., 184
Cook, John, 194n19
Cook, R. G., 38
Copple, Mrs. E. L., 151
Cortelyou, George B., 153
Cottonwood Falls, Kans., 196n31
Cripple Creek, Colo., 30, 66–81, 82, 84, 85, 86, 91, 98, 100, 103, 104, 114, 115, 119, 120, 171, 208n15, 209n15
Cromwell, Okla., 205n6
Crosby, Arthur, 94
Crumley, Grant, 71, 77, 78, 79
Crumley, Newt, 71, 77, 78
Crumley, Sherman, 71, 77, 78
Cuba, 82, 84, 86, 90–93, 95, 100, 102, 103, 105, 117, 125, 140, 159, 206n36, 207n54
Curry, George, 89, 125, 212n2,
Curtius, Augustus, 116
Czolgosz, Leon, 107

Dahlman, Jim, 130
Daiquiri, Cuba, 91
Daniels, Aaron, 3–4, 21, 193n4
Daniels, Aaron, Jr., 193n3
Daniels, Albert, 193n7
Daniels, Annie Evalina Stakebake Seayrs, 157, 167, 187, 189, 220n56
Daniels, Annie Laura Ware, 53, *54,* 152
Daniels, Ben (of N.Dak.), 205n7
Daniels, Ben (of Tex.), 41, 44, 46–50
Daniels, Benjamin Franklin, 18, 83, 105, 107, 108, 115, 118, 121, 126, 137, 141, 155, 158, 159, 160, 162, *167,* 168, 169, 175, *186,* 191, 195n1, 197n43, 198n1, 201n28, 212n48; arrested, 10, 17, 63, 143, 170; as buffalo hunter, 5–9, 194n11; as convict, 3, 19–21, 23, 114, 116, 117, 119, 129, 135, 136, 176; as cowboy, 4–5, 94, 176; death of, 187–88; described, 17, 19, 20, 82, 85, 94, 98, 130, 131, 161; early life, 3–4; as gunfighter, 22, 32, 34–41, 49, 56, 57, 59–63, 66, 120, 154, 190, 197n43, 203n22, 211n35; illnesses, 4, 8–9, 100, 185; as Indian fighter, 5–8, 194n19; as inventor, 122–23; as lawman, 3, 25–33, 49, 51, 52–53, 55–56, 67, 71, 75, 77, 80–81, 111–12, 133–36, 138–51, 171, 181–85, 198n7, 202n6, 204n5, 207n54, 216n54, 217n24; marriages of, 53, 54, 153, 157; as miner and mining speculator, 80, 104, 106, 122, 164, 165, 170, 174, 177, *178;* as outlaw, 11, 16, 17, 21, 116, 170, 176, 180, 189; as saloonkeeper, 34–40, 50, 199n9; as prison warden, 124, 127, 129, 131, 133, 138, 141, 176, 177, 189, 213n13; as professional gambler, 55, 67, 69, 78, 102, 109, 110, 113, 114, 117, 119, 211n45; quoted, 81, 98–99, 103–104, 106, 156–

Daniels, Benjamin Franklin (*cont.*)
  57, 163, 166, 172–73; as Rough Rider, 82, 84–95, 98–104, 125, 192; trials of, 17, 19, 38, 64–65, 197n38
Daniels, Edward (Ben's brother), 193n3
Daniels, Edward (Ben's half-brother), 193n7
Daniels, Elizabeth, 4, 193n3
Daniels, Esther Stickley, 4
Daniels, Flora, 193n7
Daniels, George, 193n7
Daniels, Henry, 193n7
Daniels, Jonathan, 193n3
Daniels, Judith, 193n3
Daniels, Maria (Ben's mother), 3–4
Daniels, Maria (Ben's sister), 4, 21, 193n3
Daniels, May, 193n7
Daniels, Menewa, 193n3
Daniels, Ruth, 193n3
Daniels, Stephen, 193n7
Daniels, Thomas E., 143, 214n18
Daniels, William A. ("Bill"), 198n1
Davis, Richard Harding, 95
Deadwood, S.Dak., 126, 130
Delaney, William, 197n1
Denver, Colo., 59,73, 74, 76, 77, 114, 116, 119, 166, 167
Denver City Hall War, 73
Devereau, Horace K., 86, 90, 95, 105, 208n6, 209n22
Dickson, J. E., 8, 171
"Ding Dong Bell" (melodrama), 209n15
Dixon, Charles J., 60
Dodge, Fred, 102, 107, 141, 150, 166, 167
Dodge City, Kans., 5, 10–11, 14, 15, 16, 21, 22–40, 24, 41, 49, 50, 52, 53, 56, 57, 59, 60, 63, 64, 66, 67, 75, 80, 85, 87, 89, 95, 107, 116, 119, 130, 133, 137, 142, 154, 160, 170, 171, 190, 191, 196n31, 197n43, 198n7, 198n9, 202n2, 217n19
"Dodge City War," 22
Donohue, Frank, 59
Double Lakes, Tex., 7
Douglas, Ariz., 162
Dowd, "Big Dan," 198n1
Drachman, S. W., 116
Draper, George W., 197n37
Dunlap, "Three-Fingered Jack," 138
Dunn, George W., 65

Eagle Pass, Tex., 43
Earp, Wyatt, 3, 10, 23, 32, 128
Eaton, Howard, 130
Edie, John S., 21
Elks Lodge, 80, 104
El Paso, Tex., 126, 143
Emporia, Kans., 151, 215n37
English, J. W. ("Will"), 60, 62, 63, 64, 65, 120, 203n23
Evans, A. J., 63
Evergreen Cemetery (Tucson, Ariz.), 187, 188

Fairhurst, Ed, 61
Fisher, J. W., 17
Fitch, Clarence A., 79
Fletcher, Charles ("Oklahoma Charley"), 182
Flood, Jack, 55
Flood, Mrs. Jack, 55
Florence, Ariz., 168, 176, 184, 185, 212n4
Finlay, J. H., 38, 39
Forbes, Albert W., 218n31
"Forlorn Hope" campaign, 7
Fort Griffin, Tex., 8, 9

INDEX

Fort McKavett, Tex., 44, 45, 46, 48, 49, 50, 201n28
Forts: Concho, 7; Laramie, 16; Lyon, 11, 13, 17; Whipple, 84; Yuma, 128
Fort Smith, Ark., 16
Foster, John, 125, 138, 150, 214n6
Fowler, Charles, 143, 214n20
Frantz, Frank, 125, 129, 212n2
Frost, Daniel M., 27, 37

Gangs: "Dutch Henry," 14, 16; "High Five," 89; "Saloon," 23, 25, 36, 38, 40
Garfield, James A., 216n45
Garfield, James R., 153, 155, 156, 216n45
Garrett, Pat, 9, 126, 194n18
Garten, Ellis, 64, 65; quoted, 52, 57, 64
Gates, Thomas, 128
Gatling guns, 72
Geronimo, 84
Gibson, James, 78
Glenn, Willis Skelton, 194n18, 194n19
Globe, Ariz., 138, 143
Goodwin, James C., 125
Granada, Colo., 53
Grand Canyon, 155
Gray County Seat War, 55, 67, 116, 120
Greathouse, "Whiskey Jim," 194n19
Greenwald, Samuel, 138, 168, 214n6
Greenway, Charles Campbell, 173, 174, 175, 218n28
Gregory, Walter T., 138, 213n13
Griffith, W. M., 127
Gryden, Harry, 15
Gunnison, Colo., 206n36

Guthrie, Okla., 66, 67, 171, 204n5, 217n19

Hagerman, J. J., 69, 74
Hallowell (district attorney), 196n31
Hamer, D. C., 178, 180
Hamilton, Robert, 19
Hanna, Mark, 121
"Happy Jack" (Rough Rider), 88
Harrington, Henry, 61
Harris, J. D., 139
Harris, William H., 25
Hart, "Mollie," 29
Hart, "Ollie," 29
Hart, Pearl, 128
Hart, Walter, 28, 29, 198n10
Harvard University, 83, 90
Harvey, James, 7
Havana, Cuba, 82
Hay, John, 124, 127
Hays City, Kans., 14
Haywood, C. Robert, quoted, 39
Haywood, William Dudley ("Big Bill"), 205n11, 209n15
Heard, Dwight N., 174
Heard, George, 217n24
Hearst, William Randolph, 82
"Hell Hole of Yuma," 128
Hess, O. G., 53
Hickok, "Wild Bill," 3, 11
Hill, John Thomas, 44
Hill, Wesley A., 213n9
Hillman, "Six-Shooter Bill," 194n19
Hinan, Bill, 53
Hines, Ben, 53
Hinkle, George, 22, 25
Hitchcock, Frank H., 155–56
Hoar, George F., 109, 111, 121
Hoggett, Volney, 204n5
Hoover, George, 25, 27, 30
Hopkins, Arthur A., 150

240　INDEX

Hotels: Copper Queen, 175; National, 80; Raleigh, 131, 153
Hot Springs, Ark., 133
House, A. J., 19
Hoyt, W. M., 150, 151
Hudson, Sadie, 28
Hughes, Charles Evans, 175, 176
Hughes, David, 138
Hughes, L. C., 116, 146
Hughes, P. C., 17
Hunter, J. Marvin, 48; quoted, 41, 46–47
Hunter, John Warren, 42, 43; quoted, 41, 44–46, 47–48, 49

Indian tribes: Apache, 84; Cheyenne; 11, 13; Comanche, 5, 6, 194n16; Menomonee, 162, 164, 216n4; Papago, 177; Yaqui, 150, 151, 154
Irwin, John N., 84

Jackson, Joe, 7
Jefferson, Thomas, 83
Johnson, Junius J., 73, 74, 75, 206n36
Jones, C. B., 15
Jones, Clabe, 81
Jones, "Conk," 59
Jones, Thomas S., 38, 196n31
Julian, J. E. ("Ed"), 34–41, 50, 51, 116, 119, 120, 142, 191

Kane, Woodbury, 90, 130
Kansas City, Mo., 95, 102, 104, 122
Kansas counties: Clark, 52; Coffey, 21; Ellis, 13; Ford, 10, 15, 16, 17, 25, 32, 40, 52, 63, 107, 191, 217n19; Franklin, 4; Gray, 60, 63, 64; Osage, 21; Pawnee, 17; Scott, 202n6; Shawnee, 15
Kansas Supreme Court, 59

Kelley, James H. ("Dog"), 25
Kent, Edward, 141
Keshena, Wisc., 164
"Kettle Hill," 95
Key West, Fla., 98
Key West, Kans., 21
Kibbey, Joseph H., 141
Kinkaid and Riner (law firm), 17
Kit Carson, Colo., 11
Klondike Gold Rush, 81
Knox, Philander Chase, 108, 115
Krag-Jorgensen rifle, 90
Kress, "Wild Bill," 194n19

La Junta, Colo., 114
Lake, Stuart, 32
Lamar, Colo., 57, 85, 98, 202n6
Laramie, Wyo., 17, 67, 115, 129
Laramie County, Wyo., 19
Larned, Kans., 17
Larsen, Hans, 143
Lasalle County, Ill., 3
Las Guasimas, Cuba, 84, 91, 95
Layman (prosecutor), 17
Lehman, Herman, 194n17
Leslie, "Buckskin Frank," 128
Lincoln, Abraham, 83
Lincoln County, N.Mex., 89
Llano Estacado, 7
Llewellyn, William Henry Harrison, 89, 108, 124
Lockwood, Bertha, 28
Lodge, Henry Cabot, 127
Loeb, William, 213n21, 216n54
Loomis, John A., 42, 201n25; quoted, 43, 201n22
Los Angeles, Calif., 139
Love, Henry K., 94
Luther, Frank, 63

Madsen, Chris, 158–60, 216n56
Manitowac, Wisc., 11

INDEX   241

Martin ("Hurricane Bill"), 11
Martin, John A., 63
Martinez, Manuel, 183, 184, 185
Masonic Lodge, 157, 188
Masterson, Ed, 5, 9, 10, 23
Masterson, Jim, 5, 9, 10, 23, 56–57, 60, 62, 63, 66, 67, 204n6
Masterson, W. B. ("Bat"), 3, 5, 9, 10, 15, 17, 23, 55, 56, 57, 59, 66, 85, 98, 102, 126, 133, 136, *137*, 142, 148, 153, 154, 158, 159, 160, 168, 170, 190, 198n7, 198n10, 202n2, 203n17, 204n5, 217n19; quoted, 170–71, 194n11
Mather ("Mysterious Dave"), 14, 23, 27–28, 202n2
McCamey (Texas pioneer), 8
McClintock, James H., 4, 5, 83, 84, 109, 113, 129, 168, 193n5, 211n44; quoted, 3, 30–31, 161
McCord, Myron H., 108–10, 122, 133, 138, 211n44
McGarr, Charles, 125
McGarry, Harvey M., 37–38
McGaw, Charles E., 150
McGinty, William, 92, 93
McKaskill, K., 138
McKinley, William, 105, 107, 108
Meade, William K., 128
Mears, J. W., 44, 50, 202n32
Menardville, Tex., 42, 44
Mesabi Range, 173
Mexican Revolution, 157
Miami (vessel), 100
Middleton, Cliff, 213n13
Middleton, "Doc," 16, 89
Miles, J. T. ("Rye"), 178, 180, 181
Military units: Arizona National Guard, 84; Colorado National Guard, 75, 209; Fifth U.S. Army Corps, 95; First Territorial Regiment, 109; First U.S. Volunteer Cavalry, 83, 84, 86, 91, 95, 207n1; Kansas National Guard, 63; Nineteenth U.S. Infantry, 17; Tenth U.S. Cavalry, 7
Millay, Jerry, 139
Mills, Tom, 185
Milner ("California Joe"), 11
Milton, Benjamin F., 38
Milton, Jeff, 138
Milwaukee, Wisc., 164, 169, 172
Mix, Tom, 130, 132
Moffat, David, 69, 74
Montauk Point, N.Y., 100
Mooney, Thomas, 138, 168
Moody, W. H., 133
Moore, "Smoky" (Rough Rider), 88
Morrow, "Prairie Dog Dave," 14
Mossman, Burt, 125
Mount Rushmore, 218n28
Moyer, Charles H., 205n11
Mullen, Oscar J., 125
Munson, J. B., 61
Murphy, "Eat-'Em-Up Jake" 57
Myers, Murray, 63
Myton, Howell P., 23, 107, 141, 195n1

"Napoleon" guns, 72
Nash, Fannie, 29
Nash, Jay Robert, 197–98n1, 201n28
National Republican Convention, 123, 156, 172, 212n48
Neill, Charles P., 153
Neville, John B., 79
New Orleans, La., 26
Newspapers and magazines: *Albuquerque Journal*, 148; *Arizona Daily Republican*, 119, 122, 127–28, 144, 150; *Arizona Daily Star*, 116, 146, 182, 188; *Arizona Weekly Republican*, 147; *Atlanta*

242   INDEX

Newspapers and magazines (cont.)
Constitution, 113, 120, 130;
Boston Herald, 134, 135; Boulder Daily Camera, 76; Buffalo Evening News, 153; Cheyenne Leader, 115; Cimarron Jacksonian, 52, 57, 62, 64; Cripple Creek Morning Times, 79, 82, 85, 98, 102; Dallas Morning News, 22, 66; Denver Post, 166, 167; Denver Republican, 77, 115, 119; Denver Tribune, 15; Dodge City Democrat, 29, 40; Dodge City Times, 6, 10, 14; Ford County Globe, 27; Fort Worth Register, 121; Frontier Times, 48; Globe Live Stock Journal, 37, 38; Gray County Echo, 157; Greeley Tribune, 76; Kansas City Journal, 40; Kansas City World, 95; Lamar Register, 53; Larned Optic, 17; Macon Daily Telegraph, 134, 135; Milwaukee Journal, 164; Montgomery Advertiser, 144; New York Times, 135; New York World, 142; Outlook Magazine, 168; Phoenix Gazette, 109; Prescott Morning Courier, 146; San Angelo Standard, 48; San Angelo Standard Times, 46; Tombstone Epitaph, 188; Tucson Citizen, 129, 157, 170; Tucson Daily Star, 116, 182, 188; Tucson Post, 145, 176, 189; Washington Post, 110, 131, 135, 144, 147
Newton, Kans., 38, 198n10
"New United Monster Railroad Show," 30
New York City, N.Y., 26, 90, 93, 101, 126, 133, 153, 170
Nixon, Tom, 9, 11, 23, 25, 27, 198n7

Nogales, Ariz., 104, 106, 109, 120, 143, 150, 184
Nolan, Nicholas, 7
Nolon, Johnny, 81
Noon, Edward E., 104

Ohl, Joseph, 113, 114, 119
O'Neill, William Owen ("Buckey"), 89
Orchard, Harry, 205n11
Organ, Perry, 16
Oro Blanco mining district, 183
Ottawa, Kans., 4
Overlock, Charles A., 162

Page, Leonard S., 150, 201n28
Palmer, W. J., 72
Panic of 1893, 69
Panic of 1907, 167
Parker, Isaac C., 16
Parker-Grimshaw Undertaking Parlors (Tucson, Ariz.), 187
Parmenter, M. D., 53
Parmer, Oliver, 184, 185
Payne, Deputy Sheriff, 10
Peabody, J. H., 208n15
Pearson, Frank J.,183, 184
Pearson, Myrtle, 183, 184
Penitentiaries: Arizona Territorial, 126, 127–28, 129, 131, 133, 138, 139, 176, 177, 184, 212n4, 215n33; Kansas State, 64; Wyoming Territorial, 17, 18, 19, 21, 113, 116, 119, 197n38, 211n35
Pernot, P. H., 67
Pettibone, Charles A., 205n11
Phoenix, Ariz., 109, 110, 122, 127, 133, 144, 168, 175, 176, 218n28
Pike's Peak, 67
Pilot Knob, 128
Poe, John, 9

Political Parties: Citizen's, 40; Democratic, 109, 158, 159, 162, 168, 170, 172, 176, 178, 180, 212n48, 217n24; Populist, 71; Progressive ("Bull Moose"), 169, 179, 171, 172, 174, 215n37, 218n25; Republican, 105, 109, 113, 114, 115, 123, 161, 162, 168, 170, 172, 174, 175, 176, 178, 180, 182, 185, 189, 212n2, 218n25
Prather, Ed, 59
Prentice, Charles, 79
Prescott, Ariz., 89, 143
Priest, D. T., 45
Princeton University, 90
Purdy, Aaron, 79
Purcell, Elizabeth, 183

Quackenbush, Mrs., 78

Railroads: Atchison, Topeka & Santa Fe, 52; Chicago, Rock Island & Pacific, 183; Denver & Rio Grande, 72; Florence & Cripple Creek, 73, 78; New Mexico & Arizona, 138; Southern Pacific, 180; Wisconsin & Northern, 163
Raine, William McLeod, 213n19
Ramsey, Alexander, 13
Rath City, Tex., 5, 6, 7
"Rattlesnake Pete" (Rough Rider), 88
Reconstruction era, 41, 42
Red Cloud, Neb., 14
Reicheldeffer, Charles, 60, 61, 62, 64
Remington, Frederic, 95, 100, 117, 142
Reno, Nev., 204n5
Reynolds, C. M., 158

Reynolds, Joseph N. ("Buffalo Joe"), 59, 62, 63
Riggs, Barney, 128
Riley, A. T., 59, 60
Riley, Charles B., 65, 203n22
Riley, James M. *See* Middleton, "Doc"
Rivers: Arkansas, 11; Double Mountain Fork of the Brazos, 5; Gila, 128; Middle Fork of the American, 193n4; Salt, 168; Wolf, 217n4
Robinson, C. H., 110
Robinson, M. E., 198n4
"Rob Roy of the Plains." *See* Born, "Dutch Henry"
Roosevelt, Alice, 144
Roosevelt, Quentin, 179
Roosevelt, Theodore, 3, 20
Roosevelt, Theodore, Jr., 153
Root, Elihu, 153
Rose, D. D., 142
Roswell, N. Mex., 89
Rough Riders, 82–111, 117, 121, 124, 125, 127–30, 134–38, 147, 159, 162, 168, 173, 174, 176, 192, 207n54, 208n1, 211n44, 212n2, 213n13, 214n6, 217n24, 218n25
Rowland, R. A.,102
Ruby, Ariz., 183, 219n47
Russell, Kans., 14
Russell, R. R., 50, 202n33
Rynning, Thomas H., 89, 125, 128, 168, 212n4

Salmon, Richard, 218n25
Saloons and dance halls: Bank, 206n36; Becker's and Dolan's, 69; Big Dog, 69; Black Bill's Topic, 69; Clipper, 69; Eldorado, 199n9; Gold Dollar, 69; Green Front, 34–36, 38, 40, 50; Long Branch,

244 INDEX

Saloons and dance halls (*cont.*) 32; Mayer's, 44, 45, 46, 47, 50; Mike Whelan's, 69; Newport, 79; Novelty, 69; Old House, 26; Opera House, 27, 28; Palace, 44; Ranch, 69; White House, 68
San Antonio, Tex., 85, 86, 90, 105, 124
San Juan Hill, 103
Santa Fe Trail, 148
Santa Rita Mountains, 170, 177
Santiago, Cuba, 89, 91, 92, 93
Saxon, Harry J., 185
Schmidt, Heinie, 35, 36
Schnitger, W. R., 19, 67, 115, 197n38
Scott, "Baldy," 59
Scott, Nathan B., 121
Scottish Rite Cathedral, Tucson, Ariz., 187–88
Seayrs, Hampton, 157
Seigfreid, H. N., 116
Sener, J. B., 19
Sewell, Marshall, 5–6, 7
Shafroth, John F., 166
Sheridan, John, 57
Short, Luke, 22–23, 25
Shoup, J. Q. ("Jake"), 60
Silva, Placido, 184
Simpson, B. F., 17
Simpson, O. H., quoted, 34, 36, 37, 38
Singer, Fred, 5, 9, 10, 23, 25, 57, 59, 60, 62, 63, 64
"Slapping Jack" ("Slap Jack Bill") (outlaw), 14, 195n13
Slaughter, John, 138
Smith, Eben, 69
Smith, Hovel, 162
Smith, Jack, 73, 74, 75, 206n36
Smith, Jim, 6
Smith, John, 11
Smith, Leonard, 184
Smith, Milt, 55
Sonora, Mexico, 122, 198
Soule, Asa T., 57
Spain, 82, 83, 109
Spanish-American War, 188, 189, 206n36, 212n4
"Spotted Jack" (buffalo hunter), 6
Springfield, Colo., 56
St. Clair, Dave, 26
Stanton, Richard, 125, 168, 213n9
Stewart, Harry, 183
Stickley, Christian, 4
Stiles, Billy, 215n33
Stillwater, Okla., 92
Stoddard, Isaac T., 110, 113
Strong, Sam, 69, 73, 79
Sughrue, Michael, 25
Sughrue, Pat, 25, 27, 35, 52
Sullinger, Wilfred, 180
Sutton, Michael W., 31–32

Taft, William Howard, 153, 158, 161, 162, 168, 169, 172, 174
Talbert, Ethelbert, 153
Talbot, James, 52, 53, 202n2
Tampa, Fla., 90, 91, 208n6
Tarsney, Thomas J., 71, 77, 207n41
Tate, Thomas J., 25, 33, 40
Taylor, Bob, 71, 77, 78, 197n36
Taylor, George, 19
"Teddy's Terrors." *See* Rough Riders
Teller, Henry Moore, 117, 136
Texas counties: Concho, 42; Hopkins, 42; Maverick, 43; Menard, 44, 50, 51; Palo Pinto, 16; Runnels, 43; Somervell, 43
Texas Rangers, 42
Thomas, Heck, 216n56
Thompson ("Smokey Hill"), 194n19

INDEX

Thorp, Doctor, 93
Tilghman, Bill, 5, 9, 10, 11, 20, 23, 25, 26, 27–28, 30, 32, 34–35, 53, 57, 59, 62, 64, 66, 67, 102, 149, 158, 159, 160, 190, 198n7 198n9, 204n29, 204n6, 216n56
Tilghman, Zoe, 27, 203n29
Topeka, Kans., 14
Trinidad, Colo., 14, 15
Tromback, William, 79
Tucson, Ariz., 116, 151, 161, 164, 166, 167, 168, 171, 177, 180, 181, 183, 184, 187, 189, 211n45
Tucson Board of Education, 116
Tucson Mountains, 183
Tupper, Edith Sessions, 69

Underwood, William (Clarence), 86, 208n6
U.S. Army, 5, 13, 14, 212n4, 218n28
U.S. Senate, 108, 149; Committee on Appointments, 140, 142; Judiciary Committee, 111, 114, 117, 121, 142, 144
U.S. Secret Service, 108
USS *Maine* (warship), 82, 147, 208n12
U.S. Steel Corporation, 168
Utting, Charles, 138, 168, 214n6, 218n25

Vaden, John W., 41–50, 200n1, 201n22, 201n28
Valentine, Robert G., 164
Valley Brook Township, Kans., 21
Van Buren, Martin, 106
Vannick, Lou, 78
Van Voorhis, H. B., 17
Victor, Colo., 72, 73, 74, 75
Vikings, 140
Vilas, Colo., 56

Waite, David H. ("Old Bloody Bridles"), 71, 73, 74, 75, 76, 77
Walker, Sam, 13
Wallace, Frank ("Kid"), 71, 77, 78
Wallick, Sam, 44, 45, 46, 47
Ware, Belle, 54
Ware, John, 54
Ware, John T., 54
Ware, Susan, 54
Warford, David, 125
Warren, Ariz., 175
Washington, George, 83
Washington, D.C., 90, 108, 109, 111, 113, 116, 120, 122, 129, 130, 131, 132, 136, 143, 147, 153, 154, 155, 157, 158, 159, 162, 164, 177, 218n28
Watson, Newton F., 59, 60, 62, 63
Webb, William W., 125
Webster, Alonzo B., 22, 23, 25, 26, 32–33, 40
Webster, Daniel, 218n28
Wellington, Kans., 195n2
West Cripple Creek, Colo., 80, 85
Western Federation of Miners (WFM), 70, 130, 205n11, 209n15
West Point Academy, 73, 84, 89, 130
Wheeler, Harry, 212n4
White, George J., 184
White, Jim ("Boss Hunter"), 6, 194n19
White, William Allen, 215n37
White House, 107, 110, 121, 126, 130, 143, 144, 153, 154, 157, 159, 168, 176, 189
Whitelaw, James T., 38, 39, 65
Wichita, Kans., 5, 15, 32
Wickersham, George W., 162
Wilbert, Charles, 19, 19736
Wilcox, Ariz., 138
Wilcox, George, 129, 168, 174, 218n24

Willets, D. N., 163
Wilson (Indian agent), 164
Wilson, Charles, 86, 208n6
Wilson, Joe R., 77
Wilson, Thomas S., 116
Wilson, Woodrow, 168, 176
Winchester rifle, 44, 62
Winkler, George, Jr., 183
Winkler, George C., 183
Wood, Leonard, 83, 85, 95, 103
Wood, Samuel N., 196n31

World's Fair, 107
World War I, 172, 175, 179, 218n28
Wormwood, Sam W., 4–5
Wright, Robert M., 31–32, 39–40, 198n9; quoted, 30

Yellow House Canyon, 6, 86
Yucatan (vessel), 90
Yuma, Ariz., 126, 127, 128, 129, 131, 138, 139, 168, 176

Also by Robert K. DeArment

Bat Masterson: The Man and the Legend (Norman, 1979)
Knights of the Green Cloth: The Saga of the Frontier Gamblers (Norman, 1990)
George Scarborough: The Life and Death of a Lawman on the Closing Frontier (Norman, 1992)
(ed.) *Early Days in Texas: A Trip to Hell and Heaven* (Norman, 1992)
Alias Frank Canton (Norman, 1996)
Bravo of the Brazos: John Larn of Fort Griffin, Texas (Norman, 2002)
Deadly Dozen: Twelve Forgotten Gunfighters of the Old West (Norman, 2003)
(ed. and anno., with William Rathmell) *Life of the Marlows: A True Story of Frontier Life of Early Days* (Denton, Tex., 2004)
Jim Courtright of Fort Worth: His Life and Legend (Fort Worth, 2004)
Broadway Bat: Gunfighter in Gotham: The New York City Years of Bat Masterson (Honolulu, 2005)
Ballots and Bullets: The Bloody County Seat Wars of Kansas (Norman, 2006)
Deadly Dozen, Volume 2: Forgotten Gunfighters of the Old West (Norman, 2007)
Deadly Dozen, Volume 3: Forgotten Gunfighters of the Old West (Norman, 2010)

Also by Jack DeMattos

Mysterious Gunfighter: The Story of Dave Mather (College
   Station, Tex., 1992)
The Earp Decision (College Station, Tex., 1989)
Garrett and Roosevelt (College Station, Tex., 1988)
Masterson and Roosevelt (College Station, Tex., 1984)
(annotator and illustrator) (by W. B. Bat Masterson) *The 75th
   Anniversary Edition of Famous Gun Fighters of the
   Western Frontier* (Monroe, Wash., 1982)

www.ingramcontent.com/pod-product-compliance
Lightning Source LLC
Chambersburg PA
CBHW022109150426
43195CB00008B/337